ELIZABETH ROSE

Printed in the United States of America

First Printing, 2015

I have recreated events, locales and conversations from my contemporaneous notes as well as my memories of them. In order to maintain the anonymity of individuals referenced in this book, I have changed certain names and often genders. I may have changed some identifying characteristics and details such as physical properties, occupations and settings.

Cover design: Yasamin Rahmani
Interior design: Karen Hudson
Photo editor: Jonathan Charles Fox

Nonfiction/Memoir

ISBN 978-0-9904392-1-9

To Donnie,

Music has called...
Take me to the children, she sings,
In the South Bronx,
In rural Pennsylvania,
In South Africa,
Take me to ALL the children
Within your reach,
And beyond.

And that is where you are...
Answering the call.

In the first place, God made idiots.

That was for practice.

Then He made school boards.

—Mark Twain

Table of Contents

The Four-One-One...

"I have bad news. You won't be able to teach here anymore." The brand-new principal of "my" Manhattan high school delivered the 411 as we balanced paper plates, waiting to grab some chow at the staff buffet. It was September 1, 2011, several days before students would invade the school, annihilating any tuft of tranquility left over from summer. "No matter how much we'd love to keep you here, the DOE wants ATRs[1] off the payroll," he continued. "It's not just you. Since they can't fire them, they're going to send all ATRs to a different school every week. They'll become permanent rotating substitute teachers. They hope they'll get so miserable subbing, they'll quit. We hate to lose you," he added grabbing, some crab salad.

I'm being exiled from my home school? Just like that? After ten years? After raising $325K for the place? I'm out?

And...they're sending me to sub in a new school each week?

WTF?

My frontal lobes flashed. I can survive. I can teach guitar. Maybe my one-woman musical comedy will make it Off Broadway. I can license more of my songs to TV and film. I've saved some money. No need to panic. Rise to the challenge. Be grateful. Maybe they made a mistake.

I'd forgotten to breathe. I remembered my feet; they were still holding me upright. I breathed. I smiled. The Universe is nudging me

[1] ATR = Absent Teacher Reserve, aka, "Excessed Teachers" = a pool of about 1500 to 2500 full-time tenured teachers whose positions were cut due to budgets or school closings. (See Appendix)

out of my cozy zone. I'm all right with this. I stepped up to the buffet, scooped out the only undead offering…rice and beans…and thought back to my first day of school ten years ago.

...And The Nine-One-One

My first day of teaching dawned a bright, sunny Tuesday morning. My first class, "Literary Songwriting," was scheduled for 11 am. I was excited about introducing my students to The Great American Songbook, starting with the blues. It was September 11, 2001.

"A plane just hit the World Trade Center."

And everything shut down: schools, businesses, air travel...joy.

Schools opened Thursday. With my guitar case strapped to my back, I hiked up the four floors to my new home, one of six small schools that occupied the block-sized Upper East Side school building built in 1923 to educate girls. As I stepped into the hallway, a noisy crowd of excited students, mostly African-American and Hispanic from the projects, was changing classes. Right in the middle of the hallway, the principal was speaking privately to a skinny brown-skinned boy who was trying to hold back tears. I drew closer.

"You did not have anything to do with the planes hitting the Towers," the principal said to him. "It was not your fault. It was not your family's fault. Don't listen to anyone who tries to blame you. This is America. You are an American and a Muslim. You have every right that all other Americans have. This horrible crime has nothing to do with you. Remember that, OK?"

The young teen stared down at his feet. The principal continued.

"If any more students, inside or out of school, try to blame you or act like a bully, you let me know immediately. That kind of behavior will not be tolerated here."

The boy kept his eyes on the floor. Students were hugging and high five-ing each other as they changed classes. In the center of the melee, the principal knelt down and looked directly into the boy's eyes.

"Promise?"

The little boy nodded his head, holding his eyes to the floor.

"OK then, off to class," said the principal and he watched the boy head across the hall.

As that tormented teen slunk into room 402, I silently signed up for his and any other Muslim kids' protection squad. That was my first teachable moment of many.

Students were assigned to my class because they needed one "art" credit, required for graduation. I couldn't screen them for interest or ability, but I went with it. My first year was extremely challenging... but that's another story. Treading water, I hung in, saved by some of my students who blew me away with their creativity and unbridled enthusiasm.

Five years later, a full time position opened up. I took it and spent the year creating DVD yearbooks in three network schools. It was fun, notwithstanding the 60-hour weeks I spent editing them at year's end. Next year, I'll teach them how to edit, I vowed. "Next year," however, didn't pan out.

"They've cut your position, but don't worry. I can keep you here," my principal told me at the end of that school year in June. "BTW, you're now officially an excessed teacher."

For the next four years, I taught documentary-making and creative writing. I won grants. A couple of (Michael) Jordan Fundamentals for video and music recording equipment. Then the biggie: $248,000 for a Mac lab and one interactive white board for every classroom. Now our kids had a chance of mastering 21st century tools.

I felt like a valued member of the community...all warm and fuzzy. Even though teaching was a "B" job in my Personal Grand Design, I was comfy in the school. I could continue with my creative projects outside. Next year, with the new digital bling installed, I could teach documentary making, music recording. Students could make music videos. Next year was gonna be *wicked!!*

Until our new principal's words tainted the buffet spread out before us.

"I have bad news. You won't be able to teach here anymore."

That's it. The Universe has put a megaphone to my ear. I hear you! I'm playing my life too small. Time to get out there and *GO BIG!* I'm going to follow that dream that's been in my heart as long as I can remember...

...to become a child star.

The Night Before

My dream to join the celebrated ranks of Biebs et al notwithstanding, I spent the weekend assessing my options. I could leave the DOE altogether and go back to my freelance life. It had been a wild rollercoaster ride. The sharp turns included everything from playing Iceland with the cast of *Beatlemania* to working on a sprout farm in the Florida Keys. I'd been developing a one-woman musical comedy for the theatre about the life of a performing songwriter. The "original cast recording" was complete. Maybe it was time to go full-tilt boogie with the show. Leave teaching. Why not?

Why not? Because...I'd miss my lovely teacher's salary, that bi-monthly gift I'd come to cherish.

It's Monday night. Early tomorrow we ATR teachers must report to school. I go online to find out which school I shall grace on my first day. My assignment says:

BARUCH COLLEGE CAMPUS HS 9/6/2011	10/9/2011

Baruch. I interviewed there last year. Very impressive school. Located between Park Avenue South and Madison Avenue, it cherry-picks some of the brightest students in the city for every incoming ninth grade. There are many who would argue against this kind of "screening" of students: it's discriminatory; it creates educational apartheid. There's great validity in these arguments. However, I have to admit, I love doing creative work with bright kids who come from families who value learning. My assignment is from September 6 until October 9. The DOE site also informs me that after one month at our first school, we ATRs will begin our weekly rotations: a new school every week.

OK. That's a no-brainer. I'm staying one more month. That's two more paychecks. Also, I wonder how the DOE is going to organize the weekly rotation of 2500 teachers in the ATR pool? That's going to take up a lot of bean counter man-hours. Maybe they'll give up on the idea. Maybe I'll be lucky enough to stay at Baruch all year...

Tuesday, September 6, 2011

Baruch College Campus High School (BCCHS)

The First Day

I emerge from the subway on Park Avenue South, on the edge of the Flatiron District. There's a blue sign with the school's name stuck to the door of what looks like an office building. I pull the heavy door open, head in and stop at the security desk. Two women wearing the uniforms of NYC School Safety Officers are manning the desk.

"Good morning," I chirp.

"Good morning," the one with the blonde hair chirps back.

"My name is Elizabeth Rose. I'm an ATR teacher, assigned to this school until October 9."

"Welcome, Miz Rose!" she says. "I'm Mary."

"Hi, Mary."

It's a friendly place. She hugs a couple of students who are returning early for a pre-college program. "Didja have a nice summer?" Most students won't be here until Thursday.

Teachers report two days early. These first days are for teachers to greet each other, share hugs and summer adventure stories, meet as a staff, locate materials and books, line up for the copy machine, get their rooms ready for students and shake off any remaining complacency from the summer. It's "go" time and it's serious. Start it right and the year will go well…you hope.

"Hi. I'm Marilyn." A lovely lady behind the office desk welcomes me as I follow Mary's directions to report to the school office. "You can stay here and help us out in the office unless they need you somewhere else. We don't have students yet but we have things you can help with."

"Anything you need," I say. "I don't mind helping out with anything. Envelopes need stuffing? Collating? Just hand it over." I smile. This is going to be easy. Another woman comes into the office, beautifully put together. She is wearing khaki Capri pants, a pretty shell topped by a short jacket and the perfect understated necklace.

"I'm Angela," she says. "I'm an ATR."

"Really? I'm Elizabeth. I'm an ATR too. Wow. There are two of us here at this small school? I wasn't expecting that. Cool." As there is no task for the moment, we sit down in the empty chairs near the entrance and swap stories, how long we've been ATRs, what school we've come from and such. She's brought her Kindle reader.

"What are you reading?" I ask her.

"Oh, I don't know yet. I've downloaded a few classics. I love the Russian writers." Hmm. An intellect. I'm a little intimidated. I mean, I enjoy the classic Russian comedies. *Ivan The Terrible Punster*, for one. Best to change the subject.

"What's your license area?" I ask her. She looks smart. I'm guessing chemistry.

"Social Studies."

"Really. Me too," I reply.

"No kidding? Two social studies teachers. That's kind of funny that they'd put two of us here at the same time. So you've taught global and American history?"

"Actually," I say, "I never taught social studies. I was in a kind of progressive school—performance-based assessment. We didn't give a social studies Regents."

"That sounds interesting."

"It was great for me. I started as a teaching artist. I'm kind of…an entertainer." Oh God. She's probably thinking I was a pole dancer.

"An entertainer? That sounds exciting. What do you do?" I give her a thumbnail sketch of my exploits, my one-woman show, my recording and touring, blah blah. I watch carefully, in case her eyes start to roll. I am not fond of people blasting me with their resumes, so I try to be sensitive and keep it simple. She kind of egged me on.

"If you ever do your show again, please let me know. I'm coming."

"You'll be the first to know." If it ever gets produced again, I think.

My first day as an ATR passes uneventfully. It's 2:50 pm. As I descend into the subway for my return commute, the refrain of the Katy Perry tune touches down in my brain. *I'm an alien.*

Wednesday, September 7, 2011
The Second Day and Beyond

"Good morning!" Angela greets me when I arrive for my second day at BCCHS.

For the next few hours, Angela and I spend most of our time preparing a mailing. All the other teachers are fully scheduled for important things: professional development (PD), departmental meetings, more time at the copy machine. A part of me is grateful that I'm not starting a normal school year. Many teachers have opening-day jitters. Everybody wants to ace that first day.

As a teacher, if you do not present a well-organized front from the first day, you are asking for trouble. You need to be clear about expectations. Yours and theirs. You need to challenge them and at the same time get them excited about learning. This is no day job for dilettantes. It takes time to establish your authority. The first year or two of teaching is boot camp. No matter what grades you've gotten in your education courses, or how well you've planned your daily lessons, once you are facing your first class of teenagers, any sign of weakness and you're circling the drain. With a few years under your belt, you learn to exude indisputable authority, to make an example of the first knucklehead who tries to get over on you, while challenging them with provocative ideas that require high level thinking. And...you have to make the subtext palpable. As they sit there, assessing what they can get away with, they can discern that behind your no-nonsense shield, there's access to an open, loving heart that wants nothing more than their victory. You need to emit an invisible energy, an unspoken transmission that informs them that the muscular pontificator up front is also a gracious, compassionate soul who sees them, gets them and recognizes their extraordinary individuality, whether they're annoyingly loquacious or too shy to utter a syllable, who will lend them an ear, in private, keeping insecurities and confidences sacred.

But Angela and I are not there. We're stuffing envelopes in the office. With an open heart, I must add.

A young lady, perhaps in her mid-to-late-20s, comes into the office. She's a thin, pretty lady wearing a straight Chanel skirt and fashionable low heels. We continue tri-folding and manipulating sticky address labels as she smiles faintly and walks behind the counter to confer with Marilyn.

"Hi. I'm the principal," she says. She's a lovely, soft-spoken lady.

"Nice to meet you," we say and introduce ourselves.

"It's going to be slow this week, as you've probably figured out. Our full staff is mostly here. By next week, I hope to figure out ways you can help us out."

"Anything," I say, boldly speaking for Angela.

"A few of the teachers are taking some students on a trip in a few weeks. We'll definitely need you for coverage by then. Meanwhile, you may continue to help Marilyn."

I take my lunch to the teachers' lounge on the second floor. A few teachers come in and out to use the copy machine or sit and talk. I get a slight acknowledgement with their eyes. To the one or two who actually say hello, I introduce myself.

"Hi. I'm Elizabeth. I'm an ATR assigned to this school for the month."

"Nice to meet you." Polite. Some reticence.

Understood. I get the feeling that this ATR thing hits a little close. One strike on a school budget sheet and any teacher might enter the ATR pool. Everybody knows it. I smile, hoping they see it's not so bad.

I don't mind stuffing envelopes. After all, I'm here to serve.

Monday, September 12, 2011

But serve in the school cafeteria? That's where I'm assigned today.

"When you're not covering an absent teacher, we'd appreciate it if you would post yourself in the cafeteria," the principal had said to Angela and me last Friday.

"All day?" I asked.

"No. Just periods three through eight would be fine. But if you wouldn't mind sitting there through period eight, that would be good, too."

Sure. After all, I'm here to serve.

The students arrive on Wednesday, September 8. Everybody goes into high gear. Except me. I'm holed up in the teachers' lounge until Friday morning when I get a call from Marilyn.

"Ms. Rose. We need you to cover a physics class."

First coverage of the year. Cool. I love modern physics. My dad taught high school physics back around the time Newton came up with his second law of motion. OK, I'm exaggerating. But it was way before the discovery of quarks, string theory and the Higgs field. I get intoxicated thinking about the H-boson. The Newtonian crap? It creates friction in my neocortex. Maybe that's why I bombed on the physics Regents...I was ahead of my time.

I pick up the assigned lesson plan and head to physics class.

"Hi! I'm Ms. Rose. Your teacher left this worksheet for you." The kids politely take the worksheet and find friends to sit with. They keep pouring in. Thirty seven total. Latecomers stand in the back. Not enough chairs.

"So…I'm not a physics teacher but maybe we can discuss this first question on your worksheet, 'What is physics?' Anybody want to write ideas on the board?"

"I'll do the board!" a girl volunteers as she runs up to the front of the class.

"So—what is physics?" I ask. A small boy with glasses raises his hand.

"Science that deals with the physical world?"

"The physical world —OK. Do you mean the seen or unseen world?"

"Both," a chorus calls out.

"OK. What specifically? What do you think physicists measure… let's say, in the *seen* world?"

"Gravity?" a girl calls out from the back.

"OK. Gravity. The mass of objects. What about the unseen world?"

"Atoms."

"Black holes."

"Speed of light." The ideas come quickly as my student scribe scribbles on the board.

"Speaking of the speed of light, how many of you are familiar with Einstein's most famous equation in his general theory of relativity?"

"$E = mc^2$!" A boy clustered around a table with his pals calls out the answer. I detect some arrogance in his voice.

"And can you tell us what each of these symbols stand for?"

"Yeah. E is energy, M is mass and C is the speed of light. So energy equals mass times the speed of light."

"OK. Good. Now I can't go much further with this because I'm not a physics teacher but speaking of the speed of light, I want to ask you one thing. How many of you have looked up at the stars on a clear night?" Most hands go up, surprising me. City kids don't get to see many stars.

"So you might be looking at a star which is, say, four light years away from Earth. That means it will take the light of that star how long to travel before you can see it...anybody know?"

"Four years." A girl in the back row calls out.

"Anybody know how fast light travels?"

The wise guy calls out, "671 million miles per hour."

"Really? Or 186,000 miles per second. Anyway, here's what I think is the fascinating part. If you look up and see that star that's four light years away, it's taken four years for the light to travel to where you can see it. Right? So, you're actually looking back into time. You're actually time traveling. Cool, huh?"

The period ends and I collect their worksheets.

"Are you going to stay with our class?" a girl asks me as she leaves.

"No. Your regular teacher will be back Monday."

"I wish you could. This was fun."

"Thanks so much. But it's better that you have a teacher who actually knows something about physics."

Back in school for cafeteria duty, I notice that these students are very polite. They open doors for me. They say, "Excuse me." It's a bit of culture shock for me, having come from teaching kids for whom the "N" word simply means a "person."

I don't get to finish my day in the cafeteria at Baruch. Instead, I have to head up to North Harlem for a *mandatory* interview at the Frederick Douglass Academy. Road trip! There's a vacancy in social studies. Hmm. I could teach them to make their own documentaries. Yeah. I could get excited about that. I stuff three resumes in my bag and head uptown.

This ain't no Baruch, lemme tell ya.

After a check-in with school security, I fight my way down a crowded hall to the main office. Junior high students in uniforms are in a friendly shoving match. The security guard is on task.

"No shoving! Walk straight to class," she yells.

"Hi, I'm interviewing for the social studies position," I say to the secretary.

"Just sit down and wait. You will be called," she says and goes back to her phone call. I look around the office. My guess: it hasn't been cleaned since Abe Beame was mayor in 1974. The chairs are all broken. As I carefully sink down into one, my sinuses start to fill. I'm not allergic to anything I know of, but something in that office is stimulating those antigens.

Another lady walks in as I look for a tissue. I assume she's also an ATR. I try not to inspect the place too closely. It needs a power wash. I'm a bit of a germphobe.

"Sit down there and wait." The secretary points her to a chair on the other side of the room from me. She sinks down with effort. She looks like a nice teacher lady. Normally, I'd make an effort at polite conversation but with my immune system triggering, I don't feel like multi-tasking. She seems absorbed in her magazine.

We wait. And wait.

After about 20 minutes, the secretary answers a phone call. She hangs up and calls out in our direction, "You may proceed to room 307."

"Which one of us?" I ask her politely.

"Both of you." I guess they have another waiting room upstairs.

I get up, brush a dust bunny off my butt, head into the hall and upstairs to 307. It is an office with two desks. A tall man in a suit shakes my hand, introduces himself. He has a cultured, African accent.

"I'm an assistant principal for social studies. May I have your resume, please?" I pull one out of my bag.

The other teacher comes into the room. The AP introduces himself and asks for her resume. Then he stands and launches into what sounds like a speech he's memorized.

"I would like to tell you ladies about our school. We demand a great deal from our teachers, you know."

Wait a minute. We're being interviewed together? That's weird.

The other teacher and I are sitting next to each other. There's no introduction. I'm uncomfortable. I should have said hello when we were downstairs.

He glances over my resume and then hers. He looks down at me.

"I don't see any social studies teaching experience on your resume."

As I yada yada my "alternative" teaching experience, I notice his eyes start to roll. He seems singularly unimpressed. I try for a little respect.

"I raised over $300K for my school." That gets his attention.

He turns to me and chortles. "Really!!!? You raised $300,000 for your school and they wouldn't give you a position? How cheap they are."

He begins to cross-examine the other lady.

"I see you were working in a school that is slated to close. Do you feel you are a successful teacher?" Ouch.

"I was just laid off on Tuesday, the first day of school," she says. Then she counters with her stats. "My students had a 75% passing rate," she adds quietly. Sweet.

He begins to pontificate again but I interrupt him.

"Sorry to interrupt, but I would just like to introduce myself to this lady. Hi. My name is Elizabeth."

"I'm Ina," she says. She has a charming manner.

The AP continues his recitation.

"I wonder what you know about our school. I would like to tell you about it. At our school, our teachers must be very dedicated. They must work very long hours. It's not unusual for them to work until 5 or 7 pm. And our students are very demanding. If a teacher is under-prepared, they will let that teacher know that this is not acceptable. We come into your class every six weeks to observe and support."

I note which action comes first.

He continues. "We collect data on your teaching every six weeks and we let you know how your students are doing."

His oratory goes on for a while. Full of approbation for his school, himself and the administration, it lacks one positive word for teachers. Nada. Teachers are judged by the data collected. Teachers serve the whims of administration. Got a passion to create lifelong learners of your students? Sorry. Doesn't count. Just make sure they score high on standardized tests. Just be sure you march in lock step with the curriculum handed down to you from the top. Do not improvise, or try to personalize the instruction. Just hurry up and get through the unit. *Sorry, Tiffany, I have no time for your very insightful question. I have to finish this unit and move on to the next. Maybe you can look it up and write a paper on it in college three years from now. Hope you're keeping a diary.*

We just sit there as he drones on. He talks faster, puffing himself up more and more. He's somewhere between a soapbox orator and a small-town preacher. I have to sit on my left hand to keep from looking at my watch.

He struts stage right. "To tell you the truth," he says, pausing for a breath. *So up to now you've been lying? That would explain why your pants are on fire.* "The truth is, I'm not really happy merely being assistant principal. I would much rather be the principal. Thank you for coming. We will be in touch with you."

Ina and I walk out of the office together.

"So. Wha'd ya think?" I ask Ina as we hit the subway.

"Oh. I would never work for that man," she says with a lovely Caribbean lilt. "No respect for teachers."

Well, to be fair, his striped suit had a nice cut.

There's another email from the DOE when I get home. Report to your school tomorrow. Then report to a mandatory job fair at the Fort Washington Avenue Armory. Bring ten resumes. Road trip two days in a row! *Awe-some*!

Wednesday, September 14, 2011
Take Me To The Fair

Yesterday's road trip took me to the heights. Literally. Washington Heights: the boisterous, bodega-busy setting for Lin-Manuel Miranda's Tony award-winning musical, *In The Heights*. As I climbed out of the subway station, I noticed a number of middle-aged folks emerging at the same time. They looked a bit uncomfortable, unfamiliar with the capacity crowd of locals ramming, sauntering or hobbling across Broadway. I assumed they were ATRs. *Yo! Ma peeps.* A glance west and a giant brick building loomed up to the west of Broadway. The Fort Washington Avenue Armory.

Opened in 1920 for the 22nd Regiment, the Armory takes up the whole block. I marched down 168th Street in file with the other ATRs. The windows were covered with iron bars. As I approached the entrance in the middle of Fort Washington Avenue, I noticed a number of folks wearing tags that hung from their necks, identifying them as DOE employees. I walked over to one of them.

"You have to get in line," she said and pointed me farther down the block. I stepped back. There was a line, all right. I started to walk along the edge of the sidewalk. The line of teachers took up half of it. I continued to walk. Teachers and more teachers were standing there, waiting. They were mostly middle aged, a great diversity of size and skin color. Both genders were well represented. There seemed to be no end to this line. It continued as I turned the corner and walked east on 169th Street. Finally I arrived at the end of the line. As soon as I took my place, more teachers filled in behind me. There must have been a thousand or more.

"Hey! Hi!" A teacher in line recognized a colleague walking to the back. "How are you? It's been a while, right?"

"Yep. How are you doing?" As they continued, I saw Angela walking my way.

"Hey! Angela!" I said. She greeted me.

"Angela!" another voice called from behind. It was a pretty, 40-ish woman in tight pants. "How *are* you?"

"Hi," said Angela. She headed back and the two women hugged each other.

"Can you believe this stupid crap?" said the pretty lady. Her straight black hair was tied back into a severe ponytail. Angela shook her head.

"I know. This is ridiculous. How many jobs do you think there really are?"

"This is bullshit," the ponytail spitfire spewed. "It's a total effin' waste of everybody's time. But it's great to see you. We sure had some times together, right? Man, this whole thing is going to hell in a hand basket." Angela gave her a hug and stepped back in my direction.

"I'd better take my place in line. Can you believe this line?" she said to me.

"I've never seen so many teachers in one place. It's a dropout's nightmare. How do you know that lady? Did you guys work together?"

"No. We were both in the rubber room together."

"Really!" Another teacher, a pudgy man, ran up to the ponytail and gave her a big hug. Seeing him, Angela excused herself and went back to the two of them. Hugs all around. It's a rubber room reunion.

The rubber rooms. That's the nickname for the Teacher Reassignment Centers, created as holding places for pedagogues accused of infractions ranging from insubordination to sexual abuse. Accusations could come from administrators or students. Didn't matter. Once accused, teachers were taken out of their schools and assigned to one of these places, awaiting arbitration. Often it took a long time (months, or in some cases, years) to see an arbitrator and even longer to get your case heard. The city and union reached an agreement to disband them in 2010, just as a documentary about them went public. There were 600 teachers assigned to 15 rubber rooms placed around the city. The teachers had to report every school day. I learned of one rubber room, located in trailer outside a schoolyard in the Heights. It had no windows. You can make your own metaphor.

Judging from the camaraderie on the line yesterday, folks in the rubber rooms made friends. Waiting on this line, some of these friends began to raise their voices.

"It's not fair!"

"How dare they!" Ouch. That was loud. It's the ponytail. She was yelling at a quiet, matronly sentry from the DOE with a name tag that said "Joy." "How dare you hold us in line?" she shouted. "This is disrespectful. Disgraceful!"

"Some of the principals are just arriving," the DOE woman explained, a deer in headlights.

"Those principals should be given an 'unsatisfactory' rating for being late," the ponytail continued to rail at the top of her lungs. I felt sorry for the sentry. When the yelling stopped, I turned to the DOE lady.

"It's not your fault," I said.

"Thank you," she said and gave me a grateful smile.

Forty-five minutes later, the line in front of me started to move. DOE sentries were stationed at the front.

"Go up the stairs to the third floor," one of them directed us. A woman with a cane slowly walked up the first few steps.

"You may take the elevator."

She headed inside. Slowly. Painfully.

When I reached the third floor, teachers were lined up again.

"Please go to the desk with the letter of your last name." I walked through a glass door with a small group of teachers. The rest were held behind. A giant sign was spread out across the lobby area. It read "NYC DOE Recruitment Fair." It didn't say "mandatory." Several ladies were sitting behind desks, greeting the throngs. As each desk was occupied, another sentry stopped my group again. When the desks were clear, he let us go. I found my initial and waited my turn.

"May I see your official letter?" a woman behind the desk said. I showed her my mandatory letter. She gave me a mandatory form. "Get a signature for each school you interview with and return this form after your interviews."

"Is it mandatory?" I couldn't help myself.

"Oh yes, it's mandatory," she said with a slight frown. "Just head to your right. You'll see signs for your license." I turned right and followed a number of ATRs to the entrance of an enormous indoor running track that took up the whole interior.

This world-class track, used by several NCAA teams, was jammed with long tables. By the time I walked into the center of the track, many lines of teachers had already formed. They were waiting for their chance to interview with a school rep, usually an AP or principal. The school reps were sitting behind long tables. In front of them were signs bearing the name of their school, the positions available and the grades. Elementary school positions were on the west side. Junior high and high school positions rose in the east. I walked around the entire floor, scanning the signs for high school social studies positions. There were probably eight or nine schools interviewing. The lines for each of these positions were ten teachers deep, at least. Then I found a short line. One teacher was being interviewed. The principal must have just arrived. I took my place behind the man and before you could raise your hand, eight more teachers got in line behind me. It was like a blue-light special at Kmart. Teachers just materialized. I was lucky to be the next one in line. It was easy to eavesdrop on the interview going on two feet in front of me. The school rep, a nice looking young principal, maybe AP, was speaking to a middle-aged male teacher about the job. They talked. And they talked. Teachers on line were grumbling. Five minutes. Ten minutes. Finally I walked up to the AP and very politely excused myself. "I'm so sorry to interrupt. I just wanted to let you know that there are nine teachers on line here."

"Oh, thank you," said the young principal. She was really grateful for the info. That speeded it up. We spoke for a few minutes. She seemed interested in my eclectic background. She was quite a lovely person who needed a social studies teacher who could prepare her students for the global and American history Regents. "So you need someone to teach to the test?" I said.

"Pretty much." She winced and then smiled.

"I'm sure everyone on this line behind me is more qualified than I to do that. But we could have the kids create some amazing historical documentaries in my class. It's a great way to learn history and contrasting points of view."

"It sounds great. But we have to get everyone to pass the Regents."

"I understand. Best of luck with finding the right person." "Thank you. I'll keep your resume, though."

"Thanks—and...oh, I almost forgot. Could you please sign my interview sheet?"

And so the mandatory afternoon went on. I continued around the track, building stamina. I needed it. It took another two hours for me to get to the front of four lengthy lines of teachers. I managed to win four interviews. By 3:30 pm, I hurdled my way back to the DOE desk-people and proudly handed in my sign-in sheet with a total of five signatures. There was no trophy awaiting me at the finish line. However, for my endurance, balance, commitment and ability to doze on my feet, I was awarded a signed form letter to prove to my adopted principal that I participated in the Great DOE Recruitment Fair. I left the track filled with a sense of accomplishment, my work ethic intact. I executed a perfectly adequate routine of running in circles.

Thursday, September 15, 2011
A Love Letter

I attempt to lighten myself up by composing a letter to the DOE:

From the Desk of
Elizabeth Rose

Dear DOE:

Thank you so much for keeping me in the Absent Teacher Reserve. I am so looking forward to this year, traveling from school to school.

Thank you also for assigning us to a different school each week where we can meet lots of new people. Especially kids. With 37—40 kids per class, it's going to be amazing.

I love a fair! Fifteen hundred teachers interviewing for 40 jobs. Great idea for an academic reality show. Maybe we can pitch it to a network as partners. Interested? Have your peeps contact my peeps.

Have a nice fall.

Love,

Ms. Rose
Ms. Rose, ATR

Monday, October 3 to Friday, October 7, 2011
The Final Days

"You'll be covering Ms. D's English class for the next week." Marilyn's call shakes me from my rapt self-involvement in the teachers' lounge. "She wants to meet with you and go over her lesson plan." She and Ms. K are taking 15 students to the Johanneskolen School in Copenhagen for a week. This exchange between the two schools has been going on for several years. A group of Danish high-schoolers spent a week at BCCHS last semester. For coverage, Angela has been assigned to the Spanish class (she speaks Spanish) and I have been given the English class (I'm fairly fluent, myself).

I meet with Ms. D. I'm impressed. She's created a day-by-day schedule of materials to be covered in each class. I'm to follow her chart precisely.

The meat of the unit is contained in the two-sided, 16-page packet she's created entitled:

> Social Contracts, Social Constructs
>
> A collection of carefully created codes that help us to consider the questions:
>
> 1. What is an individual's responsibility in his/her society?
> 2. How do society's *[sic]* create social contracts that shape our lives?

I like the alliteration in the subtitle. As for the typo, no biggie. If I were heading for the land of Danish delight with a boister of teenagers and a rucksack of responsibilities, a couple of typos might be hiding in my packets. Any student who finds a typo in my worksheets gets extra credit.

"They've already read *The Lord of the Flies* and *The Lottery*," she tells me. "For this week, they need to read the packet, take notes and think about 14 fiction and non-fiction codes created by different people from different times and places. They'll work in groups and use this chart." She hands me her *CHARTS FOR ANALYZING SOCIAL CODES*. She continues, "They have to analyze two fictional codes, one school code, one religious code, one social code, one philosophical code and one underground cultural code. I've also given them one extra-credit eighth code analysis. Then, they're going to write their own social code. That's due Friday, October 14." Man. What a great unit.

"Wish I were going to be here then," I say. "I'd love to see what they come up with."

"You're not going to be here when we come back in two weeks?" she asks, genuinely concerned.

"Unfortunately not. Next week is my last week at BCCHS. Then I'm off to another school."

"Oh. That's too bad," she says kindly. "Which school are you going to?"

"I won't know until next Thursday night. They send out our assignments via a website. You have to go online to find out."

"That's crazy," she says.

"Yeah, but it'll be an adventure. Meanwhile, your plans, materials and essential questions are terrific. I'm so glad I get to cover for you."

"I'm sure you'll be wonderful. They're a great bunch of kids. One class is a little dicey...but they're good kids."

"Have a great time in Denmark."

"Thanks. And thanks so much for covering my classes. I really appreciate it."

"I shall be as thorough as possible."

"If you have any questions, please email me. I'll check it every day."

"Will do. Don't worry, now. We'll get through it all. I'll push a little."

"Thanks again so much. Wish you could be here when I get back to tell me all about it."

"I'm sure they will."

"Bon voyage."

My week as a real substitute teacher goes very well. These kids are smart, motivated and, of course, funny. I get to pick brains, ask some teasing questions and boil down some of my fav new-age aphorisms.

"What do you know about Buddhism?" I ask.

"It was started by Buddha," a short, black-haired boy with big cheeks volunteers. I laugh with some of the kids.

"OK. What do you know about Buddha?"

"He was enlightened," a quiet boy volunteers.

"What's enlightened? How did he become enlightened?"

"Umm…there are seven factors of enlightenment. They're on the bottom of the page." A studious girl indicates the seven factors printed on the packet.

"Right. We can all read them but this goes deep. Does anybody know his story?"

"He sat under a tree and meditated," an Asian boy volunteers.

"Right. It was a bodhi tree. He meditated a lot there. One night, this demon, Mara, came to him in meditation. He tempted the Buddha with gorgeous women. No go. Then he turned into a hideous monster. Didn't work. Buddha sat there through it all and Mara disappeared, Siddhartha achieved enlightenment and became the Buddha." The class is silent. "So…can anybody tell me anything more about enlightenment?" No volunteers. "All right…is there anybody in this class who is enlightened?"

A skinny boy with red hair raises his hand.

"No, you're not!" A girl at his table slaps his arm.

"OK," I say. "Here's something to think about. The Buddha said we all suffer, right? And the reason he said we all suffer…? Anybody want to guess?"

"Um…maybe because we're afraid?" a tall, self-possessed boy with long dreadlocks calls out.

"Exactly. Fear is one of the reasons. All feelings, according to the Buddha, cause suffering. And all suffering is based on ignorance. Are you guys still with me?"

"So you use the seven factors of enlightenment and you don't suffer anymore?" The studious girl is on track, searching for an academic answer.

"Maybe. At least...in the moment. It's like, we're all in this room together thinking we're all separate from each other. But the Buddha would say we're not. He would say something like, 'If the wave knew it was also the water, it wouldn't suffer.' "

Just then, the bell rings.

"I'm enlightened." The red-haired boy jumps out of his chair, dodging another slap by the girl next to him.

"Remember—the Buddha said, 'the jailer is ignorance,' " I call out after them.

Just as I'm about to leave the room, the studious girl comes over to me. She looks like she's had an "aha" moment. Oh boy! This is why we teach, I'm thinking. A young mind picks up a big idea and takes it further. Maybe she'll study comparative religions in college. This could be a life changer. I'm so pumped. "Yes?" I say with a smile. I can't wait to hear how I've contributed to her intellectual development. She steps closer to me and in *sotto voce* says,

"Do we have to memorize the seven factors of enlightenment for the test?"

We have some lively discussions as they go through the packet over the week.

"Hey, guys! Did you check out the Code of Hammurabi?" I ask them. It's become my personal fav. "Anything jump out at you with that one?"

"It's got a lot of death in it," says a bright girl.

"Yes. So...where did he live?" Keep 'em thinking.

"Babylon." A freckle-faced boy speaks up.

"Right. He was the Priest King for 43 years. Not such a nice guy, huh? Why would they put you to death back then?"

"Umm...if you steal something that's the property of the temple or the court...." I nod. The hands keep going up.

"If you ensnare another...what's that?" A dark-haired boy with thick glasses asks me. Uh oh. I'm not sure.

"Show me where you see that," I counter.

"The first one: *If anyone ensnare another, putting a ban upon him, but he cannot prove it, then he that ensnared him shall be put to death.*"

"I guess that means you can't tie up your neighbor and put him away for some crime you can't prove. If you do, it's your head," I attempt to clarify. "Anything else jump out?"

"Incest. They burn you for incest."

"Read it, please, out loud."

A sweet little girl volunteers, *"If any one be guilty of incest with his mother after his father, both shall be burned."*

"That would certainly harsh your mellow," I say.

"Does that mean you'd sleep with your mother after you slept with your father?" a boy calls out from a table of smart alecks.

"Interesting question. Anybody notice some other penalties—like what if you are somebody's son and you strike your father?" There's a pause as groups of students rustle their papers, looking for the answer. "It's number 19," I help them.

"They cut off his hands," a bright-eyed girl with dreadlocks calls out.

"Where does it say that?" I ask her.

"If a son strike his father, his hands shall be hewn off." She reads from the packet.

"Ouch," I say. "Check this one out: *If a man strike a free-born woman so that she lose her unborn child, he shall pay ten shekels for her loss. If the woman die, his daughter shall be put to death."*

"They kill his daughter! She didn't do anything," a girl protests.

"Right. Kind of an-eye-for-an-eye and a daughter-for-an-unborn child. Do you see any other code hidden in that one?" They look back at the paper. No one says anything for a moment. I prod them.

"Does this code apply to all pregnant women?"

"Free-born only," someone calls out.

"So what does that tell you?"

"That there were slaves."

"Exactly. Who will read code #25?" A boy's hand shoots up.

"If he kill a man's slave, he shall pay one-third of a mina."

"Good," I say. "I have no idea how much a *mina* is but I'd guess it's less than a *shekel*. Does this remind you of something in American history?" A pause. They're thinking. A Hispanic girl's hand shoots up.

"Slaves were considered 3/5 of a full person…"

"Excellent. We have an historian in our midst. OK, everybody. You're on track. Great stuff, right?"

"I really loved teaching you guys." I say to my last three classes. "Ms. D will be back on Monday. I hope they all had a great trip. I hope you liked this unit as much as I did. I learned a lot. I hope you did." I pause, then add, "You're all so smart. I know you will be very successful in your lives. This is a terrific school." I bid each class farewell on Friday.

"We'll miss you, Ms. Rose," say a couple of girls who come up to me after class.

"I'll miss you too."

Angela and I run into each other downstairs in the office as we sign out. We bid the two secretaries goodbye and give each other a hug.

"Best of luck next week. Stay in touch," Angela says.

"You, too. I'm heading to the Henry Street School for International Studies. It's way the heck down on the Lower East Side."

Where there's a whole new set of social codes.

Tuesday, October 11, 2011

Henry Street School for International Studies (HSSIS)

Weekly Rotation Begins

Columbus Day weekend has come and gone.

Henry Street, no, it ain't Broadway, it's Henry Street…[2]

It's also a far cry from Park Avenue South. It's a trek from the subway. There are rows of buildings, many the remnants of hundred-year-old tenements, some kept up, many ravaged by time. One six-story red-brick façade is dominated by wobbly rusted fire escapes. A few filthy air conditioners hang from its windows. There's a small satellite dish perched on a third-floor landing. The rows persist, thrown up against each other. The next three structures, a brownstone, a red-brick refurbish and a brown 60s modern are in better shape but they all have one thing in common: iron barricades surround their entrance and the windows open behind bars.

I cross Clinton Street and approach a long school building decorated with lettering that says, "Corlears Junior High School." It takes up most of the block. I see no sign indicating HSSIS, so I head into the front entrance and sign in with security.

"Is this the building for Henry Street School?"

[2] from *Funny Girl*, lyrics by Bob Merrill, music by Julie Styne.

"Fourth floor," says the guard as she checks my ID. "Take the back stairway." No *hi how're ya?* Security is serious biz here. I follow her directions down the hall. Students are buzzing past security guards. Crews of boys saunter along, slowed down by their sagging jeans belted around their thighs. Their high-top sneakers look brand new. The "N" word bounces off the drab halls indiscriminately. It's second nature. It jars my tender spirit after four weeks in the well-mannered halls of BCCHS.

Upstairs, I find the main office, a drab and dusty place. Doesn't seem to have been painted since the building opened in 1968. An unsmiling woman appears behind the counter. Maybe I can cheer up her morning.

"Hi. I'm Elizabeth Rose, your new ATR," I say with a bright smile. "I'll be here all week. Please let me know how I can help out."

"Fill out a punch card," she says and hands me a blank card. "Print your name only," she continues. "You don't have to punch in and out every day but you need to punch out and in for lunch." Huh? I have never worked in a "punch card" school. I don't get her logic but, since she seems to have woken up on the wrong side of her nest of stinging nettles, I let it go.

"Just go into the teachers' lounge. Down the hall. Someone will call you if a teacher is absent," she says, happy to get back to her sulking.

The teachers lounge is pretty big, with large dirty windows overlooking the industrial landscape. No view of the East River, even though it's only a few blocks away. There's a large table in the middle, computer stations up against the wall, a copy machine and a small area with cushioned chairs. A few teachers are talking and prepping for their classes. I sit at a computer station. Don't want to disturb any microbes inhabiting the cushions. I attempt to get on line. This old Dell seems to have less power than the Apollo 13's computer. It takes ten minutes for it to boot up. While I'm waiting, the first-period bell rings and all but one of the teachers leave. Although I have smiled at everyone who has given me eye contact, no one has found any particular reason to engage me in light conversation. Two teachers, one a handsome youngish fellow, the other an older lady, have remained behind. They are both sitting at the large table quietly reading newspapers. I decide to join them.

"Hi. I'm Elizabeth."

"I'm Barry."

"I'm Ms. Clay."

"So, I'm only here for a week," I say cautiously.

"Me, too. You're an ATR?" asks Barry.

"Yes."

"Me, too."

"So am I," says Ms. Clay. An ATR trifecta! Ms. Clay goes back to reading Page Six. Barry, a sweet, slightly gloomy guy, turns to me.

"This is so miserable," he says. "I can't believe what they're doing to us." I know he wants me to commiserate but I have never been particularly skilled at stoking negative energy.

"Well...I was just thinking about how nice the weather is and that this year could turn into a pretty interesting adventure."

"You are so right!" he says, and his entire being perks up.

"Yeah. I figure I can make something of it. When am I ever going to get a chance to see so many schools in such a short period of time, you know?"

"You have some great energy. I am so glad to meet you," he says and he shakes my hand. "I'm an English teacher," says he, "but I'm also an actor and a jazz singer."

"Nice. Me, too."

"Which one?"

"All of the above, except social studies and I wouldn't call myself a jazz singer," I say, thinking of Jolson. Singer is plenty.

"Really? What do you sing?"

"Everything from opera to hip hop," I answer. He laughs. "I have been performing a one-woman show I wrote. It has lots of styles of music." We talk about our performing careers for a minute. His energy gets progressively happier.

"I'm waiting to hear from a friend of mine who is a principal in the Bronx. He wants to hire me as dean. But he can't hire me until next month. So I guess I can just wait this out."

"This is miserable, don't you think?" Ms. Clay looks up from her tabloid. "I can't believe they are doing this to us, moving us around like this. I'm too old for this sort of thing."

"Yes, it can be difficult for some teachers," I say. She's soft-spoken, old school; a lady with lovely mannerisms. Her calf-length dress is fitted at the top. She has carefully closed the top button of her collar. A string of cultured pearls hangs from her neck.

"What is your subject area?" I ask her.

"Typing and shorthand." Wha? Is she a visitor from 1958?

"So you teach computers nowadays?" I ask her.

"No. I never learned computers," she says. "I really don't care for them. I taught in a commercial school until they closed it. Now I'm starting this terrible rotation."

"I hope it is not too difficult for you to get around," I say.

"I can do it. If I can't, I'll retire. I tell you, this profession has certainly changed since I started teaching. It's going down the drain. There's no respect anymore. The way they treat teachers…they ought to be ashamed of themselves."

"You can say that again," says Barry. I slip away to the ladies room to get away from the complaint bureau. Their points are well taken but I choose not to sing the blues, unless of course, they're paying me for the gig.

I spend the rest of the morning in the teachers' lounge, clicking on the dull Dell and growing a couple of new age spots as I wait for the next email to open. It's lunchtime. I head into the office. Several middle-aged ladies are now there, bantering happily in three languages: English, Spanish and Spanglish. It's a much cheerier place. The secretary almost smiles at me when she sees me. She hands me a paper with the school schedule blocked in.

"You have a program. Sixth grade. Seventh period."

"Sixth grade? I've never taught sixth grade. My license is for social studies, seventh through twelfth grade." Ninth graders are tough enough. I'm a little scared of sixth graders. "Well, you have to speak to Mr. A," she says, calmly pulling a stinging nettle from beneath her thumbnail with her front incisors.

I stand there. No additional information is forthcoming so I ask, "Who's Mr. A?"

"He's the dean of the middle school." I wait a moment for her to tell me how and where I can find him but again, *nada*.

"Is he nearby?"

"His office is down the hall. Turn right." I head out, turn right and find his skinny office. I introduce myself and mention the technical issue to him.

"Oh, that's all right for today. Don't worry. It's a small class. Their teacher has to go to a meeting. He left a reading for you to give them. They're special ed. You'll have a para. I'll check in with you. Don't worry. You'll do fine." Nice guy.

I go downstairs to begin my search for a nice $5 lunch. There's nothing but a *bodega*. The guy scratching himself in its doorway, sipping his *cervesa*, does not entice me to enter. Moving on, I find myself standing in front of the famed Henry Street Settlement. For the past 120 years, it has served as the heart, soul, kitchen, nurse and muse for so many immigrants who have landed in this neighborhood, often their first stop along the bumpy road to realizing their American dreams. Standing here, my stomach has stopped growling but I've got a different craving. Maybe there's a life I can touch this week. The "N" word and sagging pants notwithstanding, these kids are dealing with poverty. That's the same poverty my family faced as it crossed the Atlantic from Eastern Europe in search of freedom. We're all the same after all, right?

All of us? Really? Even this hyperactive sixth-grade lad who is racing around my classroom like an inebriated twister? There are two other adults in the room beside myself: a para and a middle-aged male teacher who is sitting in the back of the room during his prep period. They have both risen to help me. The other five sixth graders are still at their desks. I've passed out their reading material (Earth science) but the floorshow has taken their rapt attention.

"I'll take him," the nice teacher offers. "He knows me," he adds. "Come here, Dalyonell," he calls out to the boy who's just snuck up behind one of the girls, poised for some mischief. "Let's work with these puzzles. Don't run now, OK?" Dalyonell runs over to him and somehow the teacher gets him to sit down at a small table opposite him. They start working on a puzzle. I'm so grateful I want to kiss this teacher. I've been in this classroom 13 minutes. Just before his save, I was ready to run out, screaming, cursing all students, the Lower East Side and every immigrant who ever crossed over to our shores, especially my own family. If they hadn't come here, I wouldn't be chasing a maniacal midget whose name I can't pronounce. Get me out of here. I hate sixth grade. Help. Help me. Please.

A minute later, the teacher and Dalyonell are quietly putting puzzle pieces together, the rest of the students are reading and I'm waiting for my tongue to stop bleeding where I bit into it. I'm drinking my own blood and I haven't even had lunch yet. You make your own vampire joke. I'm too exhausted.

My first day at Henry Street School for International Studies ends as I drag my aching soul four interminable blocks to the East Broadway subway station. Self-incrimination arises from the detritus of desolation. The dominos start to fall: ineffective teacher, lousy classroom manager, can't even entertain 11-year-olds, stuck in a B job, not living my best life, show biz dreams light years away. That song from *Funny Girl* rewrites itself as I descend into the hole:

Henry Street has something it ain't had so far,
A frustrated, famished, & tongue-chewing, mortified,

Big finish here! Hold those notes!
Failed...Child...Star!
FAST FADE TO BLACK.

Wednesday, October 12, 2011
And the Week Drags On

I do not wish to cast aspersions on HSSIS. To anyone who might still be reading this, please allow me to reiterate: this is merely my story. I'm just reporting my first impressions. If I were a visiting dignitary or someone sent here to rate the school for its annual DOE report card, I'm sure the red carpet would be rolled out, I'd be shown the best classes and teachers and offered a nice cup of coffee. Puckered lips would be proffered to my posterior.

Given the enormous daily challenges a principal endures, you would have to be a mental case to take on a job like this without being driven by inner purpose and passion. A principal's job is 24/7. Lives are at stake. Issues are knotty. Some people will file grievances against you. Something inside you must find a way to lead even though many days are so overwhelming you're ready to bolt out of the building, fly to the Caymans and scuba dive with barracudas. Quickly, principals learn to desensitize themselves to the daily bombardments, persevere and, when the day is done, retire to the iso-cave back home where, undisturbed, they can chew on spaghetti and nails *alla diavola*.

So, to any school leaders with the stomach to plow through my sophomoric twaddle, please understand that I honor your mettle. I understand why there's no welcome wagon for the likes of my rotating ATR compatriots and me.

It's 8:45 am. I arrive at the teachers' lounge. First period starts at 9 am. The gloomy school secretary comes in and hands me a paper with a grid. Three classes are circled. They must be mine.

"Here's your schedule for today," she grunts.

"Good morning," I say, trying to acknowledge our common membership in the family *Hominidae*. Getting no reaction I continue. "Who am I subbing for?"

"I don't know. Let's see." She grabs the schedule from me. I look over her shoulder.

"It says 'Abraham.' "

"Right. Abraham." With no more info forthcoming, I ask, "What does he teach?"

"I have no idea!"

"You have no idea?"

"I have no idea."

"Well, it would be nice to have a subject and lesson plan...you know, like a normal school?" I try to keep it light. She is not amused.

"You can ask Mr. K. You know who he is?"

"I have no idea."

"The programming teacher."

"Oh...him."

Another sixth-grade class. Jeeze...

"Yo Miz. You our sub?" A small, energetic boy is excited to see me.

"Yes. Hi. I'll write my name on the board."

"Yo, you seen this Zombie commercial, Miz?"

"No. I don't think so," I say as I turn from the board. Just then, another boy sitting next to the first blurts out, "Miz! You come to my house and I'll get out my gun. I got one there."

"A toy gun?" I ask him. As a teacher, I am mandated to report anything that gives me reasonable cause to suspect child abuse or maltreatment. My ears are up.

"Naah. It's a real gun. My pop's gun."

"It's loaded?" I ask quietly.

"Yeah. He showed me how."

"You need to stay away from guns. You could hurt or kill someone or yourself."

"Naah, Miz. You should come over. I'll show it to you."

As soon as this class is over, I'm heading to the AP with my report. For now, I've got five sixth graders, special-ed kids, no lesson plan and no idea what the subject is.

"So what are you guys learning about?" I ask them. They're already starting to get restless, jumping up, moving quickly around the room.

"Nothin'."

"I'm sure you're learning something," I say, smiling. "Please come back to your desk!" I call out to the Zombie-phile.

"Naah. Our regular teacher left last week. We got our new teacher on Monday but she absent today."

"OK, then." I'm thinking fast. I've got 40 more minutes with these kids. "You must have some homework. Could you do your homework now? Then you'll have more time after school."

"I ain't got no homework."

"Me neither."

"Well...do you guys have any games or art projects you'd like to work on?"

"Yeah!!" Zombie prince runs to the back of the room.

"Please walk, don't run," I call out, trying to sound like a sixth-grade teacher.

"We got these!" He pulls some Sharpies and construction paper from a shelf.

"OK. Those of you who want to draw may do so. The others may read."

"Can we listen to music?"

"I don't think the school wants you to."

"Come on, Miz. Please."

"No. I can't let you do this." Wish I could. It's a great babysitter.

In a couple of minutes, several students have helped themselves to art supplies, one is drawing in chalk on the board and one is listening to music. I have no complaint. I make a note to give the AP immediately after class:

These students need more homework.

Latif may have a loaded gun at home.

I never did find out this class's subject.

"Thank you." The AP seems to appreciate my efforts but he doesn't seem surprised. My next class is seventh-grade Earth science. Six students. It is a lovely group who is focused on their worksheets.

For my third, and last, coverage of the day, I head across the hall. There is a teacher in the room. He's holding several students in place who seem to be rather anxious to escape into the hall. My incoming class waits in the hall. A boy arrives, obviously quite frustrated that he can't go in.

"Outta my way, nigga!" he commands, ramming into another boy.

"You don wanna be gettin' in my face." The second boy smacks the first on his arm.

"Guys. Let's calm down, please." My entreaty goes ignored. It looks like someone's head is about to meet the brick wall. "Please, guys." The first boy spins around and looks at me with daggers. *"Dirty-ass fuckin' bitch!"*

I quickly turn around and give a perfunctory look at my rear end. "Really? I thought my shower cleaned it up. Thanks for the heads-up." He is not amused, but the other kids crack up.

"*Yo*! You heard what she said?"

"Yo nigga, she crushed you."

At that moment, another teacher happening by walks over to my personal dresser.

"You're coming with me right now. Security!" And the two of them walk down the hall. The kids and I file in. The teacher who held the first group is now back in the room.

"I'll take them," he tells me. He turns to the class, already seated at their desks. They know him. They seem to respect him. "Today we're going to learn how to change fractions to *improper* fractions," he says. No irony here.

"I have an emergency coverage for you right now." The friendly AP comes into the room and hands me a schedule. Global history. I head down the hall to the classroom. The room is filled with older kids. They must be ninth and tenth grade. One look at me and they decide they're going to have some fun with the ole' substitute teach.

"You our substitute?" A couple of boys call to me from the back.

"Word." I shift to their aboriginal lexicon.

"Yo! You hear what she said!" A girl in front elbows the boy sitting on her desk. "She said 'word'!!! How you learn that, Miz?"

"Hanging out with a crew like yours."

"Fa real?"

"Word." They laugh. "So my name is Ms. Rose. Or you can call me 'yo miz'."

"Yo Miz!!! You hear???" They're calling out to each other. "She says you can call her yo miz!"

"Miz!!! Miz!!!" A boy calls out to me from the back of the room.

"Hey. I said you have to call me by *both* of my names, *Yo* and *Miz*," I counter.

"Yo, dumb ass. She playin' you." The girl in front has caught on.

"OK. Your teacher wants you to read this chapter that's on the board."

"Yo Miz!" the boy in the back calls out.

"S'up?"

"Yo—!!! You heard? She said 's'up'!" A big girl in the first row grabs her friend.

"Do I have to read this chapter?" The boy in the back is testing me.

"Are you in this class?" I ask with a smile.

"No—he ain't in this class," his buddy calls out.

"Yo Miz. Yes, I am!!"

"OK. I believe you," I say. "You're in this class."

"Thanks, Miz." He smacks his pal. "So I gotta read this, too?"

"Word," I say. More laughter.

"But Miz. I don't know how to read."

"Fa real?" I say. "I don't know how to teach you to read. I only know how to teach students who already know how to read. Perhaps you could draw pictures. Do you want crayons?" We're playin' each other. Several girls and one boy start reading. A group of boys continues to talk to each other in the back of the room. I walk over to them, stand quietly and listen to their conversation. It is rife with the "N," "F" and "S" words.

"Guys," I inject sweetly when there's a lull in the cursing. "Could you please clean up your language a bit? After all, we are in school." I speak quietly…respectfully.

"Oh…sorry, Yo Miz," a boy with a backwards Cincinnati Reds cap says.

"*Fuck yes*," says another boy whose arm is tattooed with an automatic weapon. I laugh.

"Lovely," I say. "I certainly appreciate your cooperation."

"Yo. Watch your mouth, nigga! She's respecting you." The first boy smacks the other on his arm.

"OK, guys. Let's see you start the reading, OK? If you do it all and answer the questions, I'll give you each a hundred dollars." One of the boys jumps up.

"Fa real? You heard? You gonna gimme a hundred dollars if I read?"

"*And* answer the five questions. In good English with good grammar and spelling."

"Fa real Miz?? You fa real?" Everybody in the class has now turned to us. It's silent.

"Yo! I'm gassin' you. Shhh. No explosion. Please. They'll kick my ass out of here if you yell."

"Shut up, nigga!! Don't get her in trouble." One of the girls on the side becomes my defender.

"Hey!!!" A big girl jumps out of her seat up against the wall. She looks at me, full of indignation.

"Miz!! You saw what he did?" There's a boy sitting in the seat in front of her. He's wearing a tank shirt and flashy red boxers. His pants are buckled right above his reproductive system.

"No," I say seriously. "What happened?"

"He grabbed me." She turns to him and yells in his face, "You keep your fuckin' hands off me, nigga!" All right. I look at the clock on the wall. Twenty-eight minutes left in this class. I need help. I open the door.

"I'm going to ask the dean to come in, guys. It's OD in here right now. You have to settle down."

"Yo! You heard what she said? *OD*?"

"Everybody, please take your seat, all right? Now, when the dean comes…" Right then a teacher walks by. I stop him and quietly ask him to get the dean. I turn back to the kids. "I've just asked for the dean."

"Miz!" A girl with beautiful pink and blonde extensions raises her hand.

"Yes?" I assume it's a question about the assignment.

"You married?"

"Yes," I say. "But I tell you what, I'll tell you all about my marital life after you get the assignment done."

"*Nigga*, I'm gonna kick your ass if you grab me again." The big girl jumps up again. She's about to fight the kid in the tank shirt. No dean yet. I have to take charge. I walk over to the boy.

"You need to turn around in your seat and face the front of the class." I'm serious. He does not move.

"What's your name?" I ask him. I don't expect an answer. I speak respectfully, quietly enough that the others can't hear.

"I know you are a good kid and like to have fun, right?" He nods. "I didn't see what happened. Perhaps you did something, perhaps you didn't. But you need to turn around because you look guilty, turned around in your seat, facing her." His mouth is half open, his eyes empty and hard. He's silent. I continue. "So, the thing is, it's not right to touch other students. Also, there are laws. You can get in trouble for doing that. Do you understand?"

"Uh huh."

"Good. So if I go back to the front of the class, I can trust you'll keep your hands off anyone, right?"

"Yeah, Miz." As I walk back to the teacher's desk, I turn. He's grabbed her with his arm around her neck.

"Not allowed," I say to him firmly, walking back over to him. "I have to report that to the dean."

"No, Miz."

"I'm sorry, but you said I could trust you."

"I don't give a shit." The door's still open. Another teacher comes by.

"Do you know how I can get the dean? I have a problem in here."

"I'll get him," the teacher says and takes off.

"Would you like to sit at the teacher's desk?" I ask the big girl who's the object of the grabbing. She picks up her bag, struts over to the front and plops down in the teacher's chair.

"That nigga touches me again, I'm gonna kick his fuckin' balls off him," she says to no one in particular. She opens her bag, takes out a mirror and applies lip-gloss. I walk over to the boy. With the big girl removed to the teacher's desk, he has nobody to harass. I sit down in an empty chair next to him and open a textbook to the assigned reading.

"I have an idea," I say. He's still staring across the room. "I think you're a good kid underneath all the cursing and grabbing. So I thought, maybe you and I could read together." A glance. A tiny crack in his armor. "Could we work together? Would you mind if I put this on your desk?"

"Naah, Miz. Do whatever you want."

"OK. Thanks." I put the open textbook on his desk. "Can you read the title to me?" He looks down at the title, which is, *Napoleon: Son of the Revolution or Emperor-Dictator?* He's stymied. "Maybe sound it out?"

"Naah. This is wack."

"So this guy was named Napoleon," I say. "He was a mean general. He rode a big white horse and if he had a Facebook page, you'd see his picture with his hand stuck inside his chest."

"You on Facebook?" he turns and asks me.

"Yes, but not with students. Anyway, this is about Napoleon. He was French. *Tu comprend ce que j'ai dit?"*

"Yo Miz! Wha'?"

"That's French. You know where they speak French?"

"Naah." He starts to pick up a pencil and write on the desk.

"So... here's the French Empire. Napoleon got his huge gang together and killed thousands of people. You see France?"

I point to the map. "Just point at France. See the F?" I smile at him and he looks down at the map. He slowly points to France.

"That's it! Great!" I say. "Now you see France is kind of gray. Well, right next to it is this big country, Spain. Do you see Spain?" He takes a moment and then puts his finger on Spain.

"Excellent," I say. "Now what do you notice about Spain? Is it all gray like France?"

"Naah."

"Right!" I praise him. "What does Spain look like?"

"It's got lines..."

"Excellent again. It has diagonal lines going through it. That means that France beat up Spain and got control of it. Are there any other countries with those diagonal lines going through them?" He slowly points to the countries labeled Confederation of the Rhine, Kingdom of Italy and the Grand Duchy of Warsaw.

"You got it! Very good," I say. "Do you see any other countries that are neither gray nor have the diagonal lines?"

"Yeah. This one. It's black."

"Exactly. Can you read what it's called?" He's gotten so many things right he actually makes a stab at reading.

"Aus...ti...."

"Austrian Empire. Say that. "

"Austin Empire."

"Almost. It's Aus-tri-an. So, any guess why the Austrian Empire is colored black on this map?"

"'Cause they're niggas?" He's having fun with me.

"Language, please. No. They're not African-Americans. You see that box on the right of the map?" I point to it. "What's it called?"

"Ummm...key."

"Great! So you see in the key that there's gray for the French Empire, diagonal lines for states under direct French control and black for what...?"

"Ummm..." He tries to read. "...states un...der..." He gets stuck and starts writing on the desk again.

"Pencil, please," I say and hold out my hand.

"Naah, Miz. Ma bad. I stopped." He doesn't give it to me but as he's ceased his current engraving project, I acknowledge him.

"Thank you. So the black state. You know it's not France, which is gray. You know it's not controlled by France, which is diagonal lines. Any idea what black is?"

"Naah, Miz."

"Come on. Make a guess." He looks up at the ceiling.

"I don't give a shit." He's given up.

"Language, please. You're almost there. Black is for states that are allied with France. It's like turf wars. You got your enemies and you got your allies. The black is the ally. It's the..." —and I point to the map— "Austrian Empire."

He suddenly turns and punches the boy diagonally across from him.

"Hey! Come on. OD! You were doing so well."

"This is boring."

"Actually, if you could have seen these guys shooting their guns from the back of their horses and all the dead bodies, you wouldn't think it's so boring. I'll bet if you had a Napoleon video game, you'd like it better than Grand Theft Auto."

"You play Grand Theft Auto, Miz?"

"No. It's horribly violent."

"You nice, Miz."

"So are you," I say. The bell rings. He jumps up, runs into the hall and grabs the big girl just as the dean walks up.

"I got this," the dean says to me. "You're in trouble, now..." I hear him say as he walks the kid toward his office.

Three days at HSSIS = one millennium.

Friday, October 14, 2011

Speaking of millennia, I receive an email Wednesday night asking me to report for another mandatory interview today. There's an opening for a social studies teacher at Millennium High School.

I head to school to let the principal know I have to leave for my interview. She looks up at me annoyed, as I gently knock on her open door.

"You may leave at ten and I expect you back in the building by noon," she declares. Her dark stare burns my retina.

"OK. Thanks so much." I cautiously back out. Whew! I got out of there alive. *Thank you.*

Later that night I think about the principal of my old school.

"You're a professional," he said when I asked him for a little extra time away from school to meet with a TV-network rep. I had a show to pitch and the rep was only available in the middle of the day. "I trust you." He was right. He could count on me. I wanted to prove him right. Leadership 101.

Today I'm off to Millennium by subway, emerging at Battery Park, crossing Broadway to Beaver Street. There are police everywhere. When I get to Broad Street, an officer waves me over to the east side. The west side of the street is barricaded, reserved for Occupy Wall Street protestors. Yellow police tape defines the boundaries. The air is serious. I see no protestors, but the police seem war-weary. I follow the barricades and turn left on South William. A nondescript glass door bearing the sign for Millennium High School is on my right.

"Tenth floor, elevator's behind me." The security guard smiles at me. First impression: this is a happy place. Upstairs, I see that it's also clean and airy with lots of light coming in the windows. In the office, a beautiful secretary wearing bright reds and oranges greets me with her Caribbean lilt. "He will be with you soon. Won't you please have a seat?"

In a few minutes, a tall, handsome man emerges from an office. He gives me a smile and extends his hand. "Ms. Rose?" I stand up and shake his.

"I'm Mr. R. Won't you come and have a seat?" He's a very soft-spoken, dapper chap, as my dad might have said. Respectful. He puts me right at ease. "We have a maternity leave coming up in American history. It will start in November and continue until March. So tell me a bit about yourself, if you don't mind, while I look over your resume."

I yada yada about myself for a minute and he stops me.

"You raised over $325,000 for your school and they let you go?" He looks at me quizzically.

"I guess there wasn't a position."

"They couldn't create a position for you?" He's the second principal to make note of this.

"I suppose not," I say, and we move on. He's respectful and his questions are thought-provoking and challenging. I ask him about the school.

"We are sending our students to good colleges," he says. "I'd like to schedule a demo lesson for you next week. I'll consult with my staff and get back to you."

"Oh…sure." He's interested? I'm going to have to teach something… social studies to really bright kids who are heading to Harvard. He's going to observe me. OK. I'm intimidated.

"Will you need a lesson plan from me?" Don't let 'em see you sweat.

"No. We'll email you a lesson plan," he says. Whew! That's a relief.

Sort of. I head back through the OWS barricades. Three trains later I arrive at Essex Street and find my way back to humble HSSIS. It's 12:30. Nobody cares.

The day ends with a bang. I'm suddenly given an eighth-period class in the chemistry lab. It's not a chemistry class. It's an Earth science class but I am given no lesson plan, reading or materials. These kids are tall, loud and one of them hostile enough to keep me on alert. We are way down at the end of the hall.

"I'm sorry, guys, but I wasn't left any work to give you," I announce over the din of their conversations.

"We don't do nothin' in this class nohow." A game of hangman starts on the board. A thick boy sporting a gang scarf radiates hostility. He is hanging with a couple of other tattooed boys. One has a tattoo close to his eye. Gang teardrop? They are oblivious to me. I try to joke a bit, use a little of their hip hop slang, but it's a tough room. I back off. A tall, older teacher with a permanent frown steps in. He's their regular teacher.

"Quiet down. I have a meeting. Take out your binders and do the Regents test." He's yelling; they're ignoring. He turns to me. "I doubt you'll get any work out of them. Just let the period run out. I'll try to look in on you if I can."

This one's over my head. Dark energy saturates the room. I hole up at a desk by the door, put earplugs in and pretend I'm safe. Every few minutes, I check the hallway. There are a few minor explosions for the next 25 minutes, but nothing treacherous. The final bell at HSSIS rings and I head to the office where I put my time card in the "out" rack.

Monday, October 17, 2011

MANHATTAN /HUNTER COLLEGE HIGH SCHOOL FOR SCIENCES (MHCHSS)

You May Sit in the Back With Your Teacher's License

It's been a busy weekend of emails. Friday late afternoon, the principal of Millennium emails me, confirming he'd like to have me teach a demo lesson on Monday. I confirm and he sends me the lesson plan. I'm to teach the Articles of Confederation in 45 minutes.

I also get an email from an assistant principal of the iSchool, asking me to interview for a full-time position. At the new iSchool, they're "rethinking high school education for the 21st century by using technology to facilitate student learning." Technology? My ears are up. I mention it to Angela on the phone.

"Oh. The iSchool would be a perfect place for you. It's really high tech and with your artsy-technology music, documentary-film making...you'd bring so much creativity."

OK. I'm a little excited. iSchool. Who knew?

It's Monday morning and I'm a bit uneasy as I cross town to start my second week as a teaching gypsy. Manhattan/Hunter College High School for Sciences is one of six small high schools occupying the former Martin Luther King Jr. High School. My apprehension is justified. This building has had a rep. Opened in 1975 with an ambitious dream to build a great, modern school right across from Lincoln Center, the dream became a recurrent nightmare. By the

1990s there was a shooting, gang beating and sexual assaults. With another shooting in 2002, the DOE shut the school down. Eventually, it re-opened as six small schools.

Today, as I climb the stairs to its large concrete plaza I see scads of students lined up, waiting to pass through metal detectors. It is still early morning. No one seems outraged or inconvenienced. This is what we do here. Every day.

"You don't have to wait in line," a security guard calls out to me. Darn. He doesn't think I'm a teenager.

"Welcome!" says a hefty lady security guard at the desk. She's absolutely adorable.

"Nice to meet you," the principal says when I reach the school's office. She's busy but quite gracious. "We need you to be in the room with our student teacher. The regular teacher has taken a sudden leave of absence so there must be a certified teacher in the room. It's four social studies classes."

"Terrific. That's my license area."

"Oh that's very good. Perhaps you can give her some support. She's a very good student teacher but I'm sure you'll have some input."

"Happy to," I say. "By the way, I'm scheduled to give a demo lesson at Millennium High School today at 12:45. I hope it's not a problem." She thinks for a moment.

"No. We'll cover for you. Go ahead. You can leave from there because school ends at 2:50 and you won't have time to get back. Just fill in this morning and then we'll see you again tomorrow. Good luck with your demo," she adds.

It's so nice to meet a fair person. I'll bet she's a great leader.

"Oh! Here's the teacher you'll be working with," she says to me. A pretty 20-something lady comes by in a tight skirt and 4-inch heels. "This is the teacher who will be with you this week, Ms. Teal. She's a social studies teacher," she adds.

"Great," says Ms. Teal. "See you in a few minutes."

Everyone in the office is upbeat, helpful. It's good to be back in a happy, respectful place. Maybe Dr. King's dream is getting another chance.

"Hi, Ms. Teal," the students greet her as they come in.

"Hi Danesha. Hi Sam." These kids respect her even though she's only about six years older than they are. "OK. We have a test today. Remember?" She hands out a six-page, double-sided test, packed with Regents-style questions. "You'd better know your Jainism from your Daoism, your Judaism from your Shinto..." ...yada yada.

She's in charge. Doesn't need me. I'm merely a teaching license in the back of the room. A second global class comes and goes. Time for me to head downtown to teach the Articles at Millennium.

I study my notes on the subway, navigate through the OWS barricades past crowds of tourists and Wall Street types and ride up the ten floors to Millennium. The principal is expecting me.

"Thanks so much for coming," he says. "You'll be teaching an 11th-grade class in American history. I will be there as well as our assistant principal, also a social studies teacher. I'll take you downstairs to the classroom."

I'm nervous. I've never been observed teaching social studies before. My depth of knowledge and experience are not particularly deep. But what the hell? I'm an entertainer. I write the "do now" on the board:

If colonial patriots were opposed to monarchy, what features of government might they have approved?

"Hi. I'm Ms. Rose," I introduce myself when the kids get settled. They're polite, not sure what to expect. With the principal and AP sitting in the back of the room, they're well behaved. "Today before we look at the Articles of Confederation, I'd like you to take a few minutes and write your thoughts about this." I point to the board. "Anybody need paper?"

I introduce the AOCs. I'm talking too fast. The kids are bright. They do the exercises. Before I know it, 45 minutes are up.

"OK, guys. The bell is about to ring but....whoa...there's something that really struck me today coming down to Millennium. You know, the Articles were written right after Shea's Rebellion. I'm bringing this up because the issues they were protesting back then are behind the protests right downstairs in the street. The banks loaned money to farmers during the American Revolutionary War. When the war was over, they came after the farmers for their money. Now these farmers had fought, risked their lives for their country. After the war, everything was drained. Nobody had any money. Still, the banks started foreclosing on their farms and this fellow Shea and a bunch of farmers took to the streets, protesting the greedy banks. Anybody see a parallel?" A couple of hands go up. The bell rings.

"Wait. One more second. You know that the banks issued sub-prime mortgages over the past few years? It's practically the same story. People couldn't pay. The banks started foreclosing—taking their homes away. The economy collapsed and these people are protesting in the streets, just like Shea. Think of that when you study the articles tonight. Thanks guys. You can go now." I'm sweating.

"Come with me and we'll do a post," says the principal after the kids leave. I'm breathing heavily as I sit down in the AP's office.

"So how do you think you did?" he asks me.

"Well, I could have used some more time. Also, I think I was talking too fast and...I was hoping to get a discussion going about the differences between Jefferson and Hamilton."

"I like the way you slipped in Shea's Rebellion. That made it relevant."

"Thanks. So what else did you think?" I ask him. He gives me some helpful comments and some resources on hierarchical reading strategies. He's a class act. I leave, convinced the job belongs to somebody who has actually taught social studies before.

I'm feeling pretty fine. I showed up. I taught my first demo. Nobody threw any rotten fruit at me. I like Millennium. If I decide to be a teacher when I grow up, I could dig it.

Thursday, October 20, 2011

The week has been easy. I'm amazed as I watch Ms. Teal command the room. She expects to graduate Hunter College in January. This is supposed to be her student teaching assignment but she's been shoved into the role of full-time teacher unexpectedly.

"I have no idea," she says to me when I ask her why the regular teacher took a sudden leave of absence. "Nobody seems to know."

It's more impressive when I realize that she is teaching both global *and* American history for the first time. When she's not standing in front of the class, she's grading papers, prepping or meeting with other members of the history department.

"I just want to be a teacher," she tells me. "I love teaching." At 23 years old, she's on her way to mastering the profession. I wish she would let me pitch in a bit more, but she needs to be in control. I continue to offer passive support.

She moves fast. It's her job to get her students Regents-ready. No time to stop for much thinking. Too bad. The material is so rich. In global, she speeds through the Enlightenment, the French Revolution, *A Tale of Two Cities* and the Industrial Revolution. In American history class, it's the Articles of Confederation (*Hey! May I help?)*, the Constitution, checks and balances, the Fourteenth Amendment and judicial review. My head spins as every day, she pulls another pile of worksheets from the ample file left by the disappearing teacher and steers her charges through the enormous load of info, helping them with concepts, asking a few questions about essential ideas, feeding them large serving platters filled with minutiae while reminding them they'll have a test at the end of the week. This is high-velocity instruction. I'm not used to this Regents-inflicted pressure. Regents or no Regents? Guess the arguments are strong on both sides. Regents are good: Regents prep allows them an overview. They can go into the details later in college. Versus...Regents are bad: let them study an historical topic of interest (and relevance) in depth and guide them as they develop critical thinking and scholarly writing. I lean towards the latter, but I think some testing is valuable. It teaches you to figure out what's important to the tester...an especially good skill to have, if you're planning on becoming a lifelong codependent.

Early this morning, I'm assigned another mandated interview at a small school in the Seward Park Educational Complex on Essex Street. This is a dual-language school (Mandarin) for Asian immigrant students. So it's back down to the Lower East Side. Briefly, here's how the interview goes:

"Do you have an ESL license?"

"No, social studies."

"Have you worked with ESL students?"

"Oh, yes. I've had quite a few over the years. I love working with them."

"But you don't have an ESL license."

"No."

"So you can't teach here."

"OK. I'm just wondering why you scheduled this interview?"

"We are looking for a social studies teacher."

"Right. I'm qualified for that. But you also might have mentioned the ESL requirement in your job posting."

"You need ESL to teach here."

"Xie Xie," I add in my best Mandarin. Just for fun.

Friday, October 28, 2011

Tuesday, I go to the iSchool for an interview, excited about tapping into the alchemy where technology meets the arts.

I imagine the school will resemble an Apple store with great light pouring in, students gathered in pods, creating brilliant projects while happy teachers guide them in a collaborative spirit. Instead, as I cross Soho Square Park, an ancient five-story building looms up in front of me with a cornerstone from 1848. Welcome to the iSchool, situated on the top two floors of one of the oldest buildings in the city. I guess fiber-optics do not stream through its vintage viscera.

In my quest for the AP, I'm sent to a large room, a cafeteria (?) packed with students. A giant HD screen on the wall is flashing the day's schedule. Other than that, it seems to be pretty low tech. To the right of me several makeshift offices stand, their glass partitions allowing all the student noise to bounce back into the big room, amplified. I walk over to the first office. A young, 30-ish man is sitting inside, sporting a tailored suit.

"Excuse me," I say to him. The din of the students forces me to speak louder than normal. "I'm looking for the AP."

"Are you here for an interview?"

"Yes, social studies."

"I'll be right with you. Please take a seat outside." He motions me to a small chair in front of his office. While I wait, I check out the students in the center of the big room. They seem bright and engaged. Books are out; schoolwork is being done. They are dressed in the usual tees and jeans. Notably absent are sagging pants, gang bandanas and the "N" word. Why? It's a "screened" school, another that cherry-picks the best students.

After about ten minutes, the well-groomed AP calls out to me over the din of the students in the great room.

"Ms. Rose. You may come in. Please have a seat. May I have a copy of your resume?"

"Certainly," I say. I hand one over. He scans it. I assume he'd already read it because I sent it with an enthusiastic email response to his job posting.

Never assume.

Just as I'm about to yada yada my skills, a student enters.

"Excuse me, please," the AP says to me. He turns to the student. "Yes, John?" The two of them carry on a three-minute conversation. I look over my resume. I want to be sure somebody reads it.

"Sorry about that. Now where were we?" He seems distracted.

"You were asking me about my arts background. It's pretty well covered in my resume. If you just take a look at the back page…"

He looks up and out at the students.

"I need to catch that kid. Excuse me, please," he says and steps out of the office. More and more kids are filling up the great room. Classes are changing. The din is so loud I'm ready to put in my earplugs.

"Sorry about that," he say as he returns five minutes later. "Where were we again?"

"My arts experience is on the third page. But I also have an idea about a political science class."

"What's that?" I can't tell if he wants my idea or if he hasn't heard me.

"A political science class," I repeat.

"I know," he says. "What's your idea?" Before I can yada yada double *forte,* the kid reappears.

"Excuse me please," says the AP and the two of them have another three-minute conversation. I'm happy for the break. My vocal cords are getting a little sore from yelling.

"So…let's see. You said something about an idea for a political science course. Have you taught political science before?" *WTF?*

"Yes! It's all in my resume," I yell. He looks up at me as if I am the one aunt he hoped his parents hadn't invited to Thanksgiving dinner. Just then, his phone rings. He takes the call.

"I have to go and teach a class. I'll be done in an hour if you don't mind waiting around."

This evening, there's a voicemail waiting for me from the principal of Millennium, offering me the six-week maternity leave fill-in. Wasn't expecting that. Flattered. But maybe there's still hope for a cool permanent political science position at the iSchool. We could produce a student-created faux Daily Show. I'm going to turn down Millennium's maternity leave, much as I admire them.

Today is Friday and I'm finishing my week at Manhattan Hunter. I'm still playing my role of a teacher's license sitting in the back of the room. Another hour and my days at Manhattan Hunter are over. But not my days in the MLK building. The algorithm has assigned me to report on Monday to the High School of Arts and Technology, another of the small schools in the building. Goodie. Maybe they'll give me something fun to do.

"Bye, Ms. Teal. You're going to develop into a master teacher," I say as I give her a hug.

"Thanks, Miz. Good luck," she says. I doubt she even knows my name.

Monday, October 31, 2011

HIGH SCHOOL OF ARTS AND TECHNOLOGY (HSAT)

Stuffing Donuts and Envelopes

How thoughtful of Al, the algorithm, to assign me to the same building, different school. I get to walk across Central Park and through Lincoln Center for the third week in row. I love early mornings in the great plaza. I've got the whole place to myself. As I approach the iconic fountain, I execute a light *pirouette*, taking in the great institutions that surround me. Who can suppress their dreams in such a place as this? I'm a child again. The great stages on my left, right and in front of me call to the small, tender, awestruck being just below my surface. "I'm going to sing here," she whispers. "People will love me."

"Hey, guuurl!" The security guard gives me a high five. "You back with us again?"

"Word!" I say and head upstairs to the High School of Arts and Technology.

"Happy Halloween!" A middle-aged blonde woman makes a grand entrance into the office where I'm waiting. Her arms are wrapped around a giant box of Dunkin' Donuts. *"Get 'em while they're hot!"* she says, placing them on a table. All of a sudden staff members begin to appear from all directions. One. Two. Three. Steadily, they slink toward the donuts. Determined. Five. Six. Where are all these people coming from?

"Hey! That one has *my* name on it!" The banter begins. Secretaries. Teachers. Paraprofessionals. Custodial staff. As I'm not a fan of *sodium acid pyrophosphate, sodium stearoyl lactylate, malodextrin, artificial flavor, sugar syrup, corn syrup, wheat starch, modified food starch, sodium benzoate,* I merely observe.

Five minutes later, all the donuts are gone. Sated, the teacher who brought them in comes over to me.

"Hi! You must be our ATR. Welcome!"

"Thank you."

"I don't have any coverages for you yet. I'll let you know. Meanwhile, you can hang out in the teachers' lounge."

"I'm happy to help you with any office work you might have." She looks at me. There are teachers who refuse to do anything unrelated to teaching. Me? I like to keep busy.

"Really?"

"Absolutely. Anything you need. Phones. Secretarial. I'm good with computers."

"We have a big mailing going out to parents. You could help with that."

"Sho' 'nuff."

I begin my task: stuffing envelopes, sticking on address labels and getting to know the office staff. It's fun. Once the sugar crash is over, everybody seems relaxed. After an hour or so, the principal emerges from her office. She looks at me. A flash of recognition.

"We've met, right?"

"I interviewed with you for a social studies position last year," I remind her.

"Oh, yeah. I remember," she cackles. "You should have taken it. Now look at you! You're an ATR. Ha ha." She's having fun with me.

"Actually, I'm fine, thanks."

"No, you're not. You're a teacher. You should be teaching."

"Well...actually, I'm a performer and writer. Teaching's my 'B job.'"

"You're a teacher. That's why you're here. A teacher should be teaching."

She is so in my face, but I think it's part tongue-in-cheek.

"Actually, I'd be careful if I were you," I say. "I'm writing everything down that you say to me." She gives me a look. "Just kidding," I say and head back to the teachers' lounge to take notes.

It is All Hallows Eve, the ancient Celtic New Year, a sacred time when the ghosts of the Dead are able to mingle with the Living. It is the hour when the newly deceased begin their journey to the otherworld. Some of the Living assist their transition. They harvest fruits and veggies for their trip. They sacrifice animals. Donuts notwithstanding, I'm going to watch my back.

Friday, November 4, 2011

As far as I can tell, there have been no animal sacrifices on campus this week…so far.

Most of my time has been divided between stuffing envelopes and covering a few unruly classes. My early morning trek is full of gifts. My ramble across Central Park regenerates me; my romp across *my* Lincoln Center Plaza makes me laugh. The kids give me something, too: a whole lot o' challenge. It's payback time. When I was a high school student, I enjoyed tormenting substitute teachers.

Over the week, I entertain a couple of rowdy boys who are totally unimpressed by my hip hop classroom management skills. I have to have a dean remove one of them. I also sub in a class with some lovely ELLs, always my favs. There is a beautiful girl from Ghana, who introduces me to some of her friends. In the back, five boys are gathered together. They are all from Yemen. I *salaam alechim* them and they warm right up to me. Together, we read through a hastily slapped-together lesson plan.

"Miz! You read it out loud to us, please?" I stop after each paragraph to ask them what they understand. I go over difficult passages and write words on the board. Together, we plow through the whole lesson and, with the time left, I ask the whole class for their personal memories about coming to the US.

No volunteers.

I go back to the five Arabic-speaking boys. A handsome, thin boy is smiling up at me.

"So…can you tell me your first impression of the United States?" He shrugs his shoulders.

"You came to JFK? Is that the way you came into the country?" He kind of nods so I go on.

"So… it must have been amazing after living in the desert. Can you remember any one thing about it?" He just shrugs. His friends are laughing.

"Guys!" I say, smiling. "Give him a chance!"

"Miz!!" One of his pals speaks up. "He don't understand nothin' you say to him."

"Come on, give him a chance," I say, still smiling. "Be nice."

"I am, Miz. But he don't speak no English. He just came here two weeks ago."

"Really?" I look at the boy. "You've only been in the country for two weeks?" The boy shrugs. I can see he doesn't understand me. His pal punches him in the arm and says something to him in Arabic.

"No punching!" I say.

"Sorry, Miz. It not bad. He my friend. It OK."

"Well, please tell him I'm honored to meet him. You understand? You're the first teenagers I've met from Yemen. I'd like to hear more about your country."

I leave them and go back to the front of the class.

"I'm very honored to meet you guys. You are the new Americans. Welcome. We need you in our country. Almost everyone here before you has a family member who was an immigrant like you. I want you to try to remember what it's like for you here right now. Your first impressions of coming to the United States are very important. Please keep a journal. Someday, when you are very successful, you will go back and write your stories. You'll remember the details because they are in your journal. And your stories will inspire others who came from your countries. Do you understand what I'm saying?"

"Yes, Miz. I wish you were our teacher."

"I'm sure you have a great teacher."

Tuesday, I left a message on the school's voicemail at 5:30 am. I say, "I'm unable to come in today," in my horrible early morning voice. "I'll be back tomorrow. Apologies." I know. My Ferris Bueller moment. Teachers have them, too. I split downtown to meet with a cable network rep who's looking for new shows. I've written a pilot, a classic sitcom for Gen Medicare I hope to pitch to her.

"We're not looking for scripted shows," the rep says in her opening remarks. My heart sighs as I file away my smart-mouthed nonagenarian protagonist. "We're looking for shows of general interest: travel, food, music. Our demographic is 50 years old and higher."

Today is Friday and I haven't had many coverages. I'm in the teachers' lounge, with time to plan an unscripted show about folk music from all over the world, starting in Queens.

"Ms. Rose? Can you please cover the class coming into the computer lab?" The secretary interrupts my self-absorption.

The lab is a large room, full of desktop PCs. A teacher comes in.

"It's a small class. Credit recovery. They're working on their own time, independently. Just monitor their progress. They shouldn't be doing anything but credit recovery online."

A few students saunter in, their belts buckled just below their hips. One chap's butt cheeks are draped in pink boxers with little red...I think they're guppies. The crack between them throws me a vertical smile. The fellows advance to their desktops in a deliberate meander. After some *W'sup's* they boot up and start checking out online shots of b-boy sneakers. A few more kids come in and find their stations. Some work alone; two quiet girls pair up at adjacent computers and whisper to each other in Spanish. I cheerfully introduce myself and walk around the room. I make a quick decision: leave the b-boyz alone until I can take the temperature of the room.

There's a skinny kid working dutifully at his desktop. I watch him go through a life science page with a short reading passage and a pretest. He clicks the right answers and goes on to a new passage. He reads it slowly and clicks on a multiple-choice question. He's right again.

"Good job," I say. "Thanks for letting me watch you. You seem to know what you're doing."

"I got this, Miz," he tells me with great confidence.

Unfortunately, he's the only one of the eight students who is actually working. The rest of them are surfing the web, laughing and ignoring the fact that they need to earn the credits to graduate. I walk around to the b-boy section. Another young fellow has taken a seat next to guppie sneaker researcher. His butt cheeks are folded into his chair, swathed in boxers crowded with the logo of that other NY Baseball-Squad-That-Must-Never-Be-Named.[3] The boy turns around and stares at me with his dark eyes, interrupting my hallucination of my Mets sweeping the subway series.

"Miz. I'm good. You don't have to watch me. I don't feel like doing the test. I'm just chillin' till the end of the period." His arms are covered with tattoos. He turns back to his screen, watching a video on You Tube of a swarm of high school boys trying to grab a mike from each other.

"I respect that," I say as the video cuts off suddenly. "But my bosses have told me that you can't use the computers for anything but credit recovery."

"Yo Miz, nobody gives a shit. Chill. Chill. I'm good. Don' worry. Nobody gonna come in and say nothin'. I'm cool. I ain't gonna

[3] Go Mets…'69, '86, *and* '06—when they clinched the National League East and I got to sing the national anthem at Shea Stadium on September 17, 2006, the night after.

change what I'm doin'." His quiet voice is threatening. I'm not going to pick up the rope and start pulling it.

"OK, then," I say.

"Yeah, Miz. Chill. Chill." He clicks on another video of a morbidly obese girl trying to dance on a folding chair in her apartment and falling over.

"Yo!! You seen this?" He laughs hysterically as he turns his screen towards his b-boy pal. The two of them watch the poor girl go splat and laugh till the little red guppies on b-boy's boxers begin a dive.

The period ends with a whimper. The eight kids split. The school week is over. My three weeks at Lincoln Center have come to an end and I look forward to my next assignment: Central Park East. Founded by Deborah Meier, the brilliant progressive educator and author of *The Power of Their Ideas*. Her educational philosophy, at the foundation of CPE:

> *Schools should be small, humane,*
> *democratic places where children*
> *learn how to think for themselves.*

Imagine that.

Saturday morning, November 5, 2011
The Catskills

It's the weekend and I'm ruminating about these six schools that take up the MLK Jr. campus, right across the street from Lincoln Center. I imagine their students' lives enriched with programs and partnerships...right across Amsterdam Avenue. Easy, right? Think again.

Location. Location. Location.

Dr. King...my apologies.

Monday, November 7, 2011

Central Park East High School (CPEHS)

A TV Pilot Is Born

It's a sunny, crisp morning. After a quick hop on the uptown Lexington Avenue line to 103rd Street, I walk north, underneath the ancient brick arch that supports the continually clattering Metro North trains. They tunnel underground to Grand Central at 96th Street, the invisible line separating *el barrio* from the tony Upper East Side. For the well-heeled, train noise is abated.

I could walk straight through the projects to Madison Avenue, but I feel safer on Park, heading to 104th Street. I also feel a little shame knowing that most of my students were born and, for the time being, are stuck here while I, their intrepid educator, am too uncomfortable to walk in their pathways on this gentle morning. Education, I tell myself. That's their escape route. Maybe I can help.

CPEHS appears in front of me. Her entrance is rather unimaginative, but I'm sure this vital learning lab must vibrate with creativity and collaboration. Founded in 1984, its seeds germinated into a number of progressive small schools. My home school is one of its sprouts.

After signing in, I'm sent to the office. A long desk divides the room. The place needed a paint job a long time ago. A middle-aged woman behind the desk is listening to a man in handyman jeans go on about his weekend.

"I'm tellin' you he din't seen nothin'. Craggy comes in with a rear naked choke. And my wife's yellin' at me to shop wid her at 116th. Lemme tell you, that ain't gonna happen. He won by submission. I though it was a guillotine choke but no. Rear naked. Down and *out!"*

"Ya shoulda helped yer wife," the woman behind the desk says in a dour tone. She shakes her head and turns to me. "Can I help you?"

"You women stick together," the kickboxing fan chides her. She shakes her head at him. I smile and give her my best Monday morning energy.

"Hi. I'm Elizabeth Rose, your ATR for the week. I'm excited to be here." Her head bobs a little in recognition of the initials.

"OK, you can go sit in the teachers' lounge. Here's the baf'room key." Although she exhibited some energy in her brief banter with Rear Naked Guillotine Choke Man, she has saved her best dissociative monotone for me. "Somebody will let you know when we need you."

It's a right jab to my gusto. I retreat across the hall to the teachers' lounge, sit in a hard chair and observe *Reality* seize a chunk of my enthusiasm, chew it up and toss it into the elderly wastebasket by the door. I'm alone with a pile of last week's *NY Post* tabloids, two empty coffee cups, crumbs and a menagerie of dust bunnies. The window, obfuscated by bars, looks out on the grounds of an adjacent project, now bleak under cloud cover. I readjust my expectations. This school might be pulsating with collaborative, reflective, playful energy. But for me...I'm *caught cold.*

Still, it's not a kick in the head. Not by a mile. No cage rage for me. Can't maul my fabulous energy. Reframe. This is the perfect time to work on developing my new TV pilot about global music, or, "G-Music." I'll start with composing a theme song or two.

By the end of the morning, I'm smokin' on the jingles, layering ideas on Garage Band in my iPad. I'm just about to whisper-sing the log line I just came up with...

Uncover the music...
Discover the world...

...when a couple of young teachers walk in. We nod at each other as I hide my iPad with the Post. I don't want anyone to think I'm having a good time here. Unlike me, they have actual work to do.

"Ms. Rose. Can you please cover a class down the hall seventh period? It starts in ten minutes." A woman I haven't met sticks her head in the door.

"Sure. Is there a lesson plan?"

"I'll find out," she says and walks away. Carefully watching the door, I give my new theme song one more listen. It's funky. I'm bad. I'm definitely bad.

"It's right here in this room." The woman leads me down the hall. "It's a small class. They have a reading assignment. Their books are under their chairs. The assignment is on the board. Thank you." She leaves; the classes change and four students come in.

"Where's our teacher?" says one girl.

"I'm not sure," I answer. "But I'm going to sub for you."

"Yes!!" she exclaims. "Hey! We got a sub!"

"Hi. I'm Ms. Rose. Please print your name on this paper so I know who is attending. Your teacher left a reading assignment on the board. You may go ahead and start that now." There are about six students now. Three of them actually take out their books and start reading. Two girls pull their chairs up close to a third who has taken out her nail polish. She's started to color her nails a vibrant blue black. I walk over to them.

"Hi," I say. "That's quite a striking nail color."

"You like it, Miz?"

"Um hum. I might have to do that on my toenails. I can't do my finger nails."

"Why not?" She and her friends are warming up to me.

"'Cause. Whenever I put nail polish on, it comes right off." I continue, "OK. Gals. Unfortunately, this is not a nail salon. Sorry, but I have to ask you to finish that job after school. Right now, you need to do the reading assignment on the board."

"No, Miz. Chill. It's OK. We do this in here."

"Right." I smile. "Do you really think you can play me that easily?"

"Yo. She said 'play me'! You heard?"

"OK. Come on. You want me to lose my substitute-teacher job?"

"Hey! You don't wanna get her fired. Put it away!" The third girl has become my job defender.

"Thank you. I really appreciate it." The nail polish disappears into the bottom of her giant purple bag with faux-gold handles. Two books appear on the desk. The nail polisher waves her three blue-black nails to dry. I'm satisfied. I head back to my desk.

Forty minutes later, the classes change. My six students bid me goodbye. Some reading got done.

"We gonna have you again tomorrow?"

"No school tomorrow."

"See ya, Miz." And they leave.

One more period to go. I compose an alternative theme, a kind of *raga,* using a musical loop called "Afghanistan Sand Rabab 05." It's hypnotizing. I can smell the saffron.

The rest of the week is uneventful.

Tuesday: Election Day, no kids.

Wednesday: The teachers' lounge again. Writing. Storyboarding.

Thursday: Same as Wednesday. By now, the lady in the school office is much friendlier. She lets me help out with some clerical work.

Walking home, I pass my old school on Second Avenue and run into the rookie principal on the street. We'd been friends for the 10 years we both taught there.

"How's it going?" I ask him. He's only been on the job for two months. It must be full of daunting challenges.

"Oh, it's great!" he says with enormous pride. "We've gotten the hallways under control." I wait for him to ask me how I'm doing. Hearing no such inquiry, I cheerfully fill him in.

"So I'm a rotating ATR," I chirp.

"Oh. We've had several ATRs," he says, shaking his head. "I just put them in the basement for the week. Gotta run."

Friday: I'm covering a large computer class in the basement. One girl refuses to stop looking at clothes online.

"Don't you want to move ahead with your assignment?" I ask her sweetly.

"Yo Miz. You don't need to tell me what to do. I'm gonna do what I want." Pounds of hostility packed in that petite frame. The dean, a lovely young lady, pokes her head in the lab.

"All good?" she asks.

"Yes, fine," I say. I walk out and stand in the door. "One of the girls, that one with the corkscrew extensions, is annoyed that I've asked her to do the assignment. She's shopping online. I decided not to push her."

"Good idea," says the dean. "That one's got a lot of issues."

End of day. End of week.

I came to CPE[4], excited, hoping I could participate in this creative community. Guess I did…kinda.

Dear DOE:

Thanks for the weeklong artist's residency. Next time, could we include some kids in the project?

CPE out.

[4] Half a dozen years or so after Deborah Meier, as well as a number of other teachers, left the school to start new ones, CPESS changed its name to CPE Middle School and CPE High School and gave up its affiliation with the Coalition of Essential Schools and the Consortium.

Monday, November 14, 2011

ACADEMY OF ENVIRONMENTAL SCIENCE SECONDARY SCHOOL

(AESSS)

Another sunny Monday morning. I check the online forecast. It reads:

Warm Start, Colder Ending to Week

Today, it's going to up to 60☺ degrees. All right! I'm headed uptown, back to *el barrio*. That's East Harlem, and for this assignment, I'm talkin' the Far East. The Academy of Environmental Science, my seventh high school so far, has an address mere yards from the East River off 100th Street. The Select Bus gets me to 97th Street in eight minutes. I walk to 100th Street and get a glimpse of my new school. It's a classic, built in the 1920s. A security guard stationed at the corner keeps his eyes glued on First Avenue. The East River gleams in the sunlight. The FDR Drive is caffeinated with the morning rush.

"Go to class! You are going to be marked late. Up the stairs, please!" a teacher is yelling at middle-schoolers. A blonde security guard gives me a big smile. "Third floor." A stream of students files up a stairwell, laughing, yelling. The younger ones get out on the second floor. As I emerge from the stairwell on three, a group of boys is shooting hoops in a gym. Another short staircase to the main hallway and I find the office down the hall.

"OK. I'm gonna give you this bathroom key. Don't lose it, OK?"

The school secretary is all biz. "You're gonna cover a class later today but for now, you can just sit out there on that chair in the hall."

"Sorry, I didn't get your name?"

"Sophia," she says.

"Hi, Sophia. Please call me Elizabeth, if you like."

My chair sits right where the hallway makes a 90-degree angle, next to the computer lab. The lab is filled with rows of cool new iMacs.

Students begin filing into classes down the hall. They're all straight from central casting. Boys: ball caps, golden sneakers, saggy pants. Girls: tight skirts, leggings, faux designer bags. They give me, the stranger in their hall, a quick look and continue to class. There are a couple of loud b-boys. One of them, the tallest one, chases a girl, slapping her arm.

"Yo. You askin' for it!" the girl snaps at him, smacking him in his arm with her fist. This slap fest is on the boundary. It could easily go from "good natured" to "pissed." I stand up and walk in the direction of these two kids, not sure how I am going to deal with it. Just then, another adult steps out of the office.

"Go to class," he says. He has a mop of long gray hair that lands on his road-weary pedagogical shoulders.

"Thanks," I say and introduce myself. He teaches Living Environment. "We're supposed to go on a trip today to the beach. We're going to take samples of the sand and water and see if we can determine any pollutants," he tells me. "I think you're going to cover a class for me. Some of the kids aren't going. They didn't turn in permission slips."

The first period has already started and the halls are pretty quiet. I poke my head in the office. The secretary gives me a slightly suspicious look. Is this ATR going to be a troublemaker?

"So you're grades 9-12?" I ask her.

"We were. But they're phasing the school out. We didn't get any ninth graders this year. They're gonna close the school when the tenth graders graduate in three years."

Why?"

"You know. Low scores." She shrugs her shoulders. She doesn't want to talk about it. Her job is going to disappear.

"There are some other schools in the building, right?"

"Yeah. There's a charter school and a middle school. I think you have to go back in the hall." Behind her, I can see the principal in her office. She's in deep conversation with the environmental teacher.

The hallway bell screeches. Classes are changing. My earplugs are in. Teens burst into the halls, which rebound with the "N" word and more borderline smack downs. Nothing serious. I stand up to appear more official. A thin woman dressed in a suit stands near me.

"Keep moving to class," she gently encourages the gyrating mass of unbridled hormones.

"Miz! I'm movin'," a tall, impulsive boy chides her.

"Thank you." She smiles at him and he runs after a girl. When the hall is empty again, she introduces herself to me. She's an assistant principal. "You're welcome to sit on the other end of the hall outside my room if you'd like a change of scene," she says, smiling.

"Thanks," I say. "I think I'll take you up on it." I walk down the long hallway and sit in a chair outside a science classroom, adjacent to her office. She seems friendly so I walk over to her door. She's seated behind her desk. A student sits behind her at a computer station.

"I have to put all these pictures up on the bulletin board," she says, mostly to herself. "I have no time."

"May I help you with that?" I ask.

"Can you do bulletin boards?

"Oh, yeah. I can do bulletin boards."

"That's great. Our principal wants us to keep up our bulletin boards. With all the testing and compliance, I never seem to have time for them."

For the next hour or two, I get to design a bulletin board.

"That looks great," the AP tells me. "But I'm afraid I have to ask you to cover a class.

"You mean for the teacher who went on the trip."

"No. The trip was canceled. They didn't have all the permission slips. I need you to cover the chemistry class in this room next door. The teacher needs to go to a meeting."

The piercing electronic bell rings. The classroom door bursts open. I stand aside to avoid being trampled by the rush of escaping students. It's a large, clean room with a bubbling half-filled aquarium, long teacher's desk and many charts, including the periodic table. A young, handsome teacher is telling a student what he must finish. I check the aquarium. A large turtle is unmoved by my cooing at him. The teacher joins me.

"Oh, hi. That's Speedy the Turtle. Are you going to cover my class?" I introduce myself. "Thank you very much. They're pretty good kids… most of them. There are one or two that might be rough. If you have any problem, just get some help from anyone in the hall. I'm leaving them the work. It's on the board. Thanks again so much."

He leaves and the kids start to enter. It's a mixed group, in age, race and height.

"Where's Danny?"

"He had to go to a meeting. He left the work on the board."

"Yo Miz. I ain't doin' no work if he ain't here." A short boy lets me know where he stands.

"OK. Your choice. He asked me to give you the work and I'd like you to take a stab at it. I can't really help you because I'm not a chemistry teacher."

"Whaddya teach, Miz?"

"Well…video production."

"Yo. That sounds cool, Miz. You should teach here."

"I'm trying to. Could you guys please settle down, check out the board and, you know, make your teacher proud?" The din is so loud by now, I doubt anyone has heard me. Sub = party time!

"Guys!! Please chill!" I smile at them.

"You heard what she said? She said 'chill'," one girl says to another up in the front row.

"How you learn 'chill,' Miz?" A couple of the girls eye me with some suspicion.

"I teach teenagers. Yo. Snap." That's it. They break out laughing. Classroom management-wise: not the best way to settle down a class. A few girls take out their notebooks. The rest of the kids are running around, high-fiveing each other.

"Guys! Please! Do I have to call your teacher back in?"

"No, Miz. We good."

There are about 30 students now in the room, a few at their desks. There's a group of boys hanging around a circular table in the back. I decide to walk over to them.

"Hi, guys." They keep talking. One or two notice me. "Guys. Hi." I'm smiling, not yelling. One of them decides to officially notice me.

"Yo. She's trying to talk. Shut the fuck up."

"You shut the fuck up." Another friend of his folds his arms.

"Guys, listen. You don't have to 'shut the 'f' up. I just want to say hi." I speak quietly with a little smile.

"Yo! Yo heard what she said? *Miz!* You cursed."

"Naah. I just said 'f'." Two boys go back to their conversation.

"Hey! Yo. Shut up, nigga. The teacher's trying to talk to us."

"Thanks so much," I smile at my defender. The boys all turn to me. "OK. So my name is Ms. Rose or 'Yo Miz'. Call me either one."

"Yo! You heard what she said? We can call her Yo Miz."

"Right. Now the thing is, Danny wants you guys to do this chemistry thing and I'm supposed to let you know that."

"Yeah. Yeah. We good. We know what he wants." One of the boys turns back to his pals.

"So...would you mind taking your seats? If I can't get you guys in your seats, I'm gonna look pretty bad."

"Yo nigga! Siddown. You gonna get her in trouble." Miraculously, they start to head towards their desks.

"YO NIGGAS!!!" A tall boy wearing a do rag on his head bounds into the room, yelling at the boys in the cluster. Let's say his energy is measurable on the Richter scale. The boys in the cluster all turn to him and instantly they form a multi-hydra-headed monster. My hopes for getting this class settled down? Dashed.

"Hi. I'm Ms. Rose," I walk over and say to the back of his do rag. I walk around him, hoping to catch his eye. He turns away, completely ignoring me.

"So, guys," I try to get a word in but the newly formed reptilian beast is heavily invested in gyrating and fist slapping

"OK. I'm going to take attendance," I announce. A few girls in front of the class look up but all the others are gossiping. The pulsating creature begins to bellow with some high decibel emissions. I know what I have to do. I walk over to the classroom door and open it. I stand in the doorway, hoping to see another adult, preferably of some authority.

"Hey, Miz. Whaddya doin'?" one of the boys yells over to me.

"Just looking for some assistance."

"Close the door, Miz."

"Naah, I'm chill," I say. Just then a thin, gray-haired man walks around the corner. "Excuse me," I say to him. "I'm the substitute teacher for this class. I have a group of boys I'm concerned about. Particularly that one." I point to the do rag. He nods his head. He completely gets it. Without missing a beat, he walks over to the kid.

"Come with me. Let's go."

"I ain't movin'." The do rag is defiant.

"Yes, you are."

"No, I ain't." He folds his arms.

"Fine. Then you're facing suspension. This time it will be for as long as a week. You're on the line. Close to getting a principal's suspension. Is that what you want? Or would you just prefer to come with me."

"Aiight...aiight, Mista. I'm comin'. Yo! Laata." He bids his crew farewell and steps out with the man.

"Yo Miz. Why you gotta call the dean?"

"That's the dean? I didn't know that. Cool, dontcha think?"

"Yo Miz. You didn't hafta do that."

"I did what I have to do. Now you have the assignment. Do what you have to do. Aiight?"

"That was the longest 45 minutes of my life," I say to the dean after class. He tells me his story.

"I was a professional opera singer for 20 years before I started teaching. Next year, I'm going to be an ATR like you."

"Why do you say that?"

"Because this school is being phased out. The student body will shrink by a whole grade by next September. They're not going to keep me. I became a dean because music is the first to go these days. I figured that could help me keep my job. But it's going. I'm glad my wife has a job."

Back in the AP's office, she fills me in some more. "We got a low grade after an evaluation a couple of years ago. The next eval, we improved. But they didn't care. They'd already made the decision. By the time this year's tenth grade graduates, the school is closed."

"You improved your grade and they're still closing the school?"

"Yup." She delivers the word with no emotion.

"Well, I'm sorry to hear that."

"Yes. Thanks."

"So I notice there's a charter school in the building." I tread lightly here. "Do you think that the decision to close this school has anything to do with the charter school wanting to expand into more of the building?"

She shrugs. "It could very well be. One can only guess."

Tuesday, November 15, 2011

As I enter the school for my second day, the office ladies are carrying out a spirited conversation in Spanish.

"*Hola. Como estan*?" I say and they warm up to me. The main secretary, who seems to run the place, starts speaking in Spanish to me but I can't follow her.

"OK. I'll teach you a few words while you're here this week," she offers. "Meanwhile, the principal wants you to monitor the halls today. You can go ahead and sit in that chair at this end of the hall, right next to the computer lab."

"I'll be happy to," I tell her, thinking I can work on my TV pilot. I'm going to need a one-pager.

The hall resounds with a deafening electronic noise. I'm sitting right underneath the bell. Earplugs in! Stat. Students burst, file and mosey out of classrooms. I forget my one-pager and monitor their behavior. Slapping. Kissing. Hugging. Chasing. Yelling. Sub-hoodie moping. Girls with boys. Boys with boys. Pants sagging below thighs. Corkscrews of hair extensions held with ribbons or bouncing below shoulders. A girl sporting polka-dotted leggings covered by a lacy ballet tutu. Cell phones surgically attached to ears.

"Guys. No cell phones, please," I remind them as they dance by me. No matter. I'm an invisible stranger in a hard chair.

"Make sure you don't let anybody into the computer lab," the secretary says to me after most of the kids are secure in their next class. "Come on, Jeremy! Go to class!" she hollers after a hoodie. She turns back to me authoritatively. "Nobody is allowed in the computer lab without a teacher." She heads into the staff ladies room.

The day goes by uneventfully. When it's quiet, I walk over to the closest bulletin board. It's filled with pictures and narrative about a class trip to the shore. The class studied the flora and fauna, took water samples, brought them back to class and analyzed the water for different pollutants. There are charts with levels, pictures and student narratives. I am very impressed.

The gray-haired, professorial science teacher whose class outing was canceled yesterday emerges from the office, right next to the bulletin board.

"Is this your class?" I ask him.

"Oh, yes. That was our unit on how pollutants affect our shoreline."

"It's really interesting," I say. This bulletin board could be hanging in the Jamaica Bay Wildlife Refuge Visitor Center. This is high-level academics, way above most expectations for an inner city science class in a "failing" school.

"I'm a consultant to the EPA," he says. "I get our kids involved in as many hands-on projects as possible. I was really upset we couldn't go out yesterday."

You walk into a school in the middle of *el barrio*. The school is closing. You don't expect much. Then you see a bulletin board that kind of blows you away. You realize you have a lot to learn: about water pollution *and* about your own expectations. A motivated teacher with a supportive administration can open doors of exploration for kids who rarely travel below 96th Street. Curiosity develops. Lives change.

So why are they closing this place??

It's 2 pm. I still haven't connected with any students. Other than my few acquaintances, a few teachers give me a small smile, a smirk of recognition. They are all facing ATR status. My presence in this hard chair might be disturbingly close to their hard future.

"The principal would like to see you." Sophia, the school secretary, comes out into the hall.

"Right now?" I say.

"Yes. Just go into her office. Take your things." Now what have I done?

"I see you made a nice bulletin board," the principal says to me. She's a lovely, soft-spoken lady.

"Oh. I'm glad you like it. Yes, that was fun," I say.

"I wonder if you would mind doing another one?" she says.

"Are you kidding? I'd love to." She warms to my enthusiasm.

"Here." She hands me an anti-bullying pamphlet published by the NYC DOE entitled *Respect For All*. "All schools are required to post this. I'd like you to design a bulletin board around this."

"This looks great."

"You can start tomorrow morning."

"That's great. If you don't mind, I'd like to take it home so I can print out some titles on my own computer."

The week just picked up. I'm looking forward to tomorrow.

Wednesday, November 16, 2011

"We are going to have you help with senior pictures tomorrow and Friday." The secretary greets me first thing in the morning.

"OK. Happy to help."

"You'll get more information from Naiima. She's in charge. Oh, here she comes now." A thick lady wearing a bright orange sweater and pink leggings blows into the office like a striking nor'easter.

"Can you believe we're gonna have an effin' storm?" she blusters in a highly indignant tone. *"Snow. Believe me, I am not ready for snow!"* she bellows. I step back into a corner, hoping to become invisible. If I, myself, were Snow and witnessed her fearsome power, I would bypass the city completely and drop my blizzard on Montauk.

The principal gives me her "art" cart and, for the rest of the day, I'm creating a giant bulletin board with great respect for all.

Thursday, November 17, 2011

Morning: Help the hired photographer set up as seniors line up outside for their official yearbook pictures. I try to help the kids but Naiima cuts me off saying, "I got this." Also, boys posing with the faux necktie and girls with the plastic red rose gets a bit old quickly.

Walking past the office for a bathroom break, I catch the principal's eye and head past the secretary to the inner sanctum.

"Naiima has the senior photography running as smooth as the Select Bus," I say. "Would you mind if I got back to the bulletin board? In case you need me for coverage, it would be great if I could finish it today."

"Yes, that's fine," she agrees. I happily roll her cart of graphic goodies back down the hall. It's only another half hour until lunchtime but I manage to paste up a large picture of a bulldog with a cartoon balloon saying "ouch." Get it? A bulldog on a bull-y-ing bull-y-tin board?

After lunch I am needed in the computer lab. The end of the day comes before I can do much more. I've only completed one-third of the whole board. Great art takes time, you know. Good thing this isn't great art. I still have tomorrow.

Checked my email: the iSchool thanks me for my interest but yada yada. My vocal cords are saved, thank you.

Friday, November 18, 2011

My last day at AES.

"Ms. Rose? May I see you for a minute in my office?" The principal stands in her doorway, looking straight at me. Oh, geeze. She hates my bulletin board. Maybe she'll give me constructive criticism.

"Please sit down," she says. When I do, she arranges a pile of papers on her desk for a second and begins. "You may know, one of our teachers is going out on a two-month maternity leave after next week." I had almost bumped into the enormous belly of a beautiful young teacher yesterday. I nod my head. "I was wondering if you would like to cover her leave. She teaches ESL. Her students are recent immigrants. They're very nice kids."

Wow. I wasn't expecting that.

"Sure. Thank you so much for asking me."

"All right, then. I'll send an email to Central requesting you."

I have to cover the dean's music class. He gives me a worksheet for the kids. It's entitled "An Introduction to the Woodwind Family." There's a picture of a flute and an oboe. There are a few words describing the two instruments and three questions below the narrative. They're fill-ins. No thinking involved. Just copy the answers from the narrative. I wonder if this is a fourth-grade lesson plan. I also wonder how this can be considered a "music" lesson. Wouldn't it be easy enough to listen to clips of a flute and an oboe playing solo? Wouldn't it be more fun to have them identify the sound of each instrument as they listen to a classical and then a jazz piece? Looking at a picture and copying the fact that a flute is made of silver and an oboe has a double reed...what is that teaching? How to copy words?

"There are no more positions for music teachers in the city," the dean tells me when I see him after class. "No more need for music in schools. It's all about passing tests. Kids only need one 'art' credit to graduate. Everybody here is going to be an ATR with this two-year phase-out."

Lunch comes and goes. There's one hour left until the end of school. Back to the board. I pick up some sharpies and start drawing squiggly lines around posters, hearts, and handwritten slogans. In giant black caps I write RESPECT FOR ALL! across the bottom of the blue side. I'm in a zone. A couple of girls watch me in my frenzy.

"Are you an artist they hired?" one of the girls asks me.

"Naah." I smile back at her. "I'm just a teacher with a sharpie."

I finish just before an end-of-the-day fire drill.

Next week, I'm assigned to the Heritage School, a few blocks away. Cool. I get to spend more days in *el barrio,* where people smile at you a lot. After that, it may be back to AES. An algorithm at Tweed is in charge of my destiny. A cyber-bureaucrat is my captain. Remember Monday, when the weather headline had predicted:

Warm Start, Cooler Ending to Week…?

Well…after a chilly start, I had fun with my *bully*-tin board. And…they want me back. To teach. Imagine that.

I'd say the weather headline got it backward.

Monday, November 21, 2011

THE HERITAGE SCHOOL (THS)

A Murderer Chills in the Library

As I walk north on Lexington to 105th Street, an ornamented, classic brick building rises majestically above me, spreading wide, overtaking the entire block. With arched windows trimmed in sky-blue paint, she soars toward the sky with an improbable rosy hue. Her beauty stuns me. She is lovely, unexpected. Could this be the home of the Heritage School? Students are traipsing in. This must be the place.

It certainly is. Her history matches her striking appearance. Opened in 1881, she was to serve the burgeoning clusters of immigrant children whose families were settling in the new row houses rapidly rising in East Harlem in the 1870s. Back then, she was the ultimate in modernity: neo-Greco style, windows designed to maximize light and air, four facades. Most noteworthy, she was one of the first public school buildings *ever* to provide interior plumbing. A lady, indeed.

Opening day, 1881, she was already overcrowded with mostly Jewish and Italian immigrants. They built an annex. Then another. Early 1930s, Puerto Ricans began to spice up the 'hood and by 1941, the moniker *"El Barrio"* was born. By the 1970s, East Harlem had been beaten down by deficits, race riots, urban flight, gang warfare, drug abuse, crime and poverty. The Board of Ed decided to close her down in 1975. The last day of school in June of that year, students raced down the five flights beneath her imperial stair tower. They hooted as they spiraled down the north and south double stairway, racing through the two-story arched wood-paneled doorway that terminates in a corbelled brick cornice. Summer vacation had begun. They burst onto Lexington Avenue, blissfully unaware of the lady's fate.

The grand old school shuddered as her great doors slammed shut for the last time. Her entrance pavilion, that dramatic portal opening the way into free education and unlimited possibility for new generations of young Americans, was now hidden, welcoming only the wastes of time. Her vibrant neo-Greco ornaments, pilasters and bluestone lintels, these silent sentinels from a decorated past, went unseen. Steadfast witnesses to the accelerating decline beneath them, they held, clinging to her, unaware of their fate.

She almost didn't make it. They attempted several incarnations: leased her to a college, a council, a job-training center. Ultimately, she was vacated in 1987 and put on the demolition list. It was thought to be a perfect site to construct a shelter for homeless families. However, at the last minute, that plan was defeated. The old gal was renovated and restored in 1994-5 and this rare example of a late 19th century public school building in Manhattan was saved.

How she shimmers in the morning sun as I approach, her open doors welcoming in her new generation of immigrant wards…this lovely Rose of Spanish Harlem.

"Good morning!" A tall, trim man standing in front of the great doors greets me with a big smile.

"Hi!" I enthuse back.

"You must be Elizabeth. I'm an AP. Just head to the third floor."

Wow. He knows my name.

A female security guard is checking in students. She's very friendly.

"Just wait for Ms. Wheatley, the AP. That's her door." I know Cynthia! We worked together at my old school when she was principal-in-training. She's a great laugher.

"Reporting for duty, ma'am," I say, saluting her as she comes over.

"Oh my God," she says. "You're here with us? That's great."

"Lessee," she says as she motions me into a chair in her office. "You can be our Plato teacher for today. Do you know what Plato is?" She is looking over a schedule grid.

"I know who he *was*. Ancient Greek philosopher. I believe he was gay."

She laughs a little. "I forgot you're funny. Anyway, Plato is a computer program the students use to catch up on lost credits. You'll manage the classes in the library. They're pretty small classes. Good kids. Here are your attendance sheets."

The school library is clean and bright with healthy wooden desks and plushy chairs lining the walls. There is a classically beautiful, gray-haired woman behind the desk, obviously the librarian.

"Hi. I'm Elizabeth, your weekly ATR. I'll be here for the next two weeks to help with the Plato kids." It's a three-day week. I'll be back next week after Thanksgiving. She gives me the keys to the cart so I can dole out laptops to my young charges.

The bell rings, heralding second period. Four boys wander in. With a quick glance at me, one blurts out, "I'm goin' out—let's get high!!"

"Not cool," I tell him. He sits down. I give him a laptop.

"Hi. What's your name, please?"

"Right there," he says, pointing to my attendance sheet. "Oscar."

A very quiet, small kid comes in. He takes a laptop.

"And you are…?" I ask him. He mutters something. "I'm sorry, I can't understand you," I say. He points at his name on the sheet. Victor Vidal-Lopez.

A third boy comes in wearing bright-orange headphones. He takes one look at me and says, "I'm not in this class."

"Then you have to leave," I respond. Ignoring me, he sits down and returns to his hip hop, tasked with flattening the cilia in his inner ear.

"Hi. I'm Ms. Rose. This is my first day here." I say.

"Me too!" says he.

"This is your first day here?" I ask. His buddies chortle.

"If you're not in this class, you really have to leave."

"No, Miz. I'm in this class."

I walk across the room and pick up the class attendance list. As I return to him I say,

"OK. Just to be clear—at this point I expect that nothing you say to me is the truth. So if you are in this class, please show me your ID and I'll let you stay."

"Naah, naah, Miz. Ask anyone. I'm in this class. Right? My name is Luis." I decide to drop the ID thing.

"OK. Luis. If you're telling the truth, I will make note of that. But I think you're playing me."

"Yo Miz. I'm not playin' you!" A bit wounded, he takes a laptop.

A fourth boy, Armando J. Santos, comes in. I give him a laptop and he sits right down with it. He clicks on the link and begins working on his math credit-recovery exam. Luis and Oscar are talking. Nigga this. Nigga that. I hear a "fuck."

"Guys." I speak very respectfully. "Please clean up your language in my class."

"Yo. Sorry, Miz."

A few minutes later Luis blurts out,

"...and I told him to suck my dick."

"Hey! Guys! *Please*. OD! " I say.

Oscar smacks Luis in the arm with his elbow. "Yo! She said *OD!* You heard?"

With a perfect comic pause I say, "Word."

They burst into a frenzy. They laugh. I got 'em.

"You know I rap?"

"Wha? You heard wha she said? She raps."
I spit a few teaser rhymes.

Yo…I'm your gangsta teach
It's you I wanna reach…

They are duly impressed.
"Yo! You my favorite teacher. *Ever!"* says Luis.

I sit down with them. They ask me questions about my life.
"How long you wanted to be a teacher?"
"I don't," I tell them.
They laugh. Luis gives me a high five.
"That's funny," he says.
"I been locked up," Oscar says.
"Really?" I look into his eyes. A big kid with a baseball cap, he's soft spoken, self-possessed.
"Yeah. Four months. They're trying to put me away for seven years."
"For what?" I ask him gently.
"I don' wanna talk about it." I drop it immediately.
"You ever smoke weed, Miz?" A standard question.
"Yes," I reply.
"Fa real?"
"Yes. A long time ago," I say.
"What else you tried?"
"This and that," I say. "I'm an old hippy." Another frenzy.
"You hear that??" Oscar punches Luis who's totally engrossed in his headphone hip hop. "She said she's a hippy!!"
"Used to be," I reply.
"You tried other stuff?" Luis inquires. I nod my head.
"Heroin?"
"Hell no! Nothing stupid." I shake my head.

"I murdered someone," says Luis.

I'm speechless. I look Luis in the eye. I think he's telling the truth.

I look around. The library is clear except for my four students.

"Are you telling me the truth?"

"Uh huh."

"Who'd you murder?"

"My stepfather," he says.

"Why?"

"He was bothering my mother."

"How?"

"I stabbed him in the neck with a knife."

"How old were you?"

"Seven."

Another pause. I don't think he's making this up.

"I finished counseling," he adds. "I was addicted to it."

"Addicted to what?" I ask.

"Murder," he clarifies. "I wanted to keep on killing."

"And now…?" I ask.

"I'm not addicted to it anymore. They're gonna erase the record after I'm eighteen."

He's so sweet, low key. I feel safe but I take note: I didn't see any metal detectors. I hope a) his addiction to killing is truly in remission and b) he is unarmed.

"OK, you guys. Let's go back to Plato. Want some help?" I ask.

"I'm a thug," volunteers Oscar. "I'm going to jail for seven years."

"I'm so sorry," I say. "You deserve better."

"They arrested me for robbery and—whaddya call it when you go into someone's purse—and possession of a deadly weapon…and attempted armed robbery…"

"Did you do all that?"

"Naah. Someone jumped me and I grabbed their weapon and I chased them."

"So you didn't do it?"

"Naah. They did it. Not me."

"Do you have a good lawyer?"

"I'm gonna be locked up."

"I hope not," I say. "You deserve a good life."

"Naah, Miz. I'm a thug. I'm a drug dealer. I'm good."

"I'll check with you thirty years from now and see how you feel about that." I pause. He wants to talk.

"So how did you get into this stuff?" I ask him.

"They shot my brother in front of me."

"Your blood brother?" Luis says.

"Yeah," says Oscar.

"Blood?" I ask. "You mean the gang?"

"Yeah. You know—bloods."

"You're a member?"

"Naah, Miz. I don't wanna talk about this."

"OK. Well—was it at night?"

"Yeah."

"What happened?"

"We was walkin' and some guys stopped us. They asked us if we was ABZ."

"ABZ?" I ask.

"Don't go there, Miz,"[5] he says protectively.

"OK. Sorry."

"So my brother's not ABZ but they didn't believe him. So they shot him in the face."

It seems that Oscar, low key as he is, has enlisted in the Dark Force for the balance of this incarnation.

The bell rings.

"Gotta go. Peace out, Miz."

They turn in their laptops and the murderer and drug-dealing armed robber head to their next class. I'm safe. I feel perfectly safe.

[5] Gang reference. Don't go there.

Tuesday, November 22, 2011

I'm in the library. It's 11:30 am. I'm between Plato classes, catching up on some reading. Earlier, I had given a couple of students a beautiful book of Richard Avedon's photographic portraits. They were sent to me because their class had been split up.

"I'm bored, Miz."

"Here, check this out," I said as I handed them the book.

They leafed through the gorgeous photos.

"White people." "More white people." They kept turning the pages. "More white people." We all laughed.

One of the young scholars ran over to the Toshiba copy machine, jumped on it and hit "start."

"Yo! Whatcha doin'?" one of his compatriots called out.

"Yo!" he exclaimed holding up his copy that had just printed. "Look! You can see my butt hairs."

That all happened about an hour ago. Using my best prison-guard tone I got them to refrain from their sophomoric idiocy.

"Yo Miz...my bad. Sorry. Fa real."

Their antics jolted my memory. I did the same thing at some temp job years ago. Butt hairs were absent, as I did not pull my slacks down, but my copy displayed a tasteful contour, if I say so myself. Anyway, the jolly pranksters are gone now, off to their next classes. My little slice of paradise in the library is as peaceful as a mortuary.

"Elizabeth!! What are you doing here???"

A familiar voice rings out across the library. I look up and see a teacher I know from my old school. She left two years ago.

"Naomi! OMG. You teach here?"

"Yes! I run the Resource Room[6]. Are you subbing here?"

"I'm an ATR. I'm assigned here for two weeks. How do you like this school?"

"Well...it's nothing like our old school. These kids need a lot of

[6] The resource room is a classroom set aside for Special Ed students, kids with learning or emotional disabilities. They get one-on-one help, remediation, and other assistance in a private space separated out from the rest of the school during certain class hours.

help and our principal doesn't get it. I've been pushing him a lot, creating programs, finding funds. He's leaving. We're getting a new principal next week. Thank God!"

"Really! A new principal in late November? That's a little bit of a shake up, isn't it?"

"You don't know the half of it. He's not a bad guy, but he just doesn't have a clue."

"So, knowing you, I imagine you're running things around here."

"I'm doing a lot of the professional development sessions. There aren't a lot of volunteers like we had at our old school. Teachers are pretty stressed here. Guess I'll see you later." And with that, she bursts out of the door.

A few minutes later, Cynthia, my AP pal, walks in.

"You're looking pretty comfortable. Maybe you'd like to work here full time. You could be our Plato teacher."

"Sure. I really feel for these kids," I say.

After praying my lunch *frijoles* were not marinated in the juice of a wild boar, I head back to the library. I don't have a Plato class for the rest of the day, but I consider myself on call. Clusters of rowdy students, sugared up from 16-ounce sodas and Skittles, lurch toward the back of the library for a Spanish class. I hear the *pequeña* Spanish teacher's voice ring out over a huge din of teenage laughter, chairs being moved and books crashing on desks.

"OK. Mandala. That's enough!" she yells. *Fuerte!*

"Miz! You saw what he did?" A girl's voice rings out with outrage. *Mas fuerte.*

"SETTLE DOWN!! Mandala!!!"

There's the sound of a slap, a chair is jerked across the floor.

"BITCH!!" A boy's voice. The sound of a scuffle.

"Sit in your seat." An unfamiliar woman's voice, void of any pretense of authority, chimes in. It must be the teachers' aide.

"Siéntate! Ya!!" The Spanish teacher's voice has become shrill.

"Shut up, asshole," a girl's voice rings out.

Things are escalating. I am tempted to walk past the partition that separates us to see if they need help. However, the sudden appearance of me, a complete stranger, might add to the disruption. I step back, keeping my ears up, in case things get out of hand. The librarian is standing behind her desk, also keeping her distance. She shrugs her shoulders. Been here before, I guess.

The noise in the Spanish class at the back of the library is intensifying. I peek in and see the Spanish teacher. She's about four-foot-eleven and bellowing like a behemoth. The students are yelling. At her. At each other. I'm not feeling so safe. Suddenly, the teacher's aide runs out. She shouts, "It's a fight!" and hastens into the hallway.

I walk beyond the partition where I can see the whole class. Girls and boys are pulling on one another's clothing, backpacks. A very large girl has a boy in a headlock. A circle of kids has formed around them.

"Kick him!"

"Naah. Kick *her* dumb ass."

"Get his balls!"

Some are egging them on. Some are laughing. This is not fun. The tiny Spanish teacher calls out, trying to be heard over the racket.

"Take your hands off him! *Quitale las manos de encima!!"*

Wisely, she does not try to physically break them up. Nobody is listening to her. Chaos rules. Again, I think....no metal detectors.

I stand in the back, giving silent support to the teacher and the quiet students who are standing out of the fray, afraid of the confrontation. The librarian is standing as well, observing, just to my side. Suddenly, two security guards and the tall AP who greeted me at the door yesterday burst into the library and cross to the back room to break up the fight. The yelling escalates as the security guard and AP close in. The teachers' aide returns but does not go into the class. She stands back with us, shaking her head, resigned. I step back to the other side of the partition. I can't see anything but I can hear the voices of the guard and the AP. Another security officer comes in and charges to the back. There are now three guards, an AP and a tiny teacher trying to break up the fight. I hear the PA speaker crackle right above me. Someone's about to make an announcement. I stand close to the speaker to make sure no one has set fire to the school. The melee continues in the distance.

"Attention, please," the voice on the speaker announces. *"This is your principal speaking. I apologize for the interruption."* He pauses. I'm impressed. He seems to be right on it. Maybe he's going to close the library. Just then, the AP's voice booms from the back.

"YOU WILL ALL GET SUSPENSION IF YOU DO NOT SIT DOWN AND STOP TALKING RIGHT NOW!" he roars. Several students are still hooked on the wrestling match. They ignore the AP completely.

"She gonna take him out."

"Choke hold, nigga. You see!"

The PA crackles with the principal's voice.

"Attention please. The students who came in late today will be getting detention. However, since this is my last day here...I will wave detention for those students...."

More yelling.

"Step away!" a guard commands.

"Yo! You in my face! Nobody gets in my face!"

"All right," the AP says. "You're suspended."

"I don't give a shit!"

"Take your hands off him," the guard says to the big girl.

The principal's monotone voice-over continues.

"I would like to say that it has been my pleasure to be your principal all these years at Heritage High...."

"MOTHER FUCKER!" the big girl screams. *"Keep your hands off me. This is fuckin' sexual harassment."*

"OK. Tone it down now," the guard keeps his voice low. "You will walk with me."

A big girl has applied a chokehold on the neck of a medium-size boy. Two security guards are pulling them apart. The AP has spread his arms, warning the rest of the students to stay away from the two central characters.

The principal drones on in his alternate universe...

"...continue to grow and become successful in life. I wish you all the best..."

One security guard drags the boy across the floor to the hallway, his saggy pants sweeping the library's carpet as he tries not to take steps. The other guard follows, securing the big girl's hands behind her back. The AP follows. I look into the girl's defiant eyes and note how school is preparing her for life. The disembodied voice continues over the PA,

"...in your future endeavors..."

Naomi has come in from the resource room.

"You see what I mean?" she says, pointing at the loud speaker. "He's clueless."

"You may dismiss them," the AP says to the Spanish teacher. She turns to the rest of the students and bellows, "You may quietly...and I mean, *QUIETLY!!*...leave for your next class. *EN SILENCIO*."

The rest of the class files out in groups. They don't seem traumatized.

"Yo! I'm gettin' mad sneakers for Christmas."

"You wanna chill tonight?"

"Those niggas are so outta here."

"Yo, nigga, I'm cuttin'. You comin?"

Seems it's business as usual.

They file past me as the principal's voice drones on.

"...as you emerge, college-ready, dignified, critical thinkers in our great democracy. And so, I thank you and bid you a fond farewell...

Tuesday, November 29, 2011

Thanksgiving behind us, it's the second day of my second week here. I've settled into my usual spot in the library. That same pesky Spanish class is back in session, behind the partition. They have a newbie substitute teacher. A few girls have just started yelling.

Last week, after the students were gone, I sought out one of the security guards.

"Thanks for breaking up that fight," I said.

"Lemme tell you something," she said, looking at me sternly. "The whole thing could have been prevented by calling me right when it started. Fights can be prevented. We are trained security officers. If a teacher comes for us early enough, we will not permit a fight to begin!"

This time, at the first sound of yelling, I head out to the security desk in the hall.

"That same class is starting to go nuts," I tell the officer. "They have a sub." She stands right up and walks right past me into the library while making a call on her walkie-talkie. Both APs follow in a moment. Less than three minutes later, a couple of girls are escorted out. Peace is restored.

The new principal arrives tomorrow. His identity is, thus far, a secret. Why? I ask myself. Wouldn't you give the staff a chance to review candidates for the job, to interview them about their educational philosophy, leadership experience, and collaborative skills? Wouldn't that make for a more authentic learning *community* in which everyone has a bit of the "ownership"? Hello? Anybody listening?

Last period, I have Luis, my recovering murderer, Oscar, my thug lord wanna-be and a few others. They take a long time to settle down. Two new kids signed their names (one phony) on the list I pass around. Given the pseudonym, it takes awhile but I eventually determine they are not supposed to be in this class. Evidently, word got around to class cutters that I'm laid back...and got bars.[7]

Once the comedians leave for parts unknown, several kids get down to working on their credit retrieval. Three do not. Chilly Oscar simply refuses. Sweet Luis won't take a laptop from me.

"I'm not doin' nothin' today, Miz. *Yo!* Did you ever take 'shrooms?"

"Forget about it, Luis. Let's go over your history program."

"Naah. I'm not in the mood, Miz."

The kids go on and on with their post-lunch conversation. Their ample use of the "N" word starts to drive me crazy.

"Hey, guys! *Guys!*" I have their attention for a second. "The "N" word is really hurting my ears. Do you think you could please go five minutes without using it?"

"Naah, Miz. Why should we? That's the way we talk."

"I am well aware of that. But for my generation, this is a very ugly word. It was used to degrade people of color."

"It don't mean no disrespect, Miz. Ya see this dumb ass?" Oscar grabs Luis by the arm. "He's my nigga."

"Yo. I ain't you nigga, nigga," Luis smacks him in the shoulder.

"Guys! Chill!" I say and they stop. "So do I understand that your generation has neutralized the inflammatory nature of the word?"

"Yo Miz! Would ya please speak English?"

"You know what I mean. It was a horrible word that you guys have turned into a friendly word. You just use it to refer to anybody. It basically means 'person,' to you, right?"

"Word. You got it, Miz."

"OK. I understand. But I want you guys to understand that to me, it's an ugly word. Whenever I hear it, it makes me cringe—it causes me pain."

"Yo, chill, Miz."

"I grew up when that was an evil word," the tall AP chimes in.

[7] Got bars = rap☺

He's just entered the library and is magnetized to our lively chat. "I don't want to hear that word in this school. I hear anyone say that word and I will suspend that student." I suppress a strong urge to say, *fa real, nigga?* as he stands up a little taller. I've always had issues with authority.

"Yo. There ain't nothin' wrong with that word." Luis sticks to his guns.

"It's a horrible word. I don't ever want to hear it," the librarian calls out from behind her desk.

More kids are moving closer from other parts of the library.

"It's not a nice word." A beautiful little Hispanic girl with rosy cheeks speaks up. "Nice people don't use it."

"Word," says a dark-skinned girl with long black extensions. "It's low class."

"You're low class," says Luis.

The librarian comes over to our group.

"There's a double standard around using that word," she says. "For example, if someone of my generation—a white person—referred to somebody as a 'N'...how would that go?" She looks straight at Oscar and Luis, waiting for an answer.

"It would sound stupid," Luis says.

"But you can say it and it's OK?"

"Yeah. It's different when we say it."

"So that's what I'm saying. You have a double standard. It's OK if you say it, stupid if I say it."

The AP, who had been completely involved in the conversation, suddenly turns on his heel to leave the library. As he walks out he points at me saying, "Ms. Rose. This discussion does not equal credit retrieval for these students." And he walks out, letting the door close behind him.

"Yo Miz. He disrespected you," Oscar says.

"Word," I say quietly.

My feelings bruised, at lunch, a girl named Chelsea runs over to me and cries out, "Yo Miz…I love you!" She gives me a hug.

"I love you too," I tell her. The kids are the cure.

Friday, December 2, 2011

The algorithm is sending me back to AES, starting Monday, for six weeks. I'm good to go.

Luis comes into the library for Plato.

"Yo Miz. This your last day, right? I wanna stay in touch. Gimme yer email." I give it to him.

"Next week, I'm going to work at a school that's going out of biz, several blocks from here," I tell him.

"Yo Miz. That's AES, right? My brother plays basketball there."

"Really?"

"Well, he's not my real brother. But he's like my brother. Yo Miz. I know you think I'm blowin' smoke up your ass, but you the best teacher I ever had. Seriously. I wish you'd stay here."

"Well, thanks but that smoke is running kind of cold." He gives me a high five. I'll miss him.

On my way out, I drop into Cynthia's office. She gives me a hug.

"I can't believe you're leaving. We need you here."

"Well—I'll just be three blocks away at AES. Send me a flare if a position opens up."

Naomi comes in. Another hug. Then I head down the Heritage School's three elegant flights, landing in her dramatic entrance portal.

Just before making my last exit through her great arched wood-paneled doorway, I realize I forgot one little detail. I climb back up the stairs and return to Cynthia's office.

"I forgot one little thing: Damian. I was tutoring him in American history today. He can't read big words. He stumbles all over them and has trouble sounding them out. But he's really smart. Earlier today, he wrote a two-page essay in my Plato class. I think he might be dyslexic. I told him he might want to get tested. I also told him that some of the smartest people in the world are dyslexic."

"Damian?" says Cynthia incredulously.

"You mean Damian with the foul mouth?" says the school secretary.

"I guess so," I say. "He's a smart kid who can't read so well."

"You mean 'suck my dick' Damian?" says Naomi with great conviction.

"Bingo," I reply. "The same."

"Thanks for letting me know. I'll give him some tests next week,"

"Peace out," I say and head down the Great Lady's elegant flights for the last time.

It's a beautiful, warm, early December afternoon. As I walk south on Lexington toward the subway, I realize how much I have enjoyed my time in the Heritage School's imposing shelter. The storefronts of *el barrio* seem to smile at me, indifferent to the thorny challenges attached to their zip code. New Americans conglomerate on the corners, yammering away in exquisite Spanglish. I take inventory of my two short weeks here. Ran into some old friends. Met some remarkable kids, survivors, who have seen more of the dark side than most adults I know. I laughed with them, got their pain and tried to stoke their heartfelt dreams. I listened to their inconceivable true stories that deserve to be heard.

It's the least I can do.

Monday, December 5, 2011

ACADEMY OF ENVIRONMENTAL SCIENCE SECONDARY SCHOOL (AES)

Maternity Leave Starts Today

For Ms. O, not for me. When I enter the upstairs office, everybody gives me a big warm welcome. Naiima, the stalwart "traffic manager" for the senior photo shoot, sees me, jumps up from her chair and gives me a massive hug. Sofia, the school secretary, gives me my class schedule. There are only two class sheets. I have one first-period class and one eighth-period class. That's it? Wow! Best job *ever!*

Time to meet my first class of eight. They're all ELLs, English Language Learners. The bell rings and I head into the big chemistry room, dodging the students bolting out of their class. I nod at Speedy the Turtle. Again...disdain...the chelonian's got an attitude. I have a plan. I'm going to introduce myself and then ask my kids to tell me a little about themselves. I sit at a long desk at the back of the room and wait for them to come to class. The bell rings, indicating the beginning of the period. I'm all alone. Danny, the fresh-faced chemistry teacher, comes in.

"Where are my students?" I ask him.

"Oh...they're usually late...or absent," he says. A tall boy comes in. He seems shy.

"Hi. I'm your teacher for the next few weeks," I'm warm, friendly. "Please take your seat. What's your name?"

"Akram," he says. He gives me a smile and sits down. A couple of girls with long black hair follow. I introduce myself to them and ask them to tell me their names.

"Jacinta," says the skinny one.

"Jovita," says the taller one. Oh boy. They both start with J. That makes it harder to remember which one is which. I've got my work cut out for me.

As I pronounce each of their names, a large, bubbly girl charges into the room. She shouts out, "Ms. O not here? I miss her."

"Hi. I'm Ms. Rose." This girl is gyroscoping around the room. "Could you please come over and introduce yourself?"

"Wha's your name, Miz?" she says to me as she bounds over with a high rate of spin. *"Akram! Why you sit there? You in my seat."* She thrusts herself up against the chair Akram has chosen. She outweighs him considerably.

"Miz! This my seat," Akram looks at me to settle our first international skirmish.

"Excuse me," I say to her. "Could you please tell me your name?"

"Miz! Akram in my seat. Tell him to move!" I smile at her. In my most diplomatic voice I say, "You know, it's my first day here. I'm very happy to meet you. I hope we'll have fun and learn together. So, as a polite beginning, would you mind letting Akram stay in that seat? You can sit next to me for today. Then we can decide who sits where." She plunks down in the seat next to me, flashing a bright smile.

"It don't matter, Miz. I can sit here." We have a truce. "When is Ms. O coming back?"

"In six weeks, I think. After she has her baby."

"Wha's your name, Miz?"

"Ms. Rose."

"Hi, Ms. Rose. I'm Mignon."

"OK. Now, since this is my first day here, I'm going to tell you a little about myself and then I'm going to ask you to tell me a little about yourselves."

"Akram. Why ya wearin' yellow?" Mignon is totally distracted. Just then, another big boy saunters in, his pants hanging down below his buttocks. Mignon hollers, *"Tavio! You late! Miz! You see him? He late."*

"Mignon. Please don't call out like that. This is my class and it's my job to deal with latecomers. Not yours. Besides, you were five minutes late, yourself."

"See! You late too," says Tavio who sits down next to Akram.

"Guys. You're here to learn English. For the next six weeks, I'm in charge. We have a big job here. *Mignon! Please sit in your seat."* She has jumped up and is running toward Tavio.

Mignon slaps his arm and laughs.

"Hey, Miz! She hit me."

"OK." I stand up, transforming into The Indestructable Stern Pedagogue. "I will not tolerate this kind of behavior. *Mignon.* Go right back to your seat. Tavio, do not make any contact with Mignon. Mignon, I will not wait any longer for you. You don't want to start off with me like this." I'm a foot shorter than she, but the message has gotten through. Don't mess with *Stern P.*

"Sorry, Miz," she says and returns to her seat next to me.

"OK. Now I want you all to introduce yourselves to me. Please tell me your name, what country you come from, how long you've been here in New York and anything else you'd like to add. Who'd like to go first?"

Total silence.

"Wait! I meant to introduce myself first. So…I was born here in New York City but my father was born in a different country.

"Really, Miz?" Akram looks up at me. "What country?"

"Anybody want to take a guess?"

"Europe," Jacinta says.

"That's right. A very small country in Europe. Want to try to guess again?"

"Mexico?" Tavio speaks up.

"You stoopid," Jacinta says. "She said Europe. Mexico ain't Europe."

"OK. Guys. We are all here to learn. Nobody calls anybody 'stupid' or any other name. We all support each other. That's how we succeed in this country. Anybody know any countries in Europe?"

"Naah, Miz. I just heard of Europe," says Akram.

"France?" Mignon pipes up.

"OK, Mignon. That's a good guess. France is in Europe. Do you speak French?" I thought I'd detected a French accent.

"Uh huh," she says.

"Where did you learn French?" I ask her.

"D'Ivory Coas'," she says.

"Where's that?" asks Akram.

"In Africa, *stoopid*," she fires back at Akram.

"*Mignon!!* There is no name calling in my classroom," *Stern P* says.

"Sorry, Miz. I gotta do homework for anotha class now. You mind, Miz?"

"No, that's fine, but shouldn't you apologize to Akram?"

"It's OK, Miz," says Akram.

"OK, Mignon. You can do your homework. Why don't you move to that desk across the room."

"I don' wanna go dat far. I'm good here."

Just then, a short, chunky girl makes an entrance. She shoots me a mean glance and walks over to where Tavio is sitting.

"This my seat," she says, a threatening tone in her voice.

"Miz?" Tavio looks up at me for the save.

"Excuse me." I command her attention. "My name is Ms. Rose. I'm Ms. O's sub. May I ask you your name?" She looks up at me and turns back to Tavio.

"My seat, *nigga*!"

"OK. That's enough. What is your name, please?" *Stern P* is revving up into *Piranha P*.

"Miz," she says. "That's my seat."

"Until you tell me your name, you don't have a seat. Plus, you are extremely late and you are disrupting this class. If you like, I can ask the dean to call home..."

"Naah, Miz. Foggedit." She slaps Tavio and takes a seat at the far end of the table.

"May I please have your name?" She sticks earbuds in her ears.

"Take those earbuds out. Zero tolerance for that in my class." She ignores me. I check my class list and by process of elimination say, *Yazmín*. That's your name, right? You and I will meet after school today."

"Naah, Miz. I don't need this class. I speak English good arready." I point to my ear and she takes the earbuds out.

"What part Europe you father born?" Akram asks me.

"Lithuania. It's a little country in Eastern Europe."

"I never heard of it," he says.

"I'll get us a map of the world. Then we can see where we all come from," I tell them. "So now, let's go around the room. Mignon...we know you are from the Ivory Coast in Africa. How long have you been here?"

"Four years in New York."

"Great. Now, Akram...what about you?"

"I'm from Yemen. I been here one year."

"Cool. So you and Mignon are from different continents, right? Mignon's country is the Ivory Coast on the continent of Africa. You are from Yemen. Do you know what continent Yemen is on?"

"Miz. I ain't no African," Akram says. "I'm Arabic."

"Right. So my father was born in Lithuania on the continent of Europe. Mignon was born on the continent of Africa. You were born in Yemen on the continent of...anybody know?" There is complete silence. Akram has fixed his eyes downward. I won't embarrass anyone.

"OK. I'm not going to tell you. Tomorrow, when we look at the map of the world, you'll see all the continents. You already know about two of them: Europe and Africa. Does anybody know what continent the United States of America is on?" Again, complete silence. "OK. We shall clear this all up tomorrow. By the end of tomorrow's class you will be experts in world geography. Let's finish up going around the room. Jacinta. Where are you from?"

"Miz. Me and Jovita are both from Mexico."

"Great. Did you know each other before you came to the US?"

"No, Miz!" Jacinta talks to me as if I'm completely thick. "We meet here."

"OK. Tavio. Where are you from?"

"Yo Miz...I'm from DR!!" He stands up and bows.

"OK. Everybody know DR?"

"Dominican Republic, Miz. He think he cool," says Jovita.

"Sid down," Mignon calls out. I give her a look.

"So...we got a whole world of people here. Can you tell me what you were working on with Ms. O? I expect everyone in this room is going to pass their ELA this time around."

Silence. Then Akram speaks quietly.

"My country...Yemen...is Asia." He smiles with pride.

We still have some time left in the period.

"So, until we have some lessons made up...and I apologize for that...what would you like to do?" I ask them.

"Read," says Juan. He's a boy from PR who just made it to class.

I look around. It's the science room. The only books on the shelves are textbooks.

"Where's the school library?" I ask the students.

"We're not allowed to use the library," Yazmín says.

"Really? You're not allowed to use the library? That's hard to believe."

"It's true," says Yazmín.

Right behind me is a shelf with 40 or so *National Geographics*. The front-page pictures are captivating: Polygamy. Polar bears. Panthers. I grab a few.

"OK. Everybody find a picture that intrigues you and read a little bit about it. Then each of you will share about the picture and give us one or two facts you've just learned."

By the time the period ends, everybody's pitched in. Good save.

As he gets up to leave, I say to Tavio, "Tavio, I'd appreciate your pulling up your pants in my classroom."

"Ok, Miz. I pull 'em up." He makes a tiny gesture, grabs his pants top and then lets them go again. The flowers on his boxer shorts appear to open to the light as he swaggers down the hallway.

Ms. L, the AP, is very helpful, catching me up with lesson plans after my class. She gives me my students' transcripts and the ELA teacher guide. Its first lessons are based on the novel, *The House on Mango Street*[8], by Sandra Cisneros, the brilliant coming-of-age novel about a young Latina girl growing up in Chicago, told in a series of elegant vignettes. I'm going to find the book and make copies of the lessons for my eighth-period class.

The library is on the second floor. I walk in. The librarian, a thin, neatly dressed woman wearing fashionable specs, gives me a serious once over.

"Who are you?" She has a severe tone.

"Hi," I say with great charm and gusto. "I'm Elizabeth Rose. I've just taken over Ms. O's classes for her maternity leave."

"Has she had the baby yet?"

"Yes." Baby's picture is hanging by the teachers' mailboxes.

"So she'll probably be out for the rest of this semester," she says matter-of-factly. "What are you here for?"

"I am teaching her classes."

"Are you an ESL teacher?" She's grilling me?

"No. But I'm subbing."

"Have you taught ESL?" What is she, the ESL Enforcement Squad? Angels fly 'cause they take themselves lightly, I say to myself.

"No—but," and I attempt a little joke, "I speak a few languages."

[8] *The House on Mango Street* by Sandra Cisneros, Arte Publico Press: 1984

"It's not necessary to speak other languages to be an ESL teacher."

Thud.

"What can I do for you?" she asks as I recover.

"I have some lessons that use *The House on Mango Street*. I was wondering if I might borrow it."

"Your school does not have the use of this library," she pronounces officiously. "However, I will loan you the book. Just you, though."

Very diplomatically I say, "So our school does not have the use of the library. I see…I wonder why that is. Forgive me but it's my first day here so I'm just curious…" and I shrug my shoulders lightly.

"Your principal excessed me. Your school is not paying for my salary. Therefore I am not responsible for any of their students and cannot, therefore, have them in the library."

"I understand. Sorry to hear that. But I'm glad you have a job."

"They took away my office. This all happened the first day of school. No warning. There was nothing I could do about it. I couldn't grieve it." That's "union-speak." Translation: she couldn't officially complain.

"That must have been very shocking and painful," I say.

So she issued an edict: None of our 200 students may use this library. Where'd she get her education degree, Revenge U?

"I forgot, what's your name?" I'm going to be kind.

"Joy." She's softened a bit. "Are you an ATR?" she suddenly asks me.

"Yes."

"I am too."

"Really. How's that? You seem to have a job."

"I'm six-tenths of an ATR. The other schools in this building are paying for me. Except the charter school. Your principal excessed me. She is the worst. Be very careful. She is horrible. Your school is at the bottom of the worst-performing schools in the city. She is evil. She doesn't care about anything except money." I like this principal very much, I think to myself. Her bulletin boards seem to trump bucks.

She continues, "There are so many layers to my story. But I'm going to get an investigation. The charter school in this building is evil. It's run by a bunch of 30-year-olds with no teaching experience. The teachers, who are all in their 20s, work ten hours a day. They're so happy to have a job, they'll do anything. And they don't know anything about teaching. And also...and you must promise to never tell anyone this...the charter school principal hired his own wife as the second-in-command."

"Nepotism, huh?" I encourage her. She's taken me into her confidence. I'm honored, especially since she's surrounded by so much evil in the building.

"They're horrible. They're stupid and they're mean. *The New York Times* wrote an article about this school but they didn't mention anything about these problems. They just made it look like a great school. It's not a great school. It's horrible. I hate them. I'm going to get back at your principal," she continues. "I can't tell you how, but I got something on her."

"Sounds dangerous." I don't want to know.

"This is war!" she declares.

Despite her condescending exterior, I can see that she's sensitive, wounded. Who am I to judge? She needs somebody to appreciate her. Who doesn't? I tread lightly as I say,

"So our students really can't use the library? I have to say that I certainly understand your position but...it seems so strange to me that they can't..."

"Well, maybe a few every once in a while." She's softened. A little compassion goes a long way.

"Thanks. I appreciate it. I totally understand your position."

A handsome teacher enters.

"Well, hi, stranger," she coos at him.

"Thanks again," I say and leave them to flirt. I head out with a few copies of *Mango Street* tucked under my arm. Seems she was able to scare them up after all.

Eighth period comes and three out of four students on my roster saunter in, slowly. They seem quietly suspicious of me, their new teacher.

"It's nice to meet you. We can have fun, and with some hard work, I expect you will pass the ELA Regents. OK. Let me see if I get your names and where you were born right. Yaniesy. Yanely. You must be Virgilio," I say to the only boy. So Yolanda is absent?" They nod. "Did I say your names right?"

"No, Miz. It's Yaneisy and Yanely." Yaneisy prounounces the "y" like a "j". I say their names again, with the "j" sound.

"That's right, Miz."

"And you're all from Mexico?"

"Yes, Miz."

"OK. Now we're going to do some reading and vocabulary exercises from this wonderful book, *The House on Mango Street.* Excuse me, Virgilio!"

"Yes, Miz?"

"Earbuds away. Zero tolerance. In this class, you pay attention to the work. *¿Comprendes?"* He sheepishly takes them out.

I read to them. We do vocabulary exercises. The class ends. First day of maternity leave ends. The birthing process has begun.

Tuesday, December 6, 2011
Mignon

Although she took a while to settle down, I'm impressed with Mignon's vivacious, effervescent personality. She's somewhat more mature than the others, even though she's so easily distracted.

We've just had our first-period ESL class. The kids drift in slowly but eventually, six of them make it.

"OK. I understand that you've been reading from this book." I hold up *The House on Mango Street.*

"No, Miz."

"Really? That's what I heard. Have you read any of it?"

"OK, Miz. We seen it."

"Well, I love this book. Let's take a look at this vignette, *My Name*." I've put together some vocabulary words for you. You can use them on your ELA Regents. Everybody please take a worksheet." I hand everybody a book and worksheet.

"OK. Anybody brave enough to read first?" Complete, abject silence.

"Nobody?" Everybody has their head down except Mignon.

"Nobody gonna read, Miz," she tells me. "You read to us."

"You want me to read to you?" I ask them. They nod.

"OK. Now as I read, I want you to underline with pencil only, very lightly, any word you don't understand. OK? Here goes."

I read the first paragraph slowly.

My Name

> *In English my name means hope. In Spanish it means too many letters. It means sadness, it means waiting. It is like the number nine. A muddy color. It is the Mexican records my father plays on Sunday mornings when he is shaving, songs like sobbing.*

"OK. Now I want you to copy each word you've underlined into this vocabulary worksheet. This way, you're going to learn more and more English words. Before you take the exam, you will have these vocabulary words to go over. Everybody should be copying words."

I wait and watch. Some of them are copying. Some of them just stare at the story. I have to keep simplifying this. I've given them too much at first.

"So...who will tell me just one word you've underlined?" No one volunteers. I look over at Tavio's vocabulary sheet. He's written down the word, *sobbing*.

"OK. That's a great word that Tavio has written down. It's the last word in the paragraph. Can you say it, Tavio?"

"Ummm...*so-beg*."

"Good. *Sobbing.* Anybody want to guess what it means? Tavio?"

"No, Miz. You tell us," he says.

"I'd rather you figure it out."

"Naah, Miz. You tell us then we write it down."

"Do you think it's a happy word or a sad word?"

"I dunno," he says. "Happy?"

"It's sad word," says Jacinta.

"Why do you say that?" I ask her.

"Because she says it means sadness."

"Very good. So that's right, sobbing is a sad word. It's actually a way of crying. You know what it's like when somebody cries very hard?"

"Like when my *abuela* died? I cried so hard," she says, frowning at the memory of her grandmother's passing.

And so the period goes. We try to extract meaning. I want to get to my favorite line in the story about the writer's grandmother who...

...looked out the window her whole life, the way so many women sit their sadness on an elbow...

But, given their late start, the fear of new words and speaking up, the bell rings before we get past the first paragraph.

"Miz. I don't understand. What I am suppose ta write down?" Mignon asks me.

"Just any words you don't understand. Then we will go over them, see what they mean in the story and you will learn some new words every class."

"OK, Miz. Where do I write dem?"

"On the worksheet I handed you." I go to where she's sitting and pull it out from under her large, faux-leopard pocketbook. "Right here," I say, pointing to the first box on the grid. She seems pretty articulate, I tell myself; a bit more secure than the others. Maybe she doesn't have much experience in English, but who knows, she might be a whiz kid if you remove the language barrier. I'm feeling good about her prospects of passing the English Regents.

"OK, everybody. Make sure you keep these vocabulary word lists. We'll go over them tomorrow."

"Ms. O meets me seven period," Mignon says. "You can give me pass from Plato class and I can work wid you. Juan too."

"Juan. Would you like to work with me and Mignon seventh period?"

"Sure, Miz."

Seventh period arrives and I arrive at their Plato credit-recovery class. Mignon's already booting up a school laptop while some of the other kids are booting up conversations with each other. Their teacher, the Earth-science professor, calls out names and hands out laptops.

"Mignon, hi. Are you coming with me?"

"Oh, Miz. I forgot."

"Do you want to work on your English?"

"Yes."

"How about Juan?" I look around the room for him.

"He cut out, Miz." I shrug my shoulders.

"So where do you usually work with Ms. O during seventh period?"

"I show you da room." She leads me down the hall, around the corner into a math classroom, next to my beautiful "Respect" poster. A young teacher at his desk is holding court with three students surrounding him.

"Hi. I'm Ms. Rose, subbing for Ms. O. Do you mind if Mignon and I work here?"

"No, that's fine. Sit anywhere you like," he says. "I'm Mr. Aquino."

We sit down at two old-fashioned school chairs with their built in desktops. It's just Mignon and me.

"So, Mignon," I say. "What do you need the most help with in English?"

"Reading," she says.

"You have to understand these equations," Mr. Aquino is telling his three charges as Mignon and I huddle. "They're basic and they will definitely be on the Regents."

"Come on, Mister...I don't get these at all."

"OK. I can stay with you after school today. Meet me here at 3:30."

"I can't. I gotta baby-sit."

"OK. How about tomorrow morning? 8 am?"

"I dunno, Mister."

"Look, you gotta make the commitment. I gotta go now. I'll be here after school and at 8 am. Show up if you can and I'll help you."

He leaves. The three students follow, giving Mignon and me privacy.

"OK. Let's try some reading comprehension from this Barron's English Regents study guide."

I open it to a passage.

"Mignon—why don't you read this out loud?" I point to the box labeled "Your Task." She is not eager.

"OK, let me read the directions to you."

Read the passages on the following pages....

I stop at the title: "Excavating Rachel's Room" by Robert James Waller.

"Now—this is about 'Excavating Rachel's Room.' Do you know what 'excavating' is?"

She smiles and says, "I tink so but not sure."

"So—you know how they're digging up the Second Avenue subway? Have you seen it?" She nods. "They're digging up and making a great big hole. It's kind of like excavating except they're not exactly looking for something."

She smiles. I go on.

"So—have you ever had a messy room?"

"Oh, yes!" She gets all excited. "I had to move and my room was sooo messy."

"Did you have to find anything?"

"Oh, yes. It was really hard."

"Well—that's what this story is about. Finding something in a messy room. Why don't you read the first section?"

The first section is two lines long:

Excavating Rachel's Room
by Robert James Waller
...With her eighteenth birthday near, Rachel has moved to Boston leaving her room and the cleaning of it to us...

Mignon looks at the first word: *With*. She takes a long pause, makes a "w" with her lips and says, "When."

"Actually, that word is 'with,' " I prompt her gently.

"Wit," she repeats, making a French "th."

She stumbles on the second word, "her." She tries to pronounce the first letter. Then she stops and looks up at me.

"I'm stupid," she says.

"No. You are very bright," I insist. "You just need help with reading in English."

We spend the next ten minutes with her painfully trying to sound out words. It's torture. I stop.

"OK. Mignon. I want you to help me to help you. Can you explain why it's so difficult for you to read these words?"

"I dunno, Miz."

"Do you think maybe your brain is wired a little different? Did you know there are very smart people who see letters backwards?"

"No. I don' tink dat's the problem," Mignon says.

Earlier in the day, I had discussed reading issues with Ms. A, the AP who gave me my first week bulletin board job. Mignon's name had come up.

"She's had interrupted schooling," Mrs. A had said. "I don't know the whole story." Now I need to hear it.

"Mignon," I say. "When did you come to this country?"

"When I was 16," she says.

"So you went to school in the Ivory Coast, right? Elementary school?"

"No. I dint go to no school at all."

"Really? You didn't go to school at all?" She shakes her head.

"Why not?"

"I was ready to start when I was nine."

"Nine? That's when you start school in the Ivory Coast?"

"Uh huh."

"So why didn't you start school then?"

"Because. Da war started. Too dangerous outside—so we stay in."

"You mean you didn't leave your house?"

"No, Miz. Dey was killing Muslims. Da president killing Muslims."

"Are you Muslim?"

"Yes."

"So you stayed in with whom? Your mother?"

"Yes, my mudda an' fadda."

"Well—let's see...you were nine. You mean you had to stay inside all those years?"

"Uh huh."

"Till you were 16?"

"No. When I was 13, some girl takes me to Mali."

"Why Mali?"

"I dunno. My mudda know dis girl who takes me to live with dis woman."

"Was she a nice woman?"

"Oh, yes. She very nice. She really loved me."

"What was Mali like?"

"It was...I dint understand nothin' nobody said. They speak some udda language. But I learn Mali language in a mont. Dat woman wanned me to be her second daughter." I take note: she learned a new language in a month?

"But you didn't stay there? Why?"

"My udda sista got me to come here. She lived here."

"Wait. I thought you just lived with your mother and father."

"Stepfodda. And my udda sista. She da one who took me to Mali when I was 13. She lef' widdout saying goodbye. She dint wan' me feel sad."

"You must have been sad when you discovered your sister was gone."

"Uh huh." She pauses, looking downcast.

"So how'd you get to New York?"

"My udda sista come to Mali to get me. She was 17 but she had like two kids. She got me and den we came here."

"Did you fly here? To JFK?" She nodded. "What was that like—your first time in a plane?"

"I was really scared. We change planes two time. Den dey started speaking English on the last plane. I dint understand a word. Someone give me a nasty sandwich. It was *really* nasty." She laughs. "I won' eat it even though I hungry. I din't know how to say not'ing to nobody. So I wait 'till da lady not lookin' and put my sandwich in da bag of da person sittin' next to me. I dint know how to say I don't wan' it."

"So you landed at JFK?"

"Uh huh. My udda sista who live here came dere. She take me to 116 Street to get some food. Miz, I tell you, dat food was nasty. I couldn't get used to it in my stomach." I'm trying to sort out her siblings.

"You live with her now?"

"Uh huh."

"You were 16 when you got here, right? And you'd never been to school?"

"Uh huh."

"So when you got here, where did you start school?"

"PS 45."

"What grade?"

"Eif. But they give me dis test and I fail. Some teacher yellin' at me and tells me dat I shoulda learnt all dis in fifth grade. She was very mean, pointin' her finger at me. So I left dat school."

"That must have been strange, being 16 years old in eighth grade."

"Uh huh. I left."

"And then you came here?"

"Uh huh."

"So this is the first school you've stayed at?"

"Uh huh." I'm blown away.

"Well I want you to know something, Mignon. You are an amazing person with a story that is unique and very important. Nobody has a story like you. You should be proud of your story for the rest of your life. You are smart but you have not had school. So you will have to work very hard to close the gap you have. You can do it. Listen to me. You are smart. We really have to concentrate on your reading. It will take practice. They say you learn words when you repeat them over and over 15 times. That's what we're going to do. But… I *really* want you to write your story. Can you do that?"

"Prob'bly."

"That was very difficult—what you went through. You lived in a war zone."

"De president he killing Muslims. When I call my mudda from here, I couldn't tell her much of anything on de phone because da president was listenin' in. Dey came and got my cousin and dey killed him. My mudda got stuck in Mecca."

"I'm so sorry."

"Uh huh. My moms went dere 'cuz Muslims go dere and she got stuck dere because da president din't like people who went dere. He din't wanna let her back in."

"She's back in the Ivory Coast now?"

"Uh huh." Another pause. She clearly misses her mother.

"Is it still bad?"

"No, it betta now." She perks up a bit.

"OK, Mignon. I really want to help you pass the Regents. Let's go back to the story." I decide I'm going to approach it like learning music by ear.

"Mignon. I'm going to read this first phrase—four words. Then I want you to repeat the phrase."

I read the phrase:

With her eighteenth birthday near…

"Can you say that?"

"When her eighteenth…" Miz! I'm 18!"

"Great. But the first word is *with* not *when.* Now let's say it all again. *With her eighteenth birthday near…"*

"When her eighteenth birthday…?"

"Near."

"Near," she parrots.

"OK. Just repeat after me again…the whole phrase. *With her eighteenth birthday near…"*

"When… No…I'm sorry, Miz. I tol' you…I'm stupid."

"Just say, *with."*

"When."

"*With* not *when.*" I pronounce them very slowly for her with a smile. Then I try some French. "It's *avec* not *quand. With.* Let's do it again."

"Wif," she says.

"OK. That's it. Now I'm going to read it again. Just repeat after me."

I read it again and she listens carefully. "Now you go."

She repeats it after me, reading along. She gets it! I read the next short phrase.

"…Rachel has moved to Boston…"

She repeats it. We do it again. She gets it.

"Excellent! Now we're going to connect these two phrases." I read them together. She follows me. She connects them. She gets through both of them. We do the same with the last two phrases of the first paragraph. We put all four phrases together. Two lines from a Regents practice exam. With a couple of tries, she reads them all the way through. Almost fluently. She's got a good ear. We discuss the meaning. She understands it.

"She moved and lef' her room messy," she explains to me.

The bell rings. "Tank you, Miz," she says.

"No—thank you, Mignon. It's great working with you."

Tomorrow is the 70th anniversary of Pearl Harbor. Mignon's on her way. She's got a chance. Victory beckons.

Wednesday, December 7, 2011

Given the language challenges these kids face, I wonder if there's a way they can get out of having to take Regents exams in order to graduate. I remember in my old school, we issued something called "local diplomas" to certain graduating seniors. They were given to students who did not pass Regents diploma requirements.

"That's all changed," Ms. A tells me between classes. "As of this year, all students are required to pass all five Regents exams."

"What's the passing grade?"

"65."

"So a 64 means...?"

"Failure."

"But what about students with disabilities? The ones that get IEPs?" That's Individualized Education Programs.

"They have to get a 55 on the English and math Regents."

"Well...my kids are not labeled 'disabled' but they are really struggling with English. It doesn't seem fair to require a 65 when the kids with IEPs get to pass with a 55. What happened to the local diplomas?"

"We are not allowed to give them anymore. New rules."

Thursday, December 8, 2011

The Map of the World, Romney and Gingrich

This morning, for our first-period class, I take out the beautiful *National Geographic* maps the librarian, my new BFF, gave me. I lay out maps of the world, the US and a giant map of Mexico. Gathering the kids around me, I lean over and quietly say to Akram, "I want them to find Yemen on the map. Now don't tell anyone where it is. Let them find it for themselves." He is happy to be in on the conspiracy.

"Guys!" I speak up. "Akram is from Yemen. Who's going to be the first to find Yemen on this map of the world?"

"I am!"

"Wait. Lemme!"

There's a lot of scrambling, excitement and pointing.

"I got it!"

"No, sorry," I say to Tavio who's pointing at the map. "That's Yugoslavia. It's in Europe."

Frustration ensues. Yemen is hiding.

"OK. Guys. Anybody remember what continent Akram said Yemen is on?" Nobody volunteers. "Shall we go over the continents?"

"Yes, Miz!"

"OK. Where is Africa?" We manage to get all the continents named as we point to them.

"Don't be stoopid! That is the US! That's our continent."

"Excuse me. No name-calling. What continent is the US on?"

"America."

"North America or South America?"

"South."

"No, stoopid, it's North."

"Allow me to repeat...nobody calls anyone any names here. Nobody is stupid and most importantly, there are no stupid questions!"

"Sorry, Miz."

"OK. So...is anybody ready to guess what continent Yemen is on?"

"I can't find it, Miz." They're really frustrated.

"You want me to say it?" Akram asks. I nod. "Asia, Miz."

"OK. Asia! Now can you find Yemen? You already know where Asia is, right?"

"Here!" Juan calls out. He's pointing right at it. The other kids are amazed.

"Wow, Akram...you came all the way from there?" Jovita lets her finger travel across the map.

"Go ahead, Jovita," I say. "Show us how to get from Yemen to New York." She traces her finger across Saudi Arabia, the Red Sea, Egypt,

Libya, over the Mediterranean Sea, across Spain, Portugal, and the North Atlantic Ocean to JFK.

"Excellent, Jovita. Except I don't think his plane flew over Libya."

"Why not, Miz?"

"Because we don't get along with Libya, so our planes can't fly over it."

"You mean they might shoot the plane?" Akram's eyes open wide.

"It was dangerous when Akram came here."

"How long were you on the plane?" Jocinta asks.

"About two days," Akram says.

"Fa real?"

"You sure ya not from Africa?" says Mignon.

"I not from Africa. I from Yemen," he says, a twinge of indignation in his voice.

"OK. Mignon, don't say anything. Guys. Mignon is from the Ivory Coast. Who's going to be the first to find the Ivory Coast? Look up here at the board." I write *Cote D'Ivoire* on the board as it's written on the map.

They all struggle to find it. It's not easy. They're getting frustrated again.

"Here. I got it!" Tavio calls out, excitedly. I look to where he's pointing. *Cameroon*. I shake my head.

"I can't see so good, Miz," Akram says to me, begging for a hint.

"Maybe it's because you're looking at the map upside down. Why don't you walk around the desk and try from the right side?"

"Miz...this is hard."

"Let's try to pin it down. What continent is the Ivory Coast on?"

"Africa!" says Tavio, giving Mignon a sharp look.

"Don' look at me like dat!" Mignon barks at Tavio, smacking his shoulder.

"*Mignon*. No hitting."

"Sorry, Miz." She flashes me her charming smile.

"So is Tavio right? Is the Ivory Coast on the continent of Africa?"

"You wan' me to say, Miz?" Mignon asks.

"Sure."

"OK. Africa."

"So you are right, Tavio. By the way, Cameroon is also in Africa. See if you can find *Cote d'Ivoire.*"

"I found it!!" Juan points to it before anyone can exhale.

"You're quite the geographer," I tell him.

"You also lived in Mali, right?" I ask Mignon. She nods. "OK—so who's going to be the first to find Mali?" A wild scramble ensues and, once again, Juan finds it, sitting right on top of *Cote d'Ivoire.*

"OK. Let's fly across the Atlantic Ocean and find PR and DR."

"Here, Miz." This one's easy.

Each of the boys is proud to show everyone his respective hometown.

"Mexico!" I say. Simple. Jacinta shows us her hometown of Puebla.

"Where you from, Miz?" Juan asks me. Everyone else has shared his or her birthplace on the large maps.

"I was born in Queens," I say and point to it. "In Jamaica Hospital." They laugh.

"But your parents?"

"Wait…you tell me before! I think I know." Akram thinks back to Monday's discussion. "Miz. I sorry. I forgot."

"That's fine, Akram. Not too many people know about this country."

I write "Lithuania" on the board. "That's the country where my father was born. Do you think you can find it on the map? It's a small country." There's another wild scramble at the map of the world.

"It's in Europe, right, Miz?" Juan confirms.

"Yep."

"I found it, Miz." Juan again.

"Very good. Now, my mother's parents were born in the Ukraine."

"Europe, right, Miz?"

"That's right, Juan." In a nanosecond, he points to it, just as Danny, the science teacher, walks in. The kids surround him.

"Where you from?" they ask him excitedly.

"Here. NYC. I was born on 16th Street. Beth Israel Hospital."

"What about your parents?"

"New York. But my grandparents are from Austria." I write it on the board.

"OK. I found it!!" This time it's Jocinta.

"No—that's Australia. Not Aus-tri-a." I hate to disappoint her. She was so excited to beat Juan to the punch. "What continent is Australia on?"

"Australia," says Mignon.

"You wack," Tavio fires at her.

"Actually, she's right, Tavio. Australia is the only country in the whole world that is also a continent. And not to confuse you, but Austria, where Mr. D's family is from, is in Europe." There's much laughter as they try to find Austria. They push each other's hands away.

"Move your hand. I can't see."

"Got it!" Juan again. The bell rings.

"Great!" I tell him. "Everybody...you did a great job today. We all learned a lot about where we are all from. I'm so excited to have you all here. It feels like we've just traveled around the world together. Learning about geography is fun, right?"

"See you tomorrow, Miz!" And they run out to their lockers.

"That was a great class," says Danny D, his Austrian roots shining. "So glad you joined us."

"Thanks. They just want to fit in and be Americans."

"Ya gotta love 'em."

Bingo.

"Can you help me with dis, Miz?" Mignon asks me when we're together seventh period on Thursday in the math room. Juan has cut out again. "I have to do this for class."

"Sure. Let me see." She hands me an article from NPR.org's website, "Gingrich, Romney Offer Stark Immigration Choice."

"So, Mignon...do you know who these two men are?"

"No, Miz."

"They are both running for the president of the United States."

She looks at their pictures. I describe the election, then cut to the issue at hand. "Mignon. I want you to understand that these two men have very different opinions on immigration. Do you know what immigration means?"

"Yes, Miz. It's when people come to America. Like me."

"Exactly. You came from a country that was at war. You might be called a political refugee." She's losing interest. "So Romney, this guy…" I point to his face.

"He handsome," she blurts out.

"Yes, he is," I say.

"De udda one's fat and old," she says, pointing at Gingrich.

"So Romney, the good-looking one…he doesn't want to let immigrants stay in this country who come in illegally. That means they sneak in against the law. You understand?"

"He mean, Miz. Ugly, too."

"…OK…the not-so-handsome guy wants all the illegal immigrants to leave the United States, go back home and apply for visas to come back."

"Dat's wack, Miz. I don' like dis guy."

"Now this other guy, the one you said was fat and old? You remember his name?"

"No. Sorry, Miz."

"Gingrich. Say it and you may remember it. It rhymes with 'ring' and 'rich.' Gingrich."

"Ging-rich," she repeats.

"He says that we should not break up families by sending illegal immigrants home."

"He not so fat. I like him."

Friday, December 9, 2011

It's first period and we're all having fun. Boy, am I lucky. I get to hang out with new Americans who really need me, who love to laugh, and who are from another world. On my right, Mignon is writing away, answering three questions about Mssrs. Romney and Gingrich on immigration. On my left, Juan, is reading about world parks in a *National Geographic.*

"I really want to read good," he says.

"That's great," I encourage him. I pause and quietly say, "I really want to read *well,*" hoping the correct adverb soaks into his brain. He shakes his head at me.

"Miz...you arready read good."

After dinner, I check my email. There's one from Gretchen Cryer, in whose solo performance workshop I developed my one-woman musical comedy. Subject: "Thrilling News!" I've been chosen as a finalist in the Mentor Project at the Cherry Lane Theatre. They're going to produce my show for a two-week run of twelve shows. With lights, costumes, stage direction, sound design, a director, Gretchen as my mentor. This is way cool!

Saturday, December 10, 2011

As I look up I see an eagle circling high above my Catskill mountain cottage. His white head and tail glow in the sun. It's exhilarating to watch him rise. I want to provide a thermal, an updraft on which my ELLs can soar to their heights.

As the eagle spirals out of sight, I realize I'm beginning to obsess. Regents = assault and battery for my ELLs. They're all in 11th and 12th grades. They need to pass five Regents with a 65%. I look over their scores thus far. 42. 39. 49. They've taken the same Regents over and over. They can hardly read English. How do they prepare?

"I just guess, Miz," Jocinta told me last week. She was referring to the multiple-choice part of the exams.

"How about the short answers and essays?"

"I don't write nothin', Miz. I used to but it don't make no difference. I always fail. I never gonna get outta here."

Still, students with IEPs get to pass Regents with a 55. But not ELLs.

Might I suggest that the folks who created this ridiculous rule may be, shall we say, *impaired?* If I may quote my hero, Mark Twain,

"In the first place, God made idiots.
That was for practice.
Then He made school boards."

Wednesday, December 14, 2011
Groundhog Day

I'm between classes, staring at their transcripts again, hoping for some insight, some flash of genius to hit my brain.

Every semester, on Regents week, they get up in the morning and come to school. January or June, these mornings all look the same. They slink into the classroom. A teacher gives them a test booklet and #2 pencil. At precisely 9 am the teacher says, "Begin." They have three hours to take these tests. The teacher writes the time the test ends and fills in the "time now" every 15 minutes. The kids open their test booklets to the multiple-choice questions and guess at a) b) c) or d). After a while, they close their booklets, stand up and hand them in. They expect to fail. Weeks later their expectations are met.

As their school years continue, their Regents "debt" piles up.

"Mignon is signed up for all five Regents in January," I'm told by Ms. A.

"You mean she has to take them all this semester?"

"Yep. It's the rule. She's failed every one since she's been here. Now, she has to take all of them every time they come around."

"But nobody could be expected to pass all five Regents in one week."

"I know. It's crazy. But we're required to sign her up for all of them."

"So how am I expected to prepare her for success?"

"Just have her concentrate on two of them," she counsels me.

Regents Week = Groundhog Day for Mignon and friends. Or, as the prophet Yogi Berra said, "It's *déjà vu* all over again."

Michael Moore
***God of Carnage* Academy Screening**
Upper East Side, Manhattan

In these dark days of pedagogue-bashing, there are still people who honor teachers.

Tonight, I attend an Academy screening of the new film "God of Carnage," starring Jodi Foster and Kate Winslett. Yes, *that* Academy. A good friend, an Academy member, invited me to join her. As she and I are descending the staircase towards the theatre, Michael Moore walks in.

"You're wonderful," my friend calls out to him. "I love what you are doing."

"Thank you. If only all my days started like this," he says, smiling.

We still have five minutes before the screening. Mr. Moore is sitting several rows ahead of us. I turn to my friend.

"I'm bursting. I want to tell him how I've taught *Bowling For Columbine* in my classes," I gush. It's his exploration of the causes of the Colorado high school massacre and gun violence. It won the Academy Award for Best Documentary.

"Well go ahead—tell him," she says, pushing me past my hesitation.

"I'm sorry to disturb you," I say as I disturb him in his row. "But I have to tell you...I'm a public high school teacher. I taught *Bowling For Columbine* in my documentary-making class. The best part was your three-minute animated *A Brief History of the USA."* This is a brilliant and incisive cartoon, narrated by a fast-talking bullet. "The kids really get it," I add.

"Really! That's great," he said. "You know, I've been thinking I should do more of that animation. You know—like from the Howard Zinn book?" He's referring to *The People's History of the US*. Unlike standard history textbooks, it relates US history through the lens of those who fought slavery and racism, working folks and protestors against war and militarism.

"Absolutely. We use that book in our school," I say. "Dr. Zinn taught in my department at my college."

"Really!"

"And when I was teaching my kids, I used *Bowling* as the best documentary for them to study. They love it."

"Well, yeah. It's about teens, after all."

"The boys, especially, relate to it. Unfortunately, they're fascinated by guns."

"Where do you teach?" he asks me.

"Oh. Uptown. In *el barrio*."

"Really!" he exclaims again. He reaches out his hand. "Thank you," he says as he shakes mine.

"Oh, no," I said. "I shouldn't be thanked. I'm the lucky one." I flash on Mignon as I walk back to my seat to catch the opening frames of *Carnage*.

Monday, December 19, 2011

The Mentor Project at the Cherry Lane Theatre is charging ahead into reality. It's back and forth in cyberspace. Script sent. Production calendar received. Contact sheet for staff received. Gretchen will direct. This is real. I keep pinching myself.

Wednesday, December 21, 2011
Teaching Can Be Bangin'

It's the middle of my third week here and we have settled into a comfy routine. Second period. It's just me and Tavio, a "pull out" from his Plato credit-recovery class. Plato is big in the *República del Barrio*.

"Miz. You can just leave me alone here. I do my work."

"OK, Tavio. But remember, in my classroom, you must pull up your pants."

"OK, Miz, but I sit now." I walk over to him.

"Miz. You don' hav'ta be here. I do my work." I look at the screen. It's blank. Tavio's playing with the chemistry manipulatives sitting on Danny's desk.

"Tavio—let me have the toys, please." I talk to him as if he's a first grader, to annoy him.

"Miz. Yo. I'm not a little kid," he whines. Bingo. I've got his attention.

"Did you answer any questions yet?"

"No, Miz. I just got it there." He points to the computer. Sure enough, he has booted up the program. My bad.

"OK. Let's do this first article together."

"No, Miz. I can do this myself." He would like me to disappear.

"I'm sure you can, but I'd like to make sure. Let's do it together."

Today's news article is about Hurricane Irene that swept the east coast in August 2011. Dateline: Nags Head, NC.

"You know where hurricanes generally start?" I ask him. There's a small map on the website.

"I dunno...maybe here." He points to Canada.

I take out the map of the US and the map of the world. I show him the equator. We trace the path of hurricanes on the big map of the US.

"I been through hurricanes in DR, Miz."

"Tavio. Please read these thought questions out loud."

"Miz! Why you make me do this? You driving me crazy?"

"'Cause—that's my job. I'm supposed to drive you crazy."

He reads. He doesn't know some words. I explain the words as they come up. Then I read the sentence over out loud. Slow. Clear.

"OK—now you read it again," I say.

"Miz! Why I have to read it again? I know what it means."

"I know you do. But it's like music. You repeat it a few times and you get better at it."

"Yo Miz! You driving me crazy."

"Go ahead."

He reads it. He still can't get some words: *brought, flooded, evacuated.* I repeat them. Slowly. Nicely. He gets them.

"OK—now read the whole sentence."

"Yo Miz!"

"You got it..."

He reads it again. He stumbles a bit but gets through it.

"OK. Once more," I say. "I'll bet you can read this really well this time."

"You givin' me a headache, Miz."

I smile. "Come on—you're gonna do this great."

His resistance breaks up like Irene did over Canada. He reads a sentence with some fluency.

We read the whole article together. Out loud. He clicks on the "next" tab and multiple-choice questions based on the article appear. He chooses the right answer seven out of eight times. Second time, he gets all eight right. A bell rings. He's very proud of himself.

"Yo, Miz! I got a 88%. I told you I know this." He struts out of the room with a royal stride.

Nags Head notwithstanding...

Some days, teaching is bangin.'

Thursday, December 22, 2011
Stupid Effin' Regents

I know. Enough ranting about testing. You get the point.

But yesterday, I hit a wall.

Although my eighth-period class meets every day, last week only Yanely came to class. We read "Excavating Rachel's Room" together. Out loud. She got it. We didn't finish because we spent time looking up words in the dictionary...words like *paean, vengeance and salvage.*

"We'll finish next Monday, OK, Yanely?" I said as the bell rings.

"Yes, Miz."

Last Monday, Yanely was back in class along with Yaneisy. Yaneisy, also a decent reader, needed to read the story from the beginning. She'd been comfortable sharing out loud since day one.

"Do you mind finishing the story by yourself while Yaneisy reads it for the first time?" I asked Yanely.

"No. That's fine," Yanely said.

"OK, Yaneisy. Read the story to yourself quietly while I finish up the attendance and look over the multiple-choice questions. All right?"

"OK, Miz."

"This is a story from an actual Regents exam. It'll really help you get used to taking it in January," I reminded them. BTW, Yaneisy failed the Regents several times. She hadn't broken a 43.

Five minutes later I noticed that Yaneisy was looking into space. Yanely had her attention on the story.

"Yaneisy. Are you reading it?" I asked her.

"No. Miz. I'm blocked."

"Why?"

"It's hard, Miz."

"OK. Let's do it together. Yanely. You've finished the story, right?"

"No." Was she also blocked?

"How 'bout Yaneisy reads the story out loud and Yanely, you can help with the words and ideas you already learned last week when you and I worked together? OK, Yanely?"

"OK, Miz."

I had Yaneisy read the story out loud. She had to stop every few words for help. At one point in the story, the narrator finds his daughter's old Barbie doll. As he looks it over, he reflects…

My ravings about the sexist glorification of middle-class values personified by Barbie seem stupid and hollow in retrospect…

How the hell do I break this one down? This is a mean sentence to give to an ELL. Small bites. I asked Yanely to explain a word or a phrase.

"What's 'ravings'?" I said.

"I dunno, Miz."

Yanely didn't remember what we went over last week. I skipped over the passage, a painful first. We continued with the story.

"Was this helpful?" I asked Yaneisy when the bell rang. "Do you think you could do this now for the Regents?"

"Not really, Miz. I couldn't understand it without you helping me," she said, her eyes downward. "That's why I can't never pass the Regents."

Or look forward to a high school diploma.

The Regents: A *paean* to the Educational Inquisition promulgated by the NYS Board of Regents, whom I'm sure are lovely individuals if you're meeting them for dinner and a show. My highly motivated ELLs are working with a *vengeance* to learn our language. It's my job to *salvage* their self-esteem. They are good kids. They need a victory. Don't we all? Isn't that what propels us to keep on learning?

My kids' chances of passing the English Regents? Somewhere between a long shot and a fat chance.

"*You are gonna do it!*" I make sure they hear that from me every day.

Here's an idea....

How 'bout we send the Board of Regents to Yemen and give them a standardized test in the Arabic language?

How 'bout they don't get to leave the country until they get a 65?

"Yo Miz. I'm stoopid," Tavio said to me the other day as I was teaching him the difference between *principal* and *principle*.

"No, Tavio. You're not. I have to look those two up myself."

No, Tavio. It ain't you.

It's those merciless exams:

Stupid Effin' Regents.

Latkes = Love

End of rant. The holidays are upon us. The regents (the humans) are not to be confused with the Regents (the exams). Joy to the world.

I walk into the office during my "prep" period. Ms. A, the AP, is standing near my locker, slicing onions. Peeled, sliced potatoes are sitting in a large bowl of water in the sink.

"What's going on?" I ask her.

"I'm making potato *latkes*," she says. "It's a tradition here. They should be ready right after fifth period. They're for the staff plus."

"Wow," I say as my eyes begin to well up with onion tears. "I'm impressed."

"I'm not a cook," she says. "I only make two things: *latkes* and *hamintaschen*...for Purim. That's it. When it's my night to cook, my kids look at me and say, 'Mom—what can I do?' "

"I've never been in a school where someone made *latkes*."

"The principal is making waffles tomorrow."

"Waffles. OK, that's basically a mix and a waffle iron. But potato *latkes?* Impressive."

"She's making waffles for the whole school. All the students and staff."

"OK. Now I'm impressed," I say. I don't know how to make *latkes*. My kosher friend is visiting on Christmas Eve. I gotta cop this joint. "How are you going to grate the potatoes?" I ask her.

She points to a shopping cart. It contains two open bags of white baking potatoes, large onions and a well-worn Cuisinart.

"I use my husband's Cuisinart. Mine's too big to bring in here."

"What kind of oil are you using?"

"This." She holds up a water bottle decorated with the word *Google*. "Whatever I have at home....I just put it in this bottle. Guess it's *Google Oil*."

Man, those guys are everywhere.

"I hope my kids come in tomorrow," I say to her as she transfers the first batch of grated spuds from the Cuisinart to the strainer. Tomorrow is the last day of school before vacation.

"I'm giving candy canes to the first 144 students who come to school," she says. "We're expecting a lot of absences. Some moms are taking their kids shopping."

At last Monday's staff meeting our principal gave us a heads up: The holidays can be very stressful for our kids. Some don't get to celebrate because they don't have money, live in shelters and are raising their younger siblings while their moms are working three jobs. Some of them may not get a decent meal until schools starts again ten days from now.

Gotta stretch those *latkes* and waffles out as far as they can go. Food being love...there's plenty of that around this place today.

Friday, December 23, 2011
Eve Before Christmas Eve

The staff is in early this am. They've laid out a lovely breakfast party. Secret Santa gifts are exchanged. There are bagels and good vibes all around.

With 200 total students on the school's roster, the first 144 students who come to school will get candy canes. By third period, 50 candy canes have been given out.

Who's at fault for this?

The school, of course.

Schools are rated, remember—by student performance on tests.

Students who don't come to school don't pass tests, right?

Schools like this one are shut down because of low performance on certain tests, even though they've actually improved scores.

So, if the candy canes aren't the draw, how do we get the kids to school? I know. We could have gone home with them, slept on their floor and made sure they came in. It's not impossible. There are about 15 full-time staff in this school. 150 students are absent today. If all 15 of us went home with the kids last night to ensure they came to school today, we'd have to stay overnight in ten homes.

Impossible? Think again.

Vacation is 20 minutes away...

My eighth-period class has not shown up. I continue helping Mignon complete a power point about ten current-event issues including abortion, gun control and the environment. We're alone in the Mac lab.

The school has been very quiet today. Our principal came around with a beautifully decorated bag with her homemade gingerbread cookies—one for each staff member.

I am trying to find a grant for Mignon. I google "Ivory Coast political refugee literacy grants." Google answers: *Thousands of refugees have fled from Ivory Coast to neighboring countries, including Liberia, following the political crisis after disputed elections in November 2010. Oxfam...*

How will Mignon get on in life? How will she be protected from people who want to take advantage of her?

Five more minutes to Christmas vacation. She's just completed her last slide for her power point.

"Thank you very much, Miz," she says to me.

"Happy holidays."

"You too, Miz. I don't celebrate Christmas. I go to mosque tomorrow."

May Mignon's miracle metabolize in the mosque.

HAPPY FESTIVUS!

Tuesday, January 3, 2012

It's our first day back from vacation. I'm really looking forward to seeing my kids. First period comes. Two students show up.

Jacinta is in on time. "Happy New Year's" are exchanged. She sits in her seat, ready to go. Mignon bursts in.

"Miz! I'm tired. I don' wanna do no work. Nothin!"

"Happy New Year, Mignon."

"Hi, Miz."

"What did you gals do over the holiday?"

"You know…wid my family. We eat a lot of food. Rice. Beans. Chicken. Got a new Hollister hoodie," Jacinta says.

I turn to Mignon.

"Did you go to the mosque?"

"No, Miz."

"You spent time with your family?"

"Uh huh."

"What did you do together?" It's important for them to speak out and describe their experience in English. Mignon is the most outgoing. "We watch some movies, Miz."

"Like what?"

"Oh. Dis Nigerian movie. It was all about a tribe and the chief o' de tribe he die and turn into a snake. Dat snake, he look after the whole village. Protect dem. Then somebody from de city who dunno nothin' about the snake and don' care nothin' about de village shoot de snake. When he shoot him, he give birth to his daughter…"

"The snake gave birth to a human daughter?" I ask her.

"Yes, Miz. First she a snake then she become a girl."

Mignon continues with her fascinating story. It's got revenge, complications…a real folktale.

"You gals know what a folktale is?" I ask them. Nobody does.

I write out the word *folk*. I tell them about folk songs and ask them if they heard any when they were little.

"My *abuela* used to sing one to me," Jacinta says, her glance drifting out the window, in a southerly direction, toward Puebla.

Now it's time to listen and visualize. I read them another vignette, "Those Who Don't," from *House on Mango Street,* and ask them to visualize and draw what they're hearing. It's only three short paragraphs, but bitingly brilliant.

Those who don't know any better come into our neighborhood scared. They think we're dangerous…

She goes on to describe how stupid that is. How the guy with the crooked teeth is Davey the Baby's brother. Her third paragraph reverses the situation:

All brown, all around we are safe. But watch us drive into a neighborhood of another color and our knees go shakity shake…

"Any comments?" Silence. But I think they identify. The bell rings.

"We work on dis together seventh period?" Mignon asks me.

"Sure. See you then."

None of my class shows for second period. Jacinta comes in for help with her Plato credit recovery in Living Environment. It's slow going but she's focused and dedicated.

Regents are three weeks away.

I go over the Regents list with my kids, writing down their top two preferences. I deliver this list to Ms. A, who is very happy to schedule them accordingly, if possible.

"We had a brainstorm about Mignon the last day before Christmas vacation," she tells me. "If you'd like, maybe Mignon could take the algebra Regents in French, her native language. She is close to passing each time, but she has a lot of trouble reading the instructions and understanding what they're saying. If you would be willing to read them to her and translate them word by word in French, that might help."

"Well…I'm not fluent in French…but I get along pretty well. I could certainly try." I'm thinking, I could certainly read the French instructions to her.

"It will be a long morning," the AP warns me. Mignon, like other

ELLs and kids with IEPs, will be given as much time as they need to complete the exams. It could go on for *beaucoup d'*hours.

"I'm fine with that."

Ms. A prints out a practice algebra Regents from two years ago and hands it to me. I look it over.

"It's in English," I say, a bit confused.

"Right," says the AP. "You would be reading it to her word for word from the English, translating it into French as you go."

That's a *cheval* of a different *couleur*. "Let me go over this, OK?" Looks like I'm going to have to learn some technical algebraic French. *Voila!* I'm a little intimidated, but I believe I can study the exams in English, make sure I understand the directions and use a combination of French and English to help clarify the instructions for Mignon.

I head for the math teacher. He is a bubbly Hispanic fellow who was hired from the ATR pool the first week I came here. Generally, math and science teachers get placed fairly quickly. Why? Well... as everyone knows, math and science are so much more important than the arts. So Einstein played music "to help him think about his theories," according to his second wife, Elsa. He should have been drilling on standardized test questions. Theories, schmearies.

But I digress.

Together, the math teacher and I go over a practice exam. He gives me the answer sheet. I look forward to seventh period so I can practice it with Mignon.

Mignon doesn't come to meet me for our usual tutoring session. She's left school for the day.

Three out of four students show for eighth period. We talk about career goals. Virgilio, a recent Mexican immigrant who hardly speaks English and is very shy, wants to be a dentist.

"That's great. But you really need to study your English. If you just go over your vocabulary words every day for a half hour after school, you'll learn them. Lessee...when can you schedule some study with me? How 'bout after school?"

"Naah, Miz. I have to go to work."

"What kind of work?"

"In a restaurant. I work till eight." We're talking pm.

"Every day?"

"Yeah, Miz." He has a full day of school and a full day of work every day. How're we going to move Virgilio toward his goal?

"Dental school is a wonderful goal, Virgilio. But we're going to have to find a way for you to get your English together so you can be successful in this country."

"OK, Miz," he says. But we can't find a slot of time to work together.

On the show biz front, the emails have been flying. The dates are set. My show, *Relative Pitch,* will run at the Cherry Lane Theatre from February 20 through March 3. Luckily, the first week falls during mid-winter recess when the NYC public schools are closed. The second week of the run is a regular school week. This presents a slight problem for me. I can't imagine performing a one-woman musical comedy every night after teaching all day. Also, I don't know what school I'll be assigned to. Perhaps they'll keep me here at AES. That would be great. If not, will my new temporary principal be a theatre lover or teacher baiter? I won't know until I get there. Maybe I'll just take a leave of absence. Surely the DOE will grant me five days off without pay.

This kind of thing is usually granted through a simple conversation with one's principal. In my old school, our principal was happy to allow teachers to go to enrichment programs, traveling across the country if necessary. A teacher needs a change of scene and usually returns from these short outings with renewed energy and enthusiasm, as well as some cool stuff to share with her kids. As a rotating ATR, I don't have a built-in relationship with a school's administration. My current principal is a lovely lady, but she can't give me permission for such a venture. I'm not officially "her staff." Fortunately, there's a union rep downtown specifically assigned to ATRs.

I call the teachers' union and I am referred to the ATR union rep. She's all business. I ask her if I can apply for a personal leave of absence for one week so I can do my show.

"I will be happy to take it without pay," I tell her. "They shouldn't have a problem with that, right? One week without pay?"

"You can apply but they won't give it to you." She douses my fire instantly.

"So what would you suggest I do?"

"Work your teaching job and do your show at night." Brrrrrrr. It must be chilly down there at the union.

"I'll fill out the request anyway. I appreciate your help." I keep it upbeat. Who knows, maybe the DOE will grant me leave without pay. Why shouldn't they? It's not going to cost them a cent.

"Congratulations on your show," she says as she hangs up.

At home, there's an envelope waiting for me from the Cherry Lane Theatre. It's my contract as a playwright. OMG! I'm a professional playwright!

Monday, January 9, 2012

It's 8 am. Very Important Teachers Meeting Before Regents:

"We've gotten the word this week," announces the AP, solemnly. "They're going to watch the testing very carefully. It's due to these testing scandals. They've tightened everything up and they're going to focus particularly on transfer schools. Like ours."

"So..." and she launchs into a very explicit 25-minute description of every move we are to make. "When you proctor, you must be proctoring at all times." *Ad nauseum.*

When the staff meeting ends, I head for my first class where we read an article from an old Regents about oceans in peril.

"Who will start?"

"I will," Akram volunteers. He is so motivated.

My ambitions for the story were modest, my expectations for its commercial prospects were nil.

I stop Akram after this sentence.

"What does this mean? What is the author saying?"

"I dunno, Miz," says Akram.

"OK—anybody else? Tavio? What do you think it means when he says 'my expectations for its commercial prospects were nil'?"

"I think he don't gonna make no money?" says Tavio.

"OK. That's right." Tavio puffs himself up. A thin but bright light is shining through. He has probably connected the word *commercial* with *money*. That's a start.

I get what they're facing. I learned about this in a PD for teachers several years ago. The leader handed out a lengthy reading:

Kinetics and Mechanisms of the Unimolecular
Elimination of 2, 2-Diethoxypropane and
1, 1-Diethoxycyclohexane in the Gas Phase:
Experimental and Theoretical Study

> *The gas-phase thermal elimination of 2, 2-diethoxypropane was found to give ethanol, acetone, and ethylene, while 1,1-diethoxycyclohexane yielded 1-ethoxycyclohexene and ethanol. The kinetics determinations were carried out, with the reaction vessels deactivated with allyl bromide*, and *so on…*

"Please read this article and, when you are finished, we expect you to explain its meaning to the rest of us. Do the best you can."

I can do this, I said to myself. I looked it over. I studied it. I didn't get it. I was pissed. Of the 40 teachers in the room, no one ventured forth, except for one science teacher, with an explanation she characterized as "superficial."

The object lesson was clear: when many of our ELLs and other special-needs students read English...straightforward, high school English...they see the page as we see this technical article. More importantly, they feel exactly what we do when we try to decipher this kind of technical writing. Humiliation. Frustration.

"Give up?" said the discussion leader, smiling. "Yep," I said to myself. I try to remember this PD on a daily basis. Especially how it feels.

Tuesday, January 10, 2012

Juan, my sweet student from PR, is standing at the top of the stairs when I come in about 15 minutes before class starts. He hasn't been to school since the week before Xmas vacation.

"Juan! I'm so happy to see you. We all missed you. Are you all right?"

"Hi, Miz. Yes—I fine."

"Were you sick?"

"Yes."

"May I ask what was wrong?"

"I was very sick in my body."

"Really? With what?" I know I'm prying a bit, but I am trying to diagnose what he might need.

"You know, Miz. I was tired. Deezy."

"Did you see a doctor?"

"Yes, Miz."

"So what did the doctor say? I hope you don't mind my asking you."

"No, Miz. I don' mind. I dunno what the doctor say. The doctor don't say nothin'."

"Did he take any blood tests?"

"Yes."

"Do you remember what the blood tests showed?"

"No, Miz. I'm gonna get 'em back later. Tomorrow maybe."

"OK. Well, welcome back. Let's get you back into class.

"When are Regents?"

"Two weeks away."

"I gotta take 'em?"

"Yes. So we're practicing from old Regents exams. I'll help you."

Mignon bursts in.

"Juan!! Where da hell you been?"

Jacinta opens the door, sees Juan and runs to him, giving him a big hug.

"Guys. It's great to have Juan back. Now we gotta get going on this Regents essay. It's still reading comprehension."

Mignon has taken out her mirror. Jacinta has a pink perfume spray bottle in her hand.

"Whas' dat?" Mignon asks Jacinta.

"It's from Victoria's Secret," says Jacinta.

"Guys," I interrupt them. "We have to focus." I'm gentle but firm.

"Jacinta," I continue. "No perfume. Please do not spray."

"Miz! It's Victoria's Secret."

"OK—but that's not for the classroom. Mignon, please put the mirror away. Who will read the first paragraph?"

"Miz. Whadda you put on your body?" asks Juan, quite innocently.

"I think we are getting into an area that is a bit personal," I say with a smile. Juan looks a bit embarrassed.

The radiator behind me is banging loudly, making it difficult to concentrate.

"That thing is driving me crazy," I say.

"Yo Miz," says Mignon. "There's prob'ly somebody inside dat ting tryin' to get you mad."

"OK—guys. We have to focus." The class drags on.

"I'm pushing you because I want you to be successful. I want you to graduate from high school, go to college, get a good job."

"But, Miz. You make it hard. You don't use no short cuts. You always go da long way," says Mignon.

"I know. To be successful, you have to work very hard."

"I don' like working hard. I'm lazy. You shou' jus tell us what de word means. Don' make us look it up." she says.

"Have you ever heard this? If a man is hungry, you can either give him a fish or you can teach him how to fish. You understand the difference?"

"Yes, Miz."

"So which do you think is better? Give the man a fish or teach him how to fish for himself?"

"Give him de fish," says Mignon. She flashes her electric smile at me.

"Right," I say. "This English dictionary is your fishing pole."

"It stink," says Juan.

"I gonna sleep wid my boss. That way he always take care of me," says Mignon. Everybody laughs.

Except me.

Teaching for Dummies

I'm in the computer lab, madly typing notes. There's a teacher, a frowning, middle-aged man, sitting next to me. Behind us, about 15 of his students are seated at their iMacs, working on a class assignment. A couple of boys are fooling around in the back. He gets up and walks back to them.

"Stop talking. Do your work. You're failing," he growls. He must have had his sense of humor surgically removed with his tonsils. He returns to the iMac next to me, in the "teacher only" section of the lab. I give him a little smile, a little encouragement.

"These are the dumbest kids I've ever had," he whispers to me. He goes back to his iMac.

Believe me, his students can tell what he thinks of them.

Teaching is tough. Classroom management is ridiculously difficult. These kids, with their emotional, intellectual and language challenges, are hard to reach, true. It's easy for teachers to burn out, especially lacking support from the administration. But, yo, Mister...

if you can't find a way to accept them where they are, along with the responsibility to bring them further, give them hope, tough love and some tools for success, then get the hell out of the classroom. You don't deserve to be there.

That's the dumbest thing I've ever heard a teacher say.

Friday, January 13, 2012

Ms. O is coming back next Tuesday. Mommy and child are doing beautifully.

The Regents are a week away. I'm feeling so much pressure. I've lost sleep. I stayed home yesterday. I hadn't slept two nights in a row. Spent all day Wednesday preparing sheets for these kids to memorize for writing opening sentences.

"Akram. Please sit up. You can't sleep through this. It's crunch time. You have to pass this exam. I want you to have a great feeling when you see that 65 on your transcript."

"Miz. I'm so tired."

After class, Akram stays behind.

"Miz. You can help me with this?" His anxiety = my anxiety. He shows me the essay question from the American history Regents:

Choose two historical turning points in American history. Give the historical circumstances that led up to them and the political, social and/or economic consequences of them.

"Please, Miz. I really scared about this," he says.

"OK, Akram. I understand how you feel. I'll help you write it but first, I need you to explain the idea to me first. What's a turning point?"

"I not sure, Miz."

"So…can you name some really important event in American history? Maybe a war?"

"I gonna fail again, Miz. What's the use?"

"Just do your best."

My heart is breaking, BTW.

"Have a nice long weekend," I say to him as he zips up his backpack. "Be sure you get enough sleep and eat healthy. That will help your Regents."

"Thanks, Miz. I not gonna pass. Don' worry, Miz. You help me. You nice lady."

"Bye, Akram. Don't know if I'll see you next week. Ms. O is going to be back Tuesday. Remember, school is closed on Monday…"

…to celebrate the birthday of Dr. Martin Luther King.

I have been to the academic mountaintop. None of my ELLs can see it. They don't even know it's there.

I have seen children, born into families that foster learning, work hard and make it all the way up to that mountaintop. But none of my ELLs can see it. Though they may come from loving families, they don't even know it's there.

They don't even know it's there because they are imprisoned in a windowless examination room where they are trapped by cruel and tricky tasks, so formidable, their escape is effectively impossible. They are segregated, humiliated, frustrated, frightened, intimidated and exasperated.

I pray they are emancipated.

Tuesday, January 17, 2012

The Last Day and the First Day

Even though Ms. O is expected back today, I arrive at AES first thing in the morning.

"Maybe we can hire you as a special global history teacher for our ELLs," the principal had said to me our first week back from vacation.

"I would love that," I said. Perhaps today I'll get to start this job.

I walk up the three flights of stairs. Mignon is standing at the top.

"Bonjour, Mignon! Bon weekend?"

"Oui—et vous?"

"*Bon*. See you in class," I say.

"OK, Miz. I really tired today."

I head into the office.

"*Bonjour*...I mean *hola,* everybody. *Como estan*?"

"*Bien, gracias*. But we can't find your assignment," says Sophia. "I'm calling in." She hasn't received the official email indicating my position on their staff. I've been ignoring Al Go-Rhythm online for the past six weeks. Getting comfy here at AES, I didn't think to consult my cyber boss.

"I'll check the computer," I say. I go to the lab and sign in to the "excess teacher" page. There's a page 2! I didn't know that.

LIFE SCIENCES HS 1/18/2012	1/20/2012

I'm assigned to Life Sciences High School. Starting today. It's four blocks down the street. I'm late.

"Gotta go," I tell the secretary.

"Sorry," she says. "It was nice having you here."

I step into the principal's office to say goodbye.

"I have some highly targeted prep for these kids," I tell her as I say goodbye. "I wish I could go over it with Ms. O." She nods sympathetically.

I walk out of her office, past the secretaries who are already absorbed in their morning tasks. A girl bursts in.

"Why you here? Go back to class," the secretary reprimands her.

"But Miz...I lost my Metrocard."

I walk down the hall, past the Plato classroom, where 17-year-olds are randomly clicking, guessing on their laptops, hopeful they can don a cap and gown come June. The door to the chemistry room... where we'd spread out the maps of the world and imagined each others' lives in Sana'a, Puebla, Bouake, Santiago and Ponce...where we miraculously congregated on the third floor of this "failing" school in the winter of two thousand eleven, tender new Americans, grappling with a strange, guttural language with its arcane regulations, trying to make friends, blend in, clad in Aeropostals and Hollisters, running on Nikes, laughing, learning...where we first- and second-gens, children of an exodus from Vilnus and Vienna, employed every tool in our kit to help our young charges find their land legs...the door to that room is closed now. On the other side of it, Speedy the Turtle is in his tank, holding his head slightly above water, while a young, energetic chemistry teacher named Danny, high-stakes Regents exam hovering like a storm cloud overhead, is deployed in his daily clash with classroom entropy, struggling to focus thirty-five fertile minds on the principle of conservation of energy.

My time at AES is over. Just like that.

I leave Mignon, Akram, Juan...all of them.

I didn't even get to say goodbye.

Life Sciences Secondary School (LSSS)

Four blocks down, I walk up 96th Street to the new school. It's covered in scaffolding. Dark. Foreboding.

"Lighten up," I tell myself. It's being revived. It will look beautiful someday.

This building must be a landmark. It's old and grand. I try to roll with the sudden change in my situation. OK. First day, new school. This could be interesting and fun. Why not? The school office is on the second floor. It's a large room, well lit. Several women are sitting at massive wooden desks from another era. The place is clean, but the scaffolding outside gives it a dark, insular vibe. A pretty, dark-haired lady smiles at me from her desk as I enter. Another middle-aged woman with long braids is working with files at her desk, opposite. She looks up at me and I flash her a smile. She doesn't return it.

"Hi. I'm an ATR..." I start to introduce myself to the sweet dark-haired secretary. Just then, her smile disappears and she moves her head, indicating I should pay attention to a strong presence that has just materialized behind me.

"That's the principal," she whispers to me and immediately puts her head down.

"Hi," I say, turning to the principal. She looks terrific. Dressed very fashionably in a business suit and high heels, she radiates strength and considerable energy. She reminds me of Michelle Obama.

"Sorry, I didn't see my assignment." I continue after introducing myself. "I reported to the wrong school."

"Why didn't you know? I knew you were coming last Thursday!" She actually barks at me. Like a pit bull.

"I went on line and didn't see the second page with the current assignment," I explained. I am very contrite, apologetic and warm.

"Go to room 1010. You're subbing for Mr. K, the music teacher. He's on jury duty."

"Give her the dean's number," she orders the sweet secretary. What am I in for? "They're good kids," she pronounces as I depart swiftly for the first floor. I forgot to ask for the bathroom key.

Twenty-five students are seated in the music room, boys on one side, girls on the other. There's a very high stage with keyboards and a small teacher's desk in the front of the room. The students are listening to headphones, talking quietly. I'm guessing they're ninth or tenth graders, although no one has told me. There is a young woman sitting on stage, baby-sitting.

"Hi, I'm the sub," I tell her. "Are you one of their teachers?"

"I'm a para," she says and gets up. "I stay with one student all day."

"OK. What are they doing?" I ask her. "Is there a lesson plan?"

"No," she says.

"So they have nothing to do?"

"No."

"Where's the dean's office?" I ask her.

"Right down the hall."

Good to know.

The stage that the young woman just jumped off is very high. I don't see any steps. I hoist my butt up on it and swing my legs sideways so I can stand up. It feels like a tech rehearsal.

"This stage is a little weird," I say to a couple of girls in the first row who are watching me. I climb down again and sit with them.

"So tell me—what are you doing in music class?"

"Nothing," one says.

"You must be doing something. Do you sing?"

"Naah."

"Do you play instruments?"

"No. We're just learning the notes," says a sweet bespectacled young girl next to me.

"So you're a general music class?"

"Un huh."

"And you don't sing at all?"

"We did at the beginning, but now we don't."

I go over to the boys' side and stand in front of them.

"You guys—what kind of music are you learning?"

"Opera," says one. He's trying to stump me. His friends lean back for the show. I can play him back.

"Really? Which opera? *La Traviata*?" And I sing four bars of the aria....

Sempre libera degg'io
Folleggiare di gioia in gioia.

Softly. *Piannissimo.* The boys look at me as if I have three heads. Tough room.

"Can I go to the bathroom?" one of them asks.

"What's your name, please?" I ask him.

"Alfredo."

Really? Alfredo? The hero of *La Traviata?*

"OK. Please leave your bag here." Alfredo leaves his bag and disappears.

As I've missed most of the period, I take a chair near the girls in front of the giant stage. I don't want to separate myself from them. I just listen to them talk among themselves. Five minutes before class ends, Alfredo charges in, grabs his bag and cuts out. I walk to the door. "Alfredo!" He runs down the hall and disappears around a corner. *Sempre libera.*

Bell rings. First period is history.

I head back up to the office. The principal sees me.

"Yes?" she says. Not barking.

"I don't have any lesson plan for these students."

She gets all flustered. "Ms. D, our AP, was supposed to copy one for you." She hits a button on her phone.

"I wonder where the bathroom is?" I ask her as we wait for a response.

"Hello," says a voice on the speakerphone.

"You were supposed to bring the ATR a lesson plan for Mr. K's class. *Did you bring it?"* she barks into the phone at the AP. *"Ms. Rose is going to the bathroom. Bring the lesson plan over right away,"* she continues with a slight growl.

"What's the school's cell phone policy?" I ask her.

"No electronics of any kind are allowed in the school," she snarls at me, turns on her heel and struts back into her lair...I mean, office.

"You can use my key," the sweet dark-haired secretary says, handing me hers.

"Thank you. Where am I headed?"

"Just at the end of the hall," she says sweetly and puts her head down immediately when the principal re-appears in the doorway of her office. I head down to a closet at the end of the hall.

"That's it," says a custodian, passing by.

When I return to the office, the woman with braids who couldn't get her smile muscles going earlier rises and hands me a stack of worksheets. She seems to be very annoyed.

"There are only 50. Make sure you collect them. That's all we have."

"By the way, my name is Ms. Rose. It's nice to meet you. What's your name?" I say sweetly.

"Ms. ..." She says something I can't catch as she makes a fast exit.

No hellos. No welcome. First day in a new school = lonely.

I stand there holding my 50 worksheets. I miss Mignon. I have a minute. I call AES. The school secretary answers.

"You miss us already?" She has no idea.

"I'm going to come back after school later. I'll turn in my key and pick up my stuff."

"See ya later. Sorry, gotta go," she says and hangs up. My teacher brain buzzes. Have my ELLs filled Ms. O in on what we did for the past six weeks? I'll look for her later.

Third period comes. It's a giant class. Every seat is taken. A tall, thoughtful boy helps me with the attendance. It's easier than trying to call out names over the din. Lots of cell phones are out. I take a picture of the students with my iPhone. That's how I can identify them.

"I've been told by your principal that you are not allowed to use cell phones. I've got your picture," I say.

Some indignation from a few girls who don't want to put their phones away.

"One warning and then you're written up." I mean business.

Their lesson is a one-page about John Philip Sousa. They are supposed to read a three-paragraph bio and answer ten questions.

This is a music class.

They are reading words.

There's no music.

Some of them are acting out, on cell phones, cursing away. Others are attempting to answer the questions that accompany the reading. Pick your battles, I say to myself. How can anyone expect them to be engaged in this "lesson"? They deserve more.

I look at my fourth-period class list. Whew. Only 20 students scheduled. I dread big classes. I'm counting the minutes until this period is over.

I count the rest of the students I'll have for the day: 57. The braided AP only left me 50 copies. I pick five off the floor. I still need more copies.

The dean's in his office, right off the school's entrance. I tell him I need more copies.

"You have to go to room 215," he says. I run up the stairs. Room

215 is outside the principal's office. Nobody's there. I peek into the principal's office. A large gray-haired man looks at me and says, "What's your problem?" I sense his great annoyance at my having been incarnated in the same century as he.

"I need another 50 copies," I tell him as I hand him one lesson plan.

"We'll take care of it," he gripes.

"Someone will bring them to me?" I ask for clarification. Low key. Polite.

"We'll take care of it," he repeats. He seems hungry. Perhaps he's about to strangle a live rodent for lunch.

As I head down the hall, I hear the principal growl, "Nobody's getting 50 copies. She don't need 50 copies."

What a bunch of crabby people. I'll keep turning on the charm. Hope the spigot doesn't run dry.

Whoops—now I get it. Maybe students were supposed to answer the questions in their own notebooks. That's why I only was allotted 50. Now I'm guilty of using too many papers. I'm an environmental disaster. I imagine I'll hear about this sooner or later.

I feel like resigning today. Two more classes left. Heading back down to the music room, I run into the para from period one and her student. They both cheerfully burst into an enthusiastic greeting.

"Hi, Miz Rose!!!" That little bit of joy and recognition is my fuel for today. Here comes sixth period with seventh graders shouting ear-splitting greetings to each other as they enter. If this were a recording studio, the VU meter would be pinned in the red.

A highly immature bunch, it takes ten minutes for them to settle down. Finally they do, but this is a colossal waste of an incarnation. Theirs and mine. This may be the last day I teach. Ever. I deserve better. Only one more class left after this one: eighth period—ninth graders. I compose a letter in my head.

Dear DOE,
You win. Your weekly rotation has worn me down. This is a mean place, full of barking, crabby people. My heart hurts. I want to go back to AES, to my ELLs. They need me. I need them. I didn't even get to say "Goodbye."

My current seventh graders have settled into three groups: gossip girls, boys finally doing the Sousa exercise and three girls sitting on the edge of the stage singing. One boy is tired and sacked out top of three chairs. In a moment of grace, the period ends.

It's eighth period, my last class of the day. One girl will not stop texting. Laqueesha. I have no energy for a battle. The bell rings. Can I make it through Wednesday? Thursday? Friday? I walk out the large school door, through the dark tunnel of scaffolding, and march four blocks back uptown back to AES. I greet the staff and turn in my key, unceremoniously. Nobody says much of anything. Back down the hall to my old classroom. Ms. O is sitting there, working with Mignon.

"*Hi, Miz!!!*" says Mignon. She's really happy to see me.

"Hi, Mignon. I miss you," I say.

"Miz. You got email?" she asks.

I give her my "official" DOE email. Must keep this formal to protect her privacy. She gives me hers.

"I hope you come back, Miz."

Ms. O is lovely. They're lucky to have her. I give her all my Regents prep materials, books, English-usage crib sheets, Part 3 and 4 Regents work sheets and the list of everything we did together while she was out.

"I really appreciate you're being so organized. Where did you get all this material?" she asks me.

"From the AP," I say.

"Well, that's funny. Didn't know she had it," she says.

"It's yours. Great stuff. All these lessons are already prepped for *The House on Mango Street,*" I tell her.

Mignon gets up to leave at 3:45 pm.

"Bye, Miz," she says to me and we have a little hug in the hallway, a little goodbye.

Tavio walks by.

"Hey, Miz. I thought you was gone."

"Yep. I've been re-assigned."

"Bye, Miz."

As he struts down the hall I call out to him,

"Tavio!"

"Yes, Miz?" He turns to me.

"Pull up your pants!"

Wednesday, January 18, 2012
The Marble Dungeon

It's a New Day. I'm ready.

> Dear DOE:
> I'm feeing good today. I'm back.
> Thanks for the tribulation. It made me stronger.

I arrive early to make up for yesterday's lateness. Two secretaries are present, both of them on the phone. Patiently, I stand in between their desks.

"That's your program today." The unsmiling one points to the desk across the room. "On the desk over there."

I pick up the sheet and walk to an empty corner of the room. It says:

> Periods 1 & 2: 95th Street Locker area and Exit
> Period 3: Lunch (that's 10:16 to 11:01 am)
> Periods 4 through 8: 95th Street Locker area and Exit

No comprendo. I'm subbing in the locker area? For what class... Breaking & Entering 101?

I walk back to the secretary and stand patiently by her desk again.

"I'll call you right back," she says into the phone and hangs up.

"I'm not sure what this means," I tell her.

She reads it back to me. "95th Street locker area and exit."

"Yes, I've read it," I tell her. "Can you explain it to me?"

"You have to see Mr. Ortega."

Great. That's the elderly dean who was very helpful yesterday. I surmise he's been around this education biz for a spell. I head downstairs to his office.

Mr. Ortega's door is closed. The custodian is standing by security.

"You need Mr. Ortega?" he asks me.

"Yes. But his door is closed."

"You gotta bang on it," he says, motioning me to follow him.

I follow him out to Mr. Os door. *BANG! BANG! BANG! BANG!* He hits the door hard with his hand. No answer. *BANG! BANG! BANG! BANG!* He smashes it again. No answer. He can't be in there, I'm thinking. But the custodian is unmoved by the lack of response. He raises his hand to *BANG* it again just as Mr. Ortega opens the door.

"There you are." The custodian smiles at me with the bedside manner of an otolaryngologist.

"Hi, Mr. Ortega," I greet him.

"Hello. What can I do for you?"

"They told me to ask you to explain my assignment."

"You're going to be over on the other side of the building," he says. "Follow me." He walks me across the large lobby. Past security. Past students coming in for their first period. He leads me down a long hallway lined with blue student lockers.

"This is an area of high activity," he tells me.

He opens the double door at the end of the hallway. It opens to a marble staircase that leads downstairs to an exit and the basement.

There's absolutely no activity, except for a large spider weaving in the window. There's a lone folding chair, yesterday's newspaper and an empty candy wrapper on the floor. The hallway is barely lit with an ancient florescent lamp. The ceiling is patched with primer. The wall is the color of mustard that's been in the fridge for ten years. It's about as perky as a mausoleum. I place my things on the chair and inhale the details. A classically designed wrought-iron banister lines the stairway. Years ago, someone painted its perimeter bright red. The rest of it was coated with silver paint that once shone, before it became coated with crud. The design contains scrolls that surround the spokes of, perhaps, a wagon wheel. Artisans, I'd guess, immigrants from Italy, created these ornamental wonders, testaments to the majesty of this once noble building, a shrine, a place of pilgrimage, a free American public school. They worked to perfect these banisters in their new country. Their children would attend this, or another, grand institution of learning. For *free*. Their dreams engage every ornate curl, propelling every angle, every wheel with its spokes beginning in the center, the mainstay of the banister. They're suns, radiating out, shining on their children, fortunate enough to be born in this grand new world. God is, after all, in the details.

But I wax poetic. For the moment.

"You're to guard this area," Mr. Ortega says as we stand by the student lockers. "It gets busy from periods four through seven. No one is allowed to use this exit. No students. No teachers. Only a custodian. If you need help, come and get me or a security guard."

He leaves me. There's a small window. I try it. It opens easily. Ahh... air. I'll stay on this side of the double doors after all. Private. Away from the kids and their lockers. No seventh graders today. Thank you. Glad I showed up today.

The Bathroom Key

Just as I settle down I realize that I need a bathroom key for the staff facility. I take my jacket and head across the lobby to Mr. Ortega's office. The door is closed. The custodian is nowhere to be seen. Using the palm of my hand, I hit the door firmly two times. I'm not going to BANG it. I wait. No response. I give it two more hits with my palm.

Mr. Ortega opens the door.

"You have to go to room 209 for the key. Main office."

The principal just happens to be standing on the right as I enter.

"Hi," I say sweetly, with a smile.

"Good morning," she says. I sense more warmth. She's dressed beautifully. Fitted wool jacket. Tasteful gold earrings.

"I just realized I need a bathroom key today," Suddenly, she spins on her spike heels, bares her teeth and howls,

"WHY YOU COMIN' TO ME FOR EVERY LITTLE THING? I'M THE PRINCIPAL!! YOU COME TO THE PRINCIPAL AT EVERY OTHER SCHOOL YOU WORKED AT?"

As she snarls on, I thank *Nabu*, the Babylonian god of writing, for giving me this moment. I actually thought of resigning yesterday. But Her Royal Highness is giving me *awesome* material. Bless her.

"YOU NEED TO ASK MR. MAHONEY. HE'S YOUR AP. CALL HIM ON ONE OF THESE BLACK PHONES!" She gesticulates madly and points to a phone near the window. *"DIAL 4111!! YOU DON'T NEED TO BE BOTHERING ME WITH THIS KIND OF THING. 4111!"*

I walk over to the phone, pick it up and dial 4111. As I do, the lovely secretary who was kind to me yesterday catches my eye. We have a sympathetic nanosecond. No words. No eyebrows. *Sympatico.*

Mr. Mahoney's recorded announcement comes on. I wait until it stops. I speak into the phone very quietly so as not to trigger another outburst. Michelle Obama has morphed into The Red Queen. She's still standing in the doorway. Did she just mutter, *off with her head*?

"Hi, Mr. Mahoney. It's Ms. Rose, the ATR." I'm speaking in a monotone. Don't want to rile the rottweiler. *Or do I?* "The principal told me to contact you about getting a bathroom key today. I'm stationed at the 95th Street exit. Thank you."

"DID YOU GET A RECORDING?" The Tsarina has turned on me again. She's watching my every move. Doesn't she have a school to run?

"Yes," I say politely. I am biting my tongue.

"WELL YOU HAVE TO SEE HIM AND GET A KEY LATER. YOU TALK TO HIM! NOT ME!"

She struts across the large office to the wall where the staff punches in and out. She grabs a wooden handle with a key on the end of it that sits next to the time-punching machine. She waves it at me.

"THIS IS THE STAFF'S KEY. YOU CAN'T BE TAKIN' THIS! SEE MR. MAHONEY."

"Would you mind if I used this staff key right now for a moment?"

"BRING IT RIGHT BACK!!" She is wailing. Smothered hilarity squeezes my bladder. She marches into the hall, her four-inch heels clicking like blitzkrieg boots. She turns her head right, then left, reconnoitering deftly. She turns on me, flailing her left arm.

"THERE HE IS. MR MAHONEY IS IN THE HALL!! GO TALK TO HIM!!"

I carefully walk past her into the hall. Mr. Mahoney is the very tall, sour, gray-crested guy who took my request for more Sousa copies yesterday. He's speaking quietly with a middle-aged lady standing outside a classroom. I stand back and wait patiently. After a minute or so, he turns and looks down at me.

"Hi, Mr. Mahoney. The principal told me you might be able to get me a key for the ladies room for today."

Mr. Mahoney walks into the main office. I follow him. He picks up the same wooden block with the key on the end. The principal stands ten feet away, across the office floor.

"Here's the staff key," Mr. Mahoney says, handing me the one hanging by the punching machine. "You can use this."

"SHE CAN'T TAKE THAT KEY TODAY." The Supreme Sultana's shriek shatters the room as a massive cockroach runs for shelter. The secretaries slink quietly into their front row seats, ready for Round Two.

"She can just use it when she needs it?" Mr. Mahoney flings back a question. He stands his ground, staring into her eyes, evidently, experienced in the ring.

"LET HER USE IT THEN!" She turns on me. *"MAKE SURE YOU PUT IT RIGHT BACK WHEN YOU'RE FINISHED WITH IT. IT'S THE STAFF KEY. EVERYBODY IN THIS OFFICE USES IT."*

I also thank Comus, the Greek god of comedy, as I summon all my acting skills to keep a straight face.

"Do you mind if I use it now?" I ask, innocently. Full disclosure: I'm hoping to induce a bit more drama for the record. I love improv.

"JUST USE IT THEN PUT IT RIGHT BACK!!" She spits out her afterthought, *"WHY AM I BEING BOTHERED WITH THESE TRIVIALITIES?"* She storms back into her cloister. Poor thing. She must have gotten up on the wrong side of the incarnation.

When I return to the office, I hang the key back in its sacred place and go downstairs, returning to guard duty at the 95th Street exit. I take my seat in the folding chair on the desolate landing. Suddenly, a student bursts through the double doors from the hallway. He stops short in surprise when he sees me.

"You're not supposed to use this exit," I tell him kindly.

"They kicked me out," he explains as he bolts through the outlawed exit to 95th Street.

A little later a uniformed security guard opens the double doors.

"Hi. I'm Elizabeth," I say warmly.

"I'm Mario. Just checking on things."

"Nice to meet you."

Shortly after that a stocky middle-aged man comes through the doors. I smile at him. He's obviously going to use the exit.

"Are you the custodian?" I ask him.

He laughs. "After 35 years in the building...I'm Mr. Nelson," he says. "I teach Spanish."

"Oh, hi," I say. "Sorry. Mr. Ortega told me nobody is supposed to use this exit. No students. No teachers." He laughs again and I smile. "I guess you're on top of all this," I say. He opens the 95th Street door and disappears. I forgive myself. After all, I'm a rookie guard.

Third period approaches. It's ten-fifteen.

"I'm going to lunch," I call out to Mr. Ortega as I head out to 96th Street. He's about five feet away. He doesn't hear a thing.

Back at school, I stop into Mr. Ortega's room. He's got three girls there, writing something.

"I was just wondering if you know how old this school building is?"

"1904. They had a centennial in 2004. Look in the hallway."

I do. A plaque reads, "Public School 150." The floor is covered with beautiful small mosaic tiles. In the center there is a decorated box with the letters:

MVTHS

"I just found the old school name: *Manhattan Vocational and Technical High School*," I report to Mr. Ortega. He doesn't hear me.

I realized during seventh period that I needed to tell the administration that the DOE is sending me to another mandated interview. Guess I'll go see Mr. Mahoney. Principal's probably still working on the bathroom key.

I head up to his fourth-floor office. He's twiddling with his computer screen. I stand quietly at the door. He looks up at me and goes back to his screen. Another moment and he looks up again at me. I assume it's my time to speak.

"Hi, Mr. Mahoney. I just want to let you know that I have a mandated interview tomorrow at 9:00 am. It's on Grand Street, so if it's all right with you, I'll go there and then come here. I should be back by 11."

"That's fine," he mutters. My guess is since it's 2 pm, there might be a Guinness in his near future. He seems to be in a mild fog of anticipation. He doesn't smile at me nor show any sign of human connection, but I feel his impending lightness.

I've got one more 45-minute turn in the marble stairwell and I get to call it a day. I'm alone in the stairwell. It's a perfect time to work on my script. We open in four weeks. As I run my lines, a sweaty b'boy who's been working out in the adjacent "Gymnatorium" looks through the glass window of the door to the gym. I continue. He cracks open the door.

"You singing?" he asks me.

"Actually, I'm rapping." There's one hip hop scene in my show.

"Can I hear you?

"Sure," I say. And I start at the top. He stands there transfixed, dead-ass serious. He closes the door. I continue to run my lines. A moment later he opens the door.

"C'mere," he says to a friend. "You gotta hear this." He and his buddy crowd the open door. "Can you rap for him, Miz?"

Just then his teacher comes up behind them.

"Back to class," he commands and my audience disappears back into the Gymnatorium.

I continue my rehearsal on the landing until the bell rings. It's been a productive day.

Thursday, January 19, 2012

Today it's down to Grand Street for my mandated interview. I'm not sure what I'll find. I'm still hoping Mignon's school will be able to hire me till the end of the year. The school I'm interviewing for is in the former Seward Park High School, now broken into small schools. My interview is at the Urban Assembly Academy of Government and Law.

As I step out of the elevator, I notice how clean and quiet it is. Flags from Harvard, Penn, Columbia, Syracuse and other top universities are hanging from the ceiling, tastefully separated from each other. A very sweet lady directs me to the office where I'm greeted pleasantly and asked to wait in a comfy chair. A colorful Van Gogh hangs on the wall opposite me. I've arrived at the Academy of Good Vibes. The young principal and I have a nice chat about filling in for a medical leave and I leave, thinking he might call me to give a demo lesson.

I arrive back at Life Sciences before 11. *Bring happiness,* I say to myself as I enter. *That's my job: bring happiness.* I greet the security guard and custodian with a big "Hi!"

The custodian returns my greeting with a great big smile.

Upstairs, I do a quick scan of the main office. No principal in sight. The one secretary I haven't spoken to shoves my schedule at me. I say, "Hi. I'm Elizabeth. We haven't really met yet."

"I'm just covering for somebody," she says. Very serious.

"And you are...?"

"Gladys."

"Hi, Gladys. I have a letter from the school I just came from."

"Why you go to some other school?" Gladys demands. Attitude festering.

"I'm an ATR. I had a mandatory interview." I continue to be polite.

"Oh," says Gladys.

"I wonder if I could have a copy of this letter for my files?" I ask sweetly.

"I got no time to make no copies." A little snarly.

"That's fine. No problem. I'll get one later." As I reach to take the letter back, Gladys slams her hand on my letter.

"I'll do it later," she snaps. Once something lands on her desk, back off. We're in her territory. Kind of a DMZ between her and the principal's haunt.

"Thanks so much, Gladys," I smile. *Bring happiness,* I think. "Enjoy the rest of the day," I say.

"OK," she says. A little softer.

It's a bit after 11 and I'm back in the stairwell. The old newspaper and candy wrapper are still here. There are some brand new balls of dust on the stairs. Guess the nighttime cleaning crew was off last night. Cracked marble. Crud on the banister. European artisans, the golden age of school buildings. Days of yore.

On the other side of the double doors, students have gathered at their lockers.

"Yo. That bitch..."

"He f***kin' said..."

It's 12:26 pm. Two-and-a-half hours are left till I am allowed to leave this marble dungeon.

700 students here. Mightn't there be one or two who could use my help? Ya think?

Mignon is sinking deeper into the lower depths of my thoughts. We're both rudderless as we navigate the stormy seas of free public education in these United States of America.

I smell gas. I open the little window to let in the freezing air. Could there be a gas leak? I take my coat and head to the custodian's office.

"Hi. I'm assigned to the 95th Street exit," I tell the secretary. "I believe I've been smelling gas."

"What's that?" A male voice rings out. The woman opens the door wide. A thick, middle-aged man sits behind the desk. He's obviously the boss. "I absolutely guarantee you there is no gas leak," he barks.

"It's just that I could feel it in my head a bit." I tread lightly.

"Then you should go up to the office and tell them you don't feel well." Still barking, of course. I wonder if employees of this school are required to take an entry-level course in self-righteous indignation.

"No. It's not that serious. Just thought I'd mention it," I say. "In the building where I live, they really jump if someone reports a gas smell," I add gently.

Mr. Boss puffs himself up. "I absolutely guarantee there is no gas leak in this building!" He crosses his arms and waits for me to make his day.

"OK. Thanks." And I go back to the stairwell. I leave the little window open and move my chair down to the second landing. It's 20 degrees outside. I'm cold. But I only have 25 minutes till my seventh-period break. Maybe I'll go use the restroom. That'll take up ten of them. Wish I didn't have to carry this jacket around with me everywhere I go. I wonder if other people who work here have a place to hang their coats?

Indian spice tea can cure anything. I grab a quick lunch at the local Hindu establishment. Om. Yumm.

Shortly before my seventh-period break, the friendly custodian had appeared on my stairwell.

"I know you talked to my boss," he said. "I just wanted to come down here and explain to you what you were smelling. I know people around here can be kind of tough with you. I could see you was a nice lady."

"Why, that's very kind of you. I pegged you for an upbeat guy when I first met you."

"What you're smelling isn't gas. You see...this is an old building. When they built it, the rainwater and the sewer drained into the same place. What they're doing now is separating out the two. So that's what you smelled. No need to worry. It's not gas."

Great. It's sewage. Much better.

Friday, January 20, 2012

Last day at LSSS. What should I wear to sit in the marble dungeon today? Lessee, it must be casual, not too victim-y and nothing that can't handle dirt balls and the smell of sewage. Leggings, a smart long-sleeved tee and a knock-off designer jacket that looks as if it had been cut from a tapestry on a wall of the Cloisters. Perfect. These can all be fumigated. Maybe I won't have dungeon duty. They might give me seventh graders. Honestly, I prefer the dungeon. I arrive, punch in the clock and pick up my schedule. It says:

95th Street Locker area and Exit, periods 1 through 8.

So happy I'm *prêt a porter*. I head downstairs, cross the lobby, patiently wait for a cluster of students to pause their play punching and let me pass. I take my place behind the double doors. The stairwell emits a pungent aroma. I assume the sewage transfer is proceeding swimmingly well. Opening the little window, I walk down to the basement landing. It doesn't smell so bad down here. This should be a relaxing day. I've brought my copy of *The Hollywood Reporter*. Fassbinder profile. I take out the half sandwich I've saved from yesterday's lunch and tea. The double doors open. A young man, snappily dressed in a sweater and slacks, appears.

"Mr. Mahoney wants to see you in the main office." Rats, I was just getting comfy. Just then, an actual rodent disappears into the wall.

Mr. Mahoney is seated at the computer, his back to me. Patiently, I stand to his side. I'm not sure he knows I'm here.

"Excuse me, Mr. Mahoney," I say quietly.

A quick quarter-turn of his big head. A scowl.

"A teacher just called in. I'll give you your schedule in a minute," he grunts.

I stand back and wait as he grapples doggedly with his computer. Five minutes later, he gives me the schedule. It's full of codes. He leaves without another word.

I can't decipher the codes, the subject area or the lesson plan. Perhaps Mr. Mahoney knows. Perhaps I can find him. Perhaps he will tell me. I start walking through the long and winding hallways.

"Have you seen Mr. Mahoney?" I ask a passing adult.

"No."

I walk the length of the hallway, around ancient corners, turn around at dead ends and go back in the same direction. Peeking back into the main office, I see Mr. Mahoney there, laughing with a middle-aged lady. "I missed you while you were out," he says to her. Hmmm. Maybe they're having a little academic tryst. Never mind. I have five minutes before second period. As their little verbal flirtation peters out I say, "Excuse me, Mr. Mahoney. Is there a lesson plan?"

"I'll get you one," he snarls.

The bell rings. Students blast into the hallways. I take all my belongings and find room 205. There is a pack of young students standing outside the locked door.

"Hey, Miz!! I had you for music!"

It's seventh grade.

"OH MY GOD! Ms. Vertigo's absent? HOLLER!!!"

"You students need to wait until I get a key. I'll be right back."

I leave them in the feral hallway and head back to the main office. There are two secretaries keeping it on the down low in case *Obergruppenführer* Principal Von Yellster bursts in seeking a sacrifice.

"Do you know where I can find Mr. Mahoney?" I ask one of them.

"He's right out there in the hall."

I go out the office door adjacent to the principal's office and there's Mr. Mahoney.

"TAKE THAT HOOD OFF!!!" He is screaming at two boys. *"YOU HEARD ME!!! OFF WITH YOUR HOOD."* Both boys—and we're talking six-feet-tall boys here—are laughing hysterically at him, trying to dodge him. One of them takes his hood off. Before Mahoney can stop him, the other one races down the hall.

"YOU'RE GONNA PAY FOR THAT!!" Mahoney hollers. My dental fillings rattle.

"I don't have a key to the classroom," I say with great respect.

"Follow me."

He leads me back down to the classroom. More seventh graders are clustered around the locked door. A slapping match has broken out between a girl and boy.

"SETTLE DOWN!!!"

The girl gives the boy a last slap. Mahoney glares at her. He opens the door. The students rush in.

"Yeah! No teacher!!

"I'm Ms. Rose," I tell them. Most of them can't hear me above the din of excitement. There's another adult woman in the class. A para—thank you, Jesus. Mahoney has left the room. I have about twenty seventh graders and no lesson plan. I walk from table to table.

"Hi. I'm Ms. Rose. I'm your substitute for today." Most of them don't hear me. They're too busy hitting each other, talking or texting. "I will call Mr. Mahoney if you do not behave well." *Stern Pedagogue.*

It's a long day. Low- and highlights include:

> A boy in the back jumping up, dancing and pounding on the table. Several boys at the two back tables jumping up and joining in this ritual boogie-on-down while the para stands across the room.

> An algebra class where I'm the team teacher and a girl allows me to help her to dilate a quadrangle. I coach her for 25 minutes. Dilation. Multiplying fractions.

"If you weighed 120 pounds before Thanksgiving and ate so much you got to be 180 pounds, you'd be how much bigger than when you started?"

"One and one half times?"

She gets it.

"Thank you, Miz."

"That's more work she did today than she ever did in this class," says Mr. A, her charming teacher from Africa.

"You did great," I tell her again as she leaves with a victory smile.

I feel like a teacher again. I skip out to lunch.

After lunch, I arrive back at the main office. Mr. Mahoney is gnawing on a rat he's just strangled. OK. I'm gassin' you. Just wanted to see if you're paying attention. Maybe he can explain a pile of Spanish lesson plans a plump man handed me during math class. He is, after all, my "go to" guy.

"I don't know anything about it," he snaps at me when I gently… very gently…inquire as to its meaning.

Three classes in a row coming right up. I'm scared. When I get to room 206 for my fifth period, I find I only have one student. Two sweet girls in hijabs are sent in to take a test. Whew.

Thirty-five students on the next roster. But only half show up. They're ninth graders, friendly and well behaved. Again, whew.

Seventh period. Seventh graders. Same para from this morning. It's back to student explosions, cursing, electronics. The clock moves very slowly. I sit with two boys whose Metrocards have been stolen by someone who's picked their lockers downstairs.

"You have a dollar?" one of them asks me. "I gotta get home."

"After class ends, wait around and I'll see if I have one."

Class finally ends. I have a dollar for him.

"Thanks, Miz." He is relieved.

Eighth period. It's back to the marble dungeon till day's end. Before heading downstairs, I leave my neat, well-organized attendance sheets along with student work in Mr. Mahoney's mailbox. Mahoney's nowhere to be seen. Neither is *Oberprincipaltz*.

Back in the marble stairwell. Last period of my longest week. Next week is Regents week. Maybe Mignon can pass algebra. Wish I could help.

Bonne chance, Mignon.

The bell rings. Three pm. For the last time, I drink in the thick, green serpentine colors that slink through the marble floor, walls and stairs. I conjure up the spirits of those newly arrived American craftsmen, anonymous masters, who heated, bent, twisted and shaped that magnificent wrought iron banister in 1904. Imagination at work. Creativity in every turn. That's what we expect from our students, isn't it? That's what we expect from our better selves, right?

Today our educational system, like the marble, is cracked and in need of polishing. You can't just throw a test at it and expect to fix it. You can't just give it a grade. You can't just throw money at it. Money helps but the expensive compound you bought might harm rather than restore the marble. Education is an art, a science and a work-in-progress. Improving it is a complex task...but not an impossible one. First of all, you gotta be there. With the kids. With the teachers. In the classrooms. In the hallways...

...in the stairwells.

One last look and I escape through the forbidden 95th Street exit.

Monday, January 23, 2012

High School of Arts, Imagination and Inquiry (HSAII)

Regents Week

It's back to the MLK, Jr. concrete behemoth opposite Lincoln Center. Al-Go-Rithummm, has assigned me to the High School of Arts, Imagination and Inquiry this week.

I wish I could have slept in this morning. The Giants kept me up. Overtime. Field goal attempt. The 49ers called a time out. They were trying to ice the kicker. *Foggedaboudit. We win!* I can't turn off the tube until I hear from my hero. Eli's coming—hide your heart now.

"Hi!" I say to the security guardess, as I enter the lobby. "My third time in this building!"

"Third time! Oh my!" She sends me to the school's payroll secretary.

"There's nobody out today. Just go upstairs. You can stay in the room up there they have for teachers."

I walk into the main office. I'm carrying my guitar. It needs some repair before my show opens in February. I can scoot it down to 48th Street after school.

I offer to help in the office. They have nothing. I settle in the teachers' room with my cuppa tea.

And that, my friends, is that. No classes on Regent week. Students only come to school to take the tests.

No teachers are absent.

There are no exits to guard.

No marble dungeon.

There is no clerical work.

There is no Mignon to help with her algebra Regents.

There is absolutely nobody who needs me.

But hey! I have my guitar.

Our first production meeting is tomorrow, after school. I can run lines, practice. For breaks, I can walk across the Lincoln Center Plaza, dream of performing my show at the Vivian Beaumont Theatre, *or* singing the role of Amina in *La Sonnambula* at the Met, *or* leading a blusey big band at Rose Hall, celebrating the women composers of the American Songbook for Jazz at Lincoln Center. Of all of these, the last one is the most intimidating. Not because of the music. I got that. It's Winton. Artistic director of Jazz @LC, Mr. Marsalis is more talented than most of the humans. He scares me.

I'm off to Century 21 to visit my money.

Monday, January 30, 2012

BARUCH COLLEGE CAMPUS HIGH SCHOOL (BCCHS)

Baruch Again

It's the last day of the fall semester. All ATRs have been assigned to return to their first schools. Why? To simplify the distribution of W-2 tax forms. Students are off today. Regents week is history. City teachers are scheduled for a full day of professional development.

It's old home week.

"Hey, girl!" The school safety beauties get up from the security desk and give me a couple of bear hugs.

"We missed you!"

"I missed you, too. You have no idea."

"Welcome back!" Angela, my ATR buddy from our first month together at Baruch, is happy to see me. "I was hoping you'd be here."

"Great to see you again." Ms. D, the English teacher/dean, leader of the Danish expedition in September, recognizes me after four months. "My kids really loved you."

"That was a great prep on social contracts you gave me. Love your kids!" I chirp.

"Angela. You look busy," I say.

"Angela is shredding old Regents exams," Marilyn, the school secretary, informs me.

"May I help?" I couldn't ask for a more satisfying task.

"Sorry. We only have one shredder."

After lunch, Angela heads back to the shredder and piles of Regents exams. How I envy her. I want to be on the Regents shredding team. Especially if I got to shred them a week before they were scheduled. I'd tie them up with a bow as a gift to Mignon, Akram, Tavio and the rest of my international crew.

Tuesday, January 31, 2012

It's the first day of the new spring semester.

"Hey Ms. Rose! You're back!" a couple of boys call out to me. I can't believe they remember my name.

In the first floor corridor, three seniors are sitting on the floor. One is a dark-haired girl with a black acoustic guitar. The guitar draws me in as I give them a big smile.

"Hey, Ms. Rose." I plop down next to them. The guitarist plays while the others small talk. She is playing some great blues guitar.

"You are a very good guitar player," I say. Her name is Hara. "I'm a guitar player, too," I tell her. She lets me play her guitar for a minute. We're bonding.

"I wish we had another guitar. We could play together," I tell her as I give her back her guitar. "Play some more for me." She rips into another blues. She has great time.

"So where have you guys applied to colleges?" I ask them. We're all sitting cross-legged in the narrow hall. Anyone wanting to pass has to squeeze by. I love being a teenager.

"Baruch, Binghamton, and California," the boy says.

"Anybody heard yet?"

"No. We're all waiting."

"May I have the guitar for a minute again?" Hara hands it to me. I start a blues shuffle in B flat and sing...

I'm a senior student
Don't know where I'll be next year
Yeah I'm a senior student
Don't know where I'll be next year
Binghamton, Baruch or UC
All I know is there better be some beer.

Upstairs, I walk into an advisory I'm covering for an absent teacher.

"How did you do on your report card?" an 11th-grade girl asks a boy.

"Umm...maybe 91.3 overall."

"I can't get to 90," says the girl, frustrated.

"What's your overall score?" I ask her.

"89.6...something like that," she says.

"That's very good," I tell her.

"I need to break a 90," she mopes.

In three weeks we open at the Cherry Lane Theatre, Off Broadway. I haven't heard back from the DOE whether they will give me a one-week leave without pay. I call my union rep.

"They denied it. I called them today." That's it. No leave granted. Game over.

I need a strategy. How can I perform a show five nights in a row plus two shows on Saturday and work a full-time job? My alternatives?

Do both: teach all day and do the show at night. Side effects: *Burnout: vocal, physical and comedic.*

Get a doctor's note for the whole week. *Not my style.*

Resign from the DOE.

None of these alternatives seem great. Our show opening falls on mid-winter recess when there's no school. Perfect. It's the second week of my run, when schools are back in session...that is the tricky bit. If I resign that would make the DOE bean counters sing. Goodbye, salary. Hello, freelance.

I can feel my high vibrational energy begin to dissipate. I grab it back as I compose an imaginary letter.

Dear DOE,

Thank you for denying my request for leave of absence without pay for one week. In the cosmic sense, I'm sure it's a gift. Can you please let me know where I might return or exchange it?

Friday, February 3, 2012

It's my last day here. I love Baruch. The students are so bright, the staff, solicitous.

For my last act, I get to sub for the global lit class—the same bunch I subbed for in September, when the teacher took a group of students to Denmark to complete an exchange.

I'm given a lesson plan. Students are to read the intro and author's preface to *Woman at Point Zero* by Egyptian author and psychiatrist Nasal El Saadawi. They're to take notes while they read.

"Hey, guys, remember me? Ms. Rose? Code of Hammurabi?" Yes.

"So we're going to read this book. I guess if you want to go farther than the assigned part, you can."

"Ms. D doesn't want us to read ahead," one of them tells me.

"Really?" They all nod in agreement. These kids are not playing me.

"OK. I'm going to read it with you." The entire class of 35 students goes silent as they start their reading. I'm in the *bizzarro* world of public education where all the students want to learn and are eager to follow instructions.

The author, born in 1931, was raised in an unusual family. She, along with her brothers, was given an education at a time when most girls in Egypt did not get to go to school. She went to medical school and became a psychiatrist. Given an opportunity to study neurosis of women in prison, she took it. Shocked and deeply affected by the conditions of the prison, she began to interview women prisoners, one in particular.

"Guys," I say when it's time. "Who is this woman in prison?"

"A prostitute," somebody says, raising his hand.

"Why is she in prison?"

"She murdered her pimp," another says.

"What about the author? Was El Saadawi ever in prison before when she met this woman?"

"No. But later she was arrested herself."

"Why?" I ask.

"Because she said something...I don't remember exactly...maybe against the government," a girl offers. She's on the right track.

"She criticized a government person—wasn't it the president?" says another.

"That's right. A few years later, she criticized President Sadat. Imagine for a moment, you are a little girl growing up in an Egyptian family at this time. You see your brothers go off to school and you're not allowed to—just because you're a girl. How do you think you'd feel?"

A lively discussion continues until the bell rings.

Teaching = awesome.

After bidding Angela and the staff farewell, I walk all the way home up the east side. I wonder if Mignon passed her algebra Regents last week. I think of her story. It resonates with El Saadawi's heroine. A young girl is denied an education because of war. She's shuttered in a little house in the Ivory Coast for years with her illiterate mother, never learns to read and write. Although Mignon has escaped the Ivory Coast, she's still stuck in a sort of minimum-security enclave: *el barrio*. *Los* Regents. Twice a year, she tries to escape. It's battle by battle. Defeat after defeat. The conflict will rage another three years until she's 21. Then she will be set free, into the world, a young woman without a high school diploma. Barely literate, she will be free to make her own way.

"I wanna be...whaddya call dat kind of person dat helps people wid dere problems?" Mignon said when we talked about future dreams.

"A psychologist?" I said.

"Dat's it! Dat's whad I wanna be." Her sparkling enthusiasm jolts my memory.

Monday, February 6, 2012

NORMAN THOMAS HIGH SCHOOL (NTHS)

Classroom Miz-Management

Giants win! They defeated the Patriots in the Super Bowl! People outside my window are dancing and shouting on Second Avenue. I've stayed up late. I don't care. Our first rehearsal is scheduled for tonight at 6 pm. Energy. I'm going to need lots of energy.

I check in to NTHS, a school first condemned to be phased out then given a reprieve. The school is in a posh, east-Midtown neighborhood, right off Park Avenue on East 33rd Street. Lines of students are standing in the lobby, waiting to be scanned, searched and frisked, if necessary. A school safety guard directs me to room 128. An elderly gentleman is sitting behind the desk. I introduce myself with a big smile. He has a professional demeanor with an underlying sense of humor. He gives me the bell schedule and the annualization list, whatever the hell that is. He has me sign a time card and gives me two sets of bathroom and elevator keys. The fellow is prepared. A brown-haired woman comes in and starts laughing at him. He looks at her and parts his scarf. He's wearing a New England Patriots shirt.

"What? Why are you a Patriots fan?" I ask.

"Why are you a Giants fan?" he counters.

"Because I am from New York," I say, a little derision in my tone.

"The Giants aren't from New York," he says. "They don't play here. But tomorrow they're getting a big parade and we are paying for it. It's our tax money."

"Are you from New England?"

"No."

"Then I still don't understand why you're a Patriots fan."

"The Patriots are a much better team on paper than the Giants."

"True," I say," although I haven't the slightest idea what a football stat looks like. "And Tom Brady's adorable," I add. "I'm sorry for your loss," I say, feigning sympathy.

"Don't be sorry for me. Here's your key to the *towl-id*."

"The what?" I ask.

"The *towl-id*," he drawls. "You know. The necessary room."

"Oh… the *toilet*. You have a bit of a drawl, don't you? Y'all from the South?"

"Yes I am."

"And you have a bit of an attitude." I believe I'm making a friend.

"Maybe I do but when I go back home to Georgia, I don't have any attitude. Don't need one there. Only in New York."

"When did you two start dating?" says a handsome, silver-haired male teacher who has walked in. Ignoring him, my new BFF turns to me and drawls, "You're going to be in CTT classes today. Team teaching."

"OK," I say as my heart sinks a little. That means special ed, aka, the wild bunch. At least there will be another teacher in the room. I get to play support. How bad can it be? Who knows? It might be fun.

NTHS is a large school with over 1100 students. Back in the early 2000s when the DOE closed a number of "failing" large schools, they sent a ton of "extra" students to NTHS. In 2004, they had to admit 1200 freshmen. The place was as crowded as a rush hour subway train with no stops. A big fight broke out and teachers demanded extra security. Which they got. By today, a majority of parents feel that their child is safe here.

After an economics class, my next period is American history class with Mr. Nosakhere.

"We have to practice Regents questions," he tells them. His words have a melodic African air. "Do questions one through five." He hands out a small green booklet, *US History Practice Test for Regents Examinations*. I'm beginning to think I might go into the Regents prep biz. It has, after all, become a billion-dollar business.

"I ain't doing no Regents questions." A lively girl in the front of the class speaks up. Her large necklace shows her name: Kamilah.

"Yes, you are!" Mr. N turns on her.

"You need to stop gettin' on me," she says. "I told you I ain't gonna do no Regents."

"You have to pass." He becomes strident. Kamilah picks up her voice. I walk up to Mr. N.

"Would you mind if I work with Kamilah?" I ask him quietly.

"Yes, of course."

"Would you like me to go over these questions with you?" She looks me over.

"Aiight."

I pull up a chair.

"I just want to let you know that I don't like the fact that you have to take Regents. I believe there are better ways to get you excited about learning." I speak very quietly so as not to disturb Mr. N. Kamilah shakes her head in agreement. "But unfortunately, you have to take them. It's the law. So you might just forget about how annoyed you are and focus on passing the test. Otherwise they can keep you in school till you're 21." She scowls a little but shows no resistance. I ask her to read the first question:

> Farmers in the Ohio River Valley gained the greatest economic benefit when the US acquired the:
> 1. Oregon Territory
> 2. Gadsen Purchase
> 3. Louisiana Purchase
> 4. Mexican Cession

"Any ideas, Kamilah?" She shakes her head. "Do you know where Oregon is?"

"No."

"Let's get a map." I search a nearby closet and find a textbook with maps. We look up the Ohio Valley. Then we locate Oregon. I find a good map of the Louisiana Purchase. She immediately gets it.

"That's it," she says. "Its right next to the Ohio River Valley."

Kamilah suddenly turns into the best student in the room. When Mr. N goes over the questions with the whole class, she volunteers to read them and calls out the answers. She gets most of them right.

"I don't like Africans," she tells Mr. N as she gets up to leave.

When she's gone, Mr. N shakes his head.

"Thank you," he says. "That one's got an attitude." He has a thick, musical accent.

"So, may I ask you where you come from?"

"I was born in Nigeria."

"Isn't that where the Ibo and Hausa tribes fought?" My grad school history tweaks my brain.

"You know Ibo and Hausa?" He's very excited.

"I just remember the stories about the war. I don't know any details."

"I lived through that war," he says. "When I was 14, I left for England. I got a doctorate in California."

"You have an amazing story."

"Not so amazing, considering I'm here," he says, indicating this room.

Sixth period I'm all alone with an economics class. Let's just say I survive.

The incredibly long morning ends and I'm exhausted. I go out to Park Avenue where the sun is shining. I want to resign today. I roll the numbers. I can do it. I've got enough saved for the next year. Then what? Fatigue makes me slip into negativity. I know better than this.

It's a beautiful day. I'm almost done. Ninth period is starting. One more class. I get to leave at 3:01.

But I can't go home and crash. Instead, our first rehearsal looms.

Thirty-Sixth Street Studio, 5 pm.

I'm running on fumes. I've been carrying my guitar around with me all day so I could grab a quick snack and head straight to the studio. I'll pick up my energy when I start performing. I hope.

"Oh—we just want you to run through your show. This will be the first time the team actually gets to see it. Nothing to worry about. Just have fun." Gretchen, my mentor/director, cheers me on as I stagger in flashing my "actress" smile.

Nothing to worry about unless you consider that there is an unexpected audience of the theatre's board of directors, as well as the crew. Oy.

A little nervous, I begin the first scene. It's funny. Or so I thought. The set designer chuckles softly and I think there's a tiny smirk on the stage manager. And that's all, folks. For the next 70 minutes I work the show. Scene after scene. Song after song. I tell the stories. I play all the characters. 19 songs. There's complete silence after each one. I've entertained Alzheimer's patients who've shown more enthusiasm. I'm so thrown I forget a whole verse. Sputtering, I see that some of them are taking notes. Maybe they're grading me.

An eon transpires. I finish the show. Everybody applauds. A tall, handsome man approaches me.

"Nice job," he says kindly and shakes my hand.

"I'm a little nervous, gotta admit it," I confess to him. "But thanks."

With a generous grin he says, "Well...now that you've got the first olive out of the jar, the rest of them will come out easy." We both laugh. I wonder who he is.

I find out later. He's Matt Williams, writer/producer on "The Cosby Show," "Roseanne" and "Home Improvement" to name a few. Great. I wonder if David Geffin was hiding behind him.

Wednesday, February 8, 2012

Today I'm assigned to help Ms. A as a team teacher in her global history classes. CTT. IEPs. Kids drag in with their saggy pants, the ubiquitous "N" word, cursing and emotional detonations.

Ms. A is 24 years old. After the first class, we get a chance to talk.

"I'm not a history teacher," she tells me. "I have a masters in technology education. I'm licensed for elementary school only. I'm really a sub. When I came here for my interview, they told me I could work with smart boards and tech. But the school doesn't actually have any smart boards. So now I'm stuck here. You need two years' experience to apply to teach in a charter school."

"This is crazy," she continues. "They've given me two different classes with the same kids. They're both global history classes and they have exactly the same kids. One class starts at the beginning of the global curriculum and the other in the middle. These poor kids are learning global starting with the Ancient World (4000BC-500AD) in one class and the Age of Revolution (1750-1914) in their other class at the same time."

"How do you do it, especially considering it's not your area?"

"I stay about two days ahead of them.

Thursday, February 9, 2012

I declare today my Bathrobe Day.

A good friend of mine, a physician, says that we all need to take a day to stay home in our bathrobes. A Bathrobe Day is a primary source of renewable energy. My energy is not so fabulous this morning. Last night I prepared everything for a full day of school and afternoon rehearsal at the theatre. Right now, I've got nothing. I call in lethargic.

Yesterday was tough. I was assigned to support Ms. A, the lovely elementary technology teacher who was well prepared with her "do now's," power points, and readings. Third period was our first class of the day. The students ruptured the fragile peace as they invaded.

"I like big butts," sang a skinny hooded boy with slits for eyes.

"Dominique," said Ms. A. "Will you please sit down and stop singing?"

"I LIKE BIG BUTTS, BIG BUTTS..."

Dominique got louder and louder. I walked over to him and quietly said, "Hi Dominique. It's rather difficult for Ms. A to teach if you are singing. She's being very respectful. Won't you please stop?"

Dominique would not look me in the eye. His eyes were quite red. He was high. I got it. He jumped up and joined the big explosive kid in the center of the class. Other kids were laughing and shouting, cursing, N this, N that. F this. MF that.

A tough kid in a leather jacket got up from a seat in the back of the class and walked to the double door. He opened it and started yelling at kids in the hall who came over to join him. I walked over to him.

"Hi. Are you leaving?" I asked him.

"No." He looked at me threateningly.

"I have to close the classroom door. Will you please come in so I can do that?" I'm very respectful. Quiet.

He blocked me from the hallway. Threatening.

"I'm going to have to get some help," I told him. He stood firm. "Would you mind stepping a little to the right so I can go past you?" I said again quietly.

He did not budge. He was also high. Weed. I could smell it. He looked very darkly at me. There was danger in him.

I opened the adjacent double door and walked out. Immediately, he slammed both doors, locking me out. I walked down the hall, found a young lady school safety officer and told her we had a problem.

"Get the dean to 516," she radioed immediately as she followed me back to the classroom.

She unlocked the door and we both walked in. The dean was there in a moment. I pointed out the kid who locked me out.

"I did not!" he exclaimed. "She just walked out." Ms. A corroborated my version.

The dean took him out. She's a tough little lady. Scary.

"Please write this up for me," she said as she left.

I went back into the room. Naturally, the chaos had increased because of this episode. Kids were yelling.

"Oh...did you hear what she said?"

"Snitch."

"Yo Miz. Why you call security?"

My ears hurt from the ghetto language all around me. Sleep deprived, I left my sense of humor in the subway. I am beginning to dislike these kids. I'm beginning to think negatively about their future. These kids don't have a prayer. They will be marginalized all their lives. They have no idea how great learning is. I will not make any difference in their lives. Ms. A is doing hours of preparation for each lesson and they are metaphorically urinating on her effort and hope.

I went out into the hall with the paper on which I wrote up the incident. The dean was there with the leather jacket kid.

"He wants to do work. Do you have work for him?" she asked me.

We went back into class. Our entrance was another disruption. Ms. A gave Leather Boy a handout. He and I walked out again.

"He wants to go to class," the dean said. "Can he?"

I looked at this kid. He gave me a criminal stare. I softened a minute.

"Would you like to come back to class?" I asked him.

"Yeah." Sullen but a little hopeful.

"OK. It's fine with me if you come back."

He sat back down in the back. The class continued to be disruptive, rude and ignorant.

Score: Another 45 minutes for the ghetto. Learning: zero.

There were three more classes like this one. I hit bottom.

That was yesterday.

Today...bathrobe ruminations.

I haven't resigned my position. Despite burn out, it feels good to share this journey. Recently, that is, over the last 100 years, the topic of public education has provoked a war of words, blame and anger. While everybody's hurling flame-throwers at each other, the ghetto triumphs over the kids. It skewers their brains, warps their values and puts them in danger. Take any one of these kids out of the ghetto, even for 20 minutes in a one-on-one, and with patience you'll discover a child who wants your help. Give them a little praise, they'll try a little harder. Speak to them with respect, they'll light up. Treat them like winners, they'll have small academic successes. Keep that up and you begin to pave a road with little victories. Modest victories lead to bigger ones. That's where Mignon and I were headed. Consistency. Love. Every day I spent with her, the foundation was fortified.

There may very well be a Mignon or two in Room 516, but I'm not going to find them.

Friday, February 10, 2012

One bathrobe day behind me, a great rehearsal, articles about our show published in Playbill.com, TheaterMania and Broadway.com, and I'm ready for my last day at NTHS.

"Hey Miz! Whasup?" some of the kids greet me as I walk in.

I'm actually happy to see them again. It's a wonder what a good night of sleep will do.

Ms. A has given them a fill-in worksheet about the Crusades. I interrupt a galère of four girls discussing the relative benefits of large and middle-sized penises.

"It ain't gotta be that big. I had a smaller one. It was OK. It don't make no much difference," a light-skinned little girl with a ponytail affirms.

"Anybody need help with the Crusades?"

"No, Miz. We got it."

They go back to their discussion of anatomical diversity as a girl with a baseball hat waves me over to her desk.

"Yo, Miz," she says. "When did the Age of Faith begin?"

You can make up your own joke here.

We look at the textbook and decide to call it at 910, the year the monks built their first monastery in Cluny, France.

"Is that AD or BC?" she asks me. Fair question.

Eight minutes before the period ends, the ponytail comes over to me. She's waving the paper that requires the fill-ins.

"Miz. Wha's the answers?"

"OK, let's look at the text together." I help her find the answers. She doesn't know where Europe or Jerusalem is. I show her a map of the Crusaders' routes.

"How do you spell Christianity?" she asks me. "What's a cathedral?"

"Have you ever seen St. Patrick's Cathedral? It's just a few blocks from here."

"Never heard of it, Miz."

We continue with the Crusades fill-in assignment. I hope she makes it to the Enlightenment.

As the period ends, her crew of three girls clamor around her to copy down the answers she wrote on her fill-in.

My work at NTHS is done.

Monday, February 13, 2012

Chelsea Career and Technical Education High School

(CCTEHS)

Walking Distance to the Theatre

Our show opens in eight days. Great spirit of the theatre, grant me ENERGY!

I'm back in West Soho, on the third floor of the five-story walk-up that houses the iSchool where I had that incredibly noisy interview back in October. If I see the AP, I doubt he'll recognize me. Unless, of course, I yell at him. That might trigger his memory.

He's not around. A secretary, who appears to have worked here since the Boer War, greets me with the enthusiasm of a ground sloth.

"You have no schedule today. Go to the teachers' lounge."

I head down the hall and enter the room. It's a comfortable place. I spend the whole day there.

Teachers come in and out. I get a few "hellos."

I don't seek out new friends. An actor prepares.

I silently run my lines, have lunch, run lines again.

Eighth period a lovely woman with a full head of curls and the energy of Patty Labelle bursts into the teachers' lounge. She turns to the only other teacher in the room who looks like he's just finished a marathon. "Did you know that my son—that's what I call him—my son—was just accepted as an intern at the New York Historical Society? I am so proud of him!"

"You mean Joaquin?" says the exhausted guy, perking up. "He's a good student."

"When he was getting ready for his interview, I coached him. Now don't you say any *uuhs*, or *humms*, I told him. Whatever they ask you, you come right in with an answer. Have a few questions prepared to ask the interviewer. We practiced and I got him a tie."

"I could have given him a tie," says the fellow. He's transformed from weary to perky.

"I tell you, I just love that boy," she continues. "He wants to be an entrepreneur but he doesn't know in what area. I told him—you gotta make a plan—you can't just go out there without some idea of what kind of an entrepreneur you want to be. I mean he's going to go to college and then get his MBA but he has to know what direction he's setting out in…that's what I told him."

Ms. Curls busts out of the room, overflowing with the joy of her "son's" success. Victory is sweet. Also contagious.

Tuesday, February 14, 2012

The Name Game

After a lovely walk across Spring Street, I enter the main office. "You have a schedule today," says Secretary Cranky with a frown. She hands me a pile of packets and a schedule entitled, "Teacher Emergency Assignment." Judging from the title, I wonder if I will have to perform surgery.

"Do you speak Spanish?" growls Crank.

"No." I answer. *"No puedo hablar español…pero comprendo algunas palabras,"* I show off my one Spanish sentence.

"Well, that's better than I can do. You're the Spanish teacher today. Room 210."

I'm 15 minutes early. I head into 210. It's a big, clean room, but it's very hot. Can't open the windows. The attendance sheets show I'm teaching every other period: 1, 3, 5, and 7. Not exactly a Fibonacci sequence, but, oddly, manageable. Each period at this school is one hour long. I can stretch. A few students start to drift in. By 8:30, the official start of the period, I have five students sitting at their desks, ready to work. There are 25 students registered for this class.

"Where's everybody else?" I ask the early birds.

"Everybody comes in late," one of them calls out.

As each student's entered, I've greeted them. "Hi. I'm Ms. Rose. Happy Valentine's Day."

"Hi, Miz."

I ask them for their names. They all give me Spanish names. One of them, a tall, handsome boy with a baseball cap, tells me, "Tommy De Los Angeles."

"Oh. That's a great name," I tell him. "Tommy Angel. You like that?" I ask him.

"Yeah, Miz."

"So—most of you must speak Spanish, right?" They nod their heads. "How do you say 'Happy Valentine's Day' in Spanish?"

"I dunno, Miz," says Tommy.

"Does it start with *feliz*?" I ask.

"*Feliz*—yes," says a soft-spoken girl.

"So…would it be *Feliz…*" And I write it on the board. "What else? How would you say day—isn't it *dia*?"

"I think it's *feliz dia de…*"

"I think you're right," I encourage her as she stops there. "Is it Valentine? Same word?"

"You have to go *san*," she says. I write *san* on the board. "Is that 'saint'?" I ask.

"Yes, Miz."

"So—it's *feliz dia de san…*and is it the same word, Valentine?"

"That's it, Miz."

I draw a big heart on the board next to the greeting. A beefy boy straggles in a bit late. He's got a nice smile.

"Hi, I say. "Mr. D is out today. I'm Ms. Rose. What's your name?"

"Tommy de los Angeles," he says as he walks across the room and sits down next to the other "Tommy de los Angeles." Game on.

"So...you're Tommy de los Angeles. That's funny because he's also named Tommy de los Angeles. Quite a coincidence, don't you think?"

They all burst out laughing as I don my fake outrage.

"OK. So one of you is lying." I look them both squarely in the eye.

"That's my name, Miz. Fa real." So says the beefy guy who just came in. The tall handsome one was playing me. I walk over behind him.

"So—why don't you tell me your real name."

"I did, Miz." He's lying. I'm turning into Detective Lenny Briscoe.

"No you di-int," I say, mocking him. "What's your real name? You're busted!" Everybody's laughing.

"He's Avery, Miz," says Tommy II, the beefy one. "I'm Tommy."

"So...Avery...all that stuff about being Tommy Angel. You were playing me right along, word?"

"No, Miz. I'm Tommy. He's Avery."

"'Fraid not, Avery. Now I know every word you say is not the truth."

"I'm not lyin', Miz."

"Yes, you are," one of the girls calls out. "He's Avery, Miz."

I stand over him, in a faux threatening stance.

"I don't like it when students play me...just because I'm a sub. I'm onto you, Mr. Avery. I may be mad old and I may be shorter than you...but I can take you down." I say this in ma best ghetto speak. They all laugh as some more stragglers come in.

The beefy kid decides it's his turn to mess with me.

"Yo Miz! He ain't Avery. I'm Avery."

"Yo, Tommy Angel." I give him the evil eye. "Remember. I can take you down."

Wednesday, February 15, 2012

Today, Avery walks into my second-period class.

"Avery, again? Or is it Tommy de Los Angeles?" I ask as he walks in.

"It's Avery," he says. I check my bubble attendance sheet. There's no Avery on the roster.

"Avery. You're not in this class. I don't see your name."

"Yes, I am, Miz." He walks up to the front of the class. "Right there." He points to a name. It's Moussa Diane.

"That's not your name," I say.

"Yes it is Miz," He is very emphatic.

"You know, yesterday you told me your name was Tommy de Los Angeles. Now you're telling me you're Moussa Diane. I'm sorry but you're not in this class. Bye."

"Miz," he says. He's getting frustrated. "That's my brother, Avery. I'm in this class. I'm Moussa."

I look at him. He looks at me. He looks exactly like the guy who played me yesterday.

"You have a twin brother? You expect me to believe you?"

"Word, Miz. I'm in this class."

I look out at the class. They are enjoying this. I give them a big smile. "Guys...is this Avery's brother?" I ask them. A couple of boys nod. They could be playing me too. "What color baseball cap was Avery wearing yesterday?" I know. It's a ridiculous question. If he's the same guy, he'd know what he was wearing. But I can judge the way he answers.

"Ummm..." He thinks for a minute. "Red." It's the right answer. I know it doesn't prove anything but I'll go with the twin paradox.

"OK. I'll let you stay but I'll check on the existence of your alleged twin after class."

He promptly goes to his seat in the back of the room, puts his head down and falls asleep.

Steady rehearsals start tonight. We're on a roll now, right up to next Tuesday's opening. I'm feeling jittery. I have my guitar with me.

Thursday, February 16, 2012

I'm the Spanish teacher again. The friendly AP gives me a warm hello. "Mr. D, the Spanish teacher, is absent a great deal. Twenty-seven absences already this year. He's a full-time sub. I think he may have lost his license."

"How do you lose your license?" I ask him.

"I think he just stopped fulfilling the requirements."

"Have you considered getting a young, enthusiastic student teacher?" I say. I tell him about my experience at Manhattan/Hunter College High.

"Good idea. Maybe we can try that."

Friday, February 17, 2012

Today is the last day of school before mid-winter recess begins. Schools are closed for one week. Everybody is happy and impatient, ready to break out into vacation mode after school.

I haven't planned to journal much today. We rehearsed till 7:30 last night. Tonight we rehearse till 10 pm. Saturday's schedule goes from 10 am to 10 pm. We're off Sunday. Dress rehearsal with invited guests is Monday. We open Tuesday. I'm exhausted.

I'm five minutes early when I arrive at the office. I offer Ms. Crank a cheery good morning.

"You're cutting it a bit close, aren't you?" she says. I look at her. I'm early. What's she mean? Do classes start 15 minutes early today? "Pick up your schedule." She points to the desk.

I assume I'm subbing for the Spanish teacher.

"Did he leave any lesson plans?" I ask her.

"Well, you left no time for that did you?" she says scornfully. "Look at your schedule." I start walking into the adjacent room where I've spent the last two days.

She stops me. "You're not subbing for Mr. D. Look at your schedule."

She's speaking to me as if I were just caught trying to break into George Clooney's villa in Lake Como, Italy. The schedule says "MES 44."

"Where's MES?" I ask, thinking it might be a special room.

"What does your schedule say?" *Yo Miz, you OD violatin' me*. I keep my thoughts to myself. I surmise she's not a morning person. "Is there a lesson plan?"

"There will be students waiting outside the door by now. You better get up there now. Someone will bring you the work."

I head upstairs. Three students are waiting outside the door. Mr. M, the nicest AP in the world, is opening up the door for them. I glance at my watch. It's 8:30.

"Hi," I say. "I'm on time but Her Majesty downstairs just gave me a little attitude."

"Oh, you're fine. She gets like that sometimes. This is math."

First period goes well. Second period nobody wants to do the math. I'm not going to force the issue. They get to hang out with each other and one of the kids does a pretty amazing trick flipping his iPod Nano. Seriously. I tell him to get it up on You Tube. Maybe Apple will pick it up for a commercial.

"Did you go home last night?" Ny, a bright kid, asks me.

"Yes. Why?"

"You're wearing the same jeans you wore yesterday."

True. I've been rehearsing every night late. These kids don't miss a thing…except their algebra.

2:30 pm. Mid-winter recess starts in 45 minutes. Even Ms. Crank is smiling at me in the hallway. And…it's vacation!

Bye-bye, Tommy de los Angeles, whomever you may be.

Thursday, February 23, 2012
Mid-Winter Recess Week
***Relative Pitch* opens at the Cherry Lane Theatre**

School is out this week. The weather is unreasonably warm. It's a beautiful, sunny day today. Blue sky, fluffy white clouds.

Our show opened Tuesday night, February 21, 2012, to a full house. It had been very intense, right up through the opening.

Opening night arrived. All day Tuesday, I did my best to be calm, but let's just say that I love food and Tuesday I had no appetite. When I walked into my dressing room, there was a bouquet of flowers and an envelope from Angelina Fiordellisi, the theatre's creative director, reading:

Happy Opening, Elizabeth.

Cherry Lane Theatre

Break a leg Elizabeth!!
Great work - you are
officially a Playwright, congrats!
Just fly woman! Have a great
time out there. Love,
Angelina

Angelina Fiordellisi

"I brought you something!" Gretchen burst in, brimming with joy. She handed me a pretty bag containing ginger tea, clover honey and a lovely teacup. "Have some. It will help your voice stay strong." She gave me a big hug. Now that's what I call mentoring.

"We're sold out," Erica, our stage manager, chirped as she appeared with the 10-minute warning. Best of all, the show went well. There was plenty of laughter and applause.

A Meditation on Teaching

I've got hours before I have to report to the theatre. My thoughts are on education.

As a self-proclaimed *ahrteeest*...I've viewed teaching as my "B" job but when it rocks, it rocks. What I know for sure is that you can't have a proper democracy without a well-informed citizenry. Over the course of human history, despots have understood and feared the awesome power of education. Because of this it was reserved for an entrusted, privileged few. They made it a crime to educate slaves, women, poor folks and people of certain colors. They burned books, murdered intellectuals and forced a one-size-fits-all curriculum on those privileged enough to learn to read and write. Fear in action.

As I rotate through school after school this year, I note that we're educating the privileged beautifully. But there's an appalling number of poor folks and people of certain colors who are not getting the education *we all* need them to have. Yes, it's a "WE" thang. A poorly educated populace is easily manipulated by greedy types...often the same ones who control the message. Democracy is fragile. If we don't pay attention, it can be injured. Democracy is our endowment. We need to bestow upon every student in America the wisdom to value it and the ability to participate in it.

Every student I meet deserves a great education. All of them want success. Each has big dreams. We need to provide them with a safe place where they can articulate these dreams. We need to offer them a path to achieve them. Help them create a road map. Help them build their skills. Sit down with them. Listen to them. Empower their voices. Find their light and flip that switch. This is our job.

All the good teachers I have known love and care about their students. They wrack their brains every day to figure out how to move their kids forward into success. They meet with each other during and after school to share stories, dump frustrations and laugh. They brag about their students' achievements. To each other! They reach out. They call home, keeping parents in the loop. They create field trips. They're fundraisers, investors, social directors, parent coordinators, psychologists, social workers, ski-trip leaders, curriculum developers, writers, artists, scientists, chess-club instigators. They are probation officers, endlessly talking things out with a troubled soul, forgiving and offering her chance after chance to achieve a small victory. They are valued mentors whom kids trust with their deepest secrets. They are shoulders for students to cry on. They rarely give up on a student. They are generous souls. They bring food into class for them...all kinds of food: from lasagna to great literature. They see the light. They arrive everyday, poised to power up the room.

Teachers might just be the most powerful force we have in protecting our fragile democracy.

Still Thursday, 11 pm.

The show went well. Light audience.

Friday February 24, 2012

I had fun last night with an intimate audience. The jitters were gone. I felt playful. My voice was in good shape. I'm beginning to relax.

Just checked my online algorhythm. I've been assigned to Urban Assembly for Green Careers for next week. I've also got six more evening performances: Tuesday through Saturday plus a Saturday matinee. School resumes Monday. Fortunately, the show is dark Monday night. I can teach Monday. I need a strategy for the rest of the week. I have some "sick days" left on my account. So here are my options:

1. Be a gamer. Go to work Monday and call in sick the rest of the week.
2. Be courageous. Ask UA Green's principal (whom I will be meeting for the first time on Monday morning) for three "personal days" contracted to all NYC public school teachers. The answer can be, "No, I expect you here every day."
3. Be a martyr. Work all week in the school and do the show at night. This would not be fair to the Cherry Lane Theatre. They deserve my full energy. This schedule would deplete my energy and voice.
4. Be a faker. Show up with a week of laryngitis.
5. Be straight. Tell the principal I can't use my voice this week.
6. Go directly to hell.

I like the truth. Gaming, faking and martyrdom...not my cup of tea. A desk jockey in Human Resources has denied me the chance to take the week off without pay. There's no appeal process. I compose another letter to my sponsors...

From the Desk of
Elizabeth Rose

Dear DOE,
Wouldn't you like to have a teacher in your classrooms who has just performed 12 shows Off Broadway? Wouldn't it be great for the kids and teacher to share that experience? We could have brought kids to the show. Then we could have guided them in creating their own piece, a song, a poem, a short story—a freakin' soliloquy—they'd be mining their own stories.

Have you noticed that many of us teachers are artists, writers, scientists, chess players? Wouldn't it be cool if we could teach what we're passionate about? Imagine how infectious our passion would be. Imagine how our kids would pick up on that energy and fly. BTW, the streets of NYC are crammed with creatives, drawn to our great city, from all fields. Lots of them would love to teach a few classes each week in your schools. Wouldn't your kids enjoy chillin' with teaching artists, making videos, podcasts, photography, graphic arts?

Have you noticed we share turf with some of the greatest cultural institutions in the world? Wouldn't it be great to buoy up partnerships, guaranteed for the long run? The Metropolitan Museum, the City Opera, the New York City Ballet, MOMA. the Schomburg Library in Harlem, El Museo del Barrio, the Hayden Planetarium? Couldn't we mandate full-semester or how 'bout four-year workshops on site for all our kids? Wouldn't that make a poor kid feel rich?

You're good with the mandates, right? Standardized testing, flav-of-the-year curriculum. How 'bout mandating an explosion of Creative Encounters of the First Kind with our world-class New York City institutions? Couldn't you give all our kids equal access to the arts?

Couldn't you have given me one little week off without pay?

Monday, February 27, 2012

URBAN ASSEMBLY SCHOOL FOR GREEN CAREERS (UASGC)

Mid-Winter Recess Is Over

Notes from the weekend: I performed two shows on Saturday. The matinee went well. Gretchen and I had a talkback with the audience. That was fun.

"Big crowd," Erica told me as she gave me the ten-minute warning for the evening show.

Yo! This crowd was on fire! They laughed their heads off. They found funny stuff in lines I didn't even think were funny. What a wonderful end to this first week.

Next show: Tuesday. Six more to go.

Sunday evening, faced with this upcoming week's moral dilemma, I meditated, hoping to receive an answer. Here's what came through:

"It's not a lie if you believe it[9]...

It's Monday morning.

Tell me and I'll forget...
Show me and I may remember...
Involve me and I'll understand...

[9] George Costanza, The Oracle at Seinfeld.

This brilliant poster is hanging on the wall, a few feet from me. I'm sitting in a metal chair at the end of the hall at Urban Assembly for Green Careers High School. I've been assigned to sit here all day and keep watch over the goings as well as the comings. Hall monitor.

"Here's the key. Your job is to open the bathroom door for the girls and boys."

Oh, boy. I can save my voice today. The universe delivers. In the hallway, all the teachers and most of the students greet me politely. A tall, friendly woman of about 35 comes over to me.

"Are you our ATR?"

"Yes."

"Well, you have an assignment."

"Oh. I'm not using my voice," I speak in a whisper, pointing to my throat.

"Would you rather be in the hall?" she asks me.

"Actually, that would be great."

"That's fine, then."

"Just wondering…who are you?" I ask her.

"I'm the principal, JR."

"Nice to meet you. Lovely school," I add.

Glad I showed up today.

Tuesday, February 28, 2012

"We gotta move on to Buddhism in a hurry…"

I'm assigned to support in two global history CTT classes. First one: teacher is Victoria—a perky and, judging by the students entering, a loved teacher. Her "do now" for the new unit on India:

Why would a civilization develop many gods?

Great question. After her kids are organized into groups, I tell her that I've spent some time in an ashram learning about Hinduism and if she'd like me to help with this, I'd be happy to.

"I have no experience with it," she tells me. "But all I care about is giving them enough that they can pass the Regents. It's probably only one question on the Regents. Then we gotta move right on to Buddhism in a hurry."

At the end of a well-structured, if rushed, period she announces, "Tomorrow we're going to do Buddhism. No more group work. I hate group work," she tells them.

After lunch, I rush back to American history class. Victoria asks them what propaganda is. A fairly lively discussion ensues. She shows them a "If you see something, say something" poster. They discuss its meaning. She brings up a picture of Rosie the Riveter and plays them the famous song of the same title. Then she passes out posters of ration cards, as well as posters asking Americans to ration. One displays punching gloves made of rationed paper smacking both Hitler and Hirohito. The kids dig the aggression.

I'm looking forward to tomorrow's sprint with Siddhartha.

Thursday, March 1, 2012

Couldn't get out of bed yesterday am. Called in sick. The principal answered the phone at 6:09 am. I told her I expect to be in tomorrow.

"Tomorrow we are having Quality Review," she said. That's when outside evaluators visit the school. The school then gets a report card with its grades.

I spent most of yesterday in bed. Happily, last night a great crowd filled the theatre. I got nervous during my performance when I realized that Steve Flaherty[10] was there. Yes, I'd invited him but wanted to be "perfect." I wasn't.

[10] Steve composed the music to many shows including *Ragtime*, *Seussical*, and most recently, *Rocky* on Broadway. One of our Great American Composers, he's a sweetheart.

Now, it's Thursday, 10 am. I'm back in Victoria's global history class. The superintendent is expected to visit this class. It's Quality Review Day. The heat is on. Students arrive.

"Maybe you should be walking around," Victoria suggests to me.

"Absolutely," I say. At least it's not Steve Flaherty. I can handle a super.

Victoria is heading into a discussion of Ashoka, the ancient ruler of India. The question on the board is:

Should rulers promote a specific religion?

There are ten minutes left in the one-hour-and-twenty-minute period. I guess the QR has bypassed us. Too bad. It's a good lesson—well organized and it engaged the students.

Suddenly, the door opens and the principal walks in with two other people—a middle-aged woman and young man. The woman is a district superintendent of high schools, I've been told. They smile, take a seat in the back of the room, pull out some notebooks and observe. Victoria and I are walking to each group of students around their tables, to monitor progress and offer help. Without exception, all of the students are writing their paragraphs. What are the administrators reviewing? The principal walks around and reads students' work in progress. Then she sits with a student group quietly. Two minutes before the bell, Victoria says, "OK. Time to clean up." The kids comply and leave for lunch. The QR team leaves without a word, to write their high-stakes review.

But they were only in the class for ten minutes, after the entire lesson was taught. Here's what they observed: students writing, stapling and putting their papers in a purple box. They missed the excellent teaching, organization, and lively discussion. What can they say about Victoria? Good use of purple?

At lunch, there's an email from Steve Flaherty.

Dear Elizabeth,

Congratulations again! The evening was YOU—funny, endearing, touching, and a perfect portrait of what it means to be a working musician. And you really ROCKED OUT, which was thrilling to hear!

Famous people like me ☺.

I'm wiped out. I go home sick at one pm, take antibiotics and go to bed. Turns out, I'm not Superwoman.

Monday, March 5, 2012

BUSINESS OF SPORTS SCHOOL (BOSS)

The Moneyball School

I'm in Hell's Kitchen—in a clean, quiet 300-student school on the fifth floor of an old school building. First period I'm free.

Yesterday, Sunday, I reveled in the warm glow of the last two days performing my one-woman musical comedy, *Relative Pitch,* at the Cherry Lane Theatre.

We had a great audience Friday night. Saturday's matinee was quite good. Saturday night, our final show, the house was packed. They began to laugh at my first twitch. They hung on every word, every nuance. Guffaws. Sympathetic silence through the sadder parts. I kept myself completely attuned to my character's journey. They came all the way with me. When the audience was gone, I packed up my five guitars, amp, cables, stands, clothing, makeup, backstage tulips. Angelina offered me a ride home and by 10 pm I was ready for bed. Success. Very sweet indeed.

Between shows, my sister-in-law took me out for a quick sandwich. She's an elementary music teacher in the North Bronx. Recently, the admin took away most of her music classes and re-assigned her.

"I heard you're teaching math," I said.

"And reading," she added.

"How's that going?" I asked.

"Not great. I asked the principal if they would give me some training on how to teach these subjects. He hasn't—yet."

"I thought you had a principal who supported you."

"She left a couple of years ago. This one is data-driven. He doesn't have any interest in the arts. We've always put on at least one full-scale musical each year. But he's given me so many other teaching jobs—completely out of my license—that I have no time to rehearse the kids. I told him we need to have a musical this year. He said, 'Well...just put one together. *It doesn't have to be great*.'" She paused.

I was saving my voice for the 7 pm show, but I could still shake my head.

"I'm teaching my student chorus the American Songbook," she continued. " 'Accentuate the Positive,'[11] 'Fascinating Rhythm.' The vocabulary they learn through these songs is so rich. That's how I learned great language."

"Me too," I nodded.

Oh, yeah. And the school musical should be great. The kids and their families deserve *GREAT*.

Here at BOSS, the "Moneyball school," it's been a long day. I've had five classes. The absent teacher emailed lesson plans; however, four out of my five classes don't have the materials for the lesson plans he emailed.

It's a long way from the Cherry Lane Theatre.

Dear DOE,
I believe I didn't lie.
Sincerely,
Elizabeth Rose
Playwright

[11]"You've got to accentuate the positive, eliminate the negative, latch on to the affirmative and don't mess with Mister In-Between." Lyrics /Johnny Mercer, music/Harold Arlen. Good advice, right?

Tuesday, March 6, 2012
Earth and Space Science

I'm assigned as a team teacher in Mr. O'Malley's Earth science class all day today.

"These are some tough classes," Mr. O says to me as the students walk in smacking each other's body parts. He's prepared a very interesting packet on climate. The kids won't settle down. Mr. O has projected images of air masses on the front board but the classroom remains somewhat chaotic.

A kid named Julio needs to be evicted after he charms me into thinking he's in this class. He isn't. For some reason, I had quietly spit a couple of bars of my *Gangsta Teach* rap before his eviction, trying to get him focused. Or was it my post-performance audience addiction?

Our second class arrives.

Suddenly Julio bursts in spinning like a cyclone.

"Yo Miz! You gotta spit some rhymes. Hey—she got bars," he announces to the rest of the students, pointing at me. I look at Mr. O. He nods at me.

"Yes. This is Julio's class."

"Julio. Sit down and start working on your packet," I say. I glower at him, summoning my most staid, sober and humorless muse.

"Aiight, Miz. Chill. See? I'm taking out my packet. I gonna finish it and then you gonna rap, right?"

"Right," I assure him. "But you need to show me you understand what you're learning, aiiight?"

"You hear what she said? She said 'aiiight,'" he calls out. Again, my bad.

For some reason, Julio settles down to his work. He completes page two of the packet. I think it's because I'm working with the entire table and they're all doing the work. I look up at Mr. O. I know he'll be happy this table is progressing.

"Mr. O. We have completed page 2," I tell him. He comes over and stamps each student's page. His stamp is a picture of a pink bunny. "Everybody at this table gets a bunny," he says.

"Yo Miz. Look! I got a bunny!!" says Julio proudly.

"Very nice," I tell him. "Now let's continue. You have to complete all six pages."

"Yeah, but I got a bunny! Check it out, Miz. See my bunny?" I look down. Julio has added something to the bunny's image. He has drawn a sizeable joint coming out of the little pink bunny's mouth. A cloud of smoke is wafting upwards from the joint.

"Very creative," I say. I don't want to laugh. Mr. O is doing everything he can to explain to the students how you classify air masses.

However, I'm hysterical. I turn and face the back of the class so they can't see me. When I regain my composure, I turn around again.

"You like my bunny, right, Miz?" says Julio. He's been watching me.

"Word," I admit.

Mr. O's third Earth science class moves in like a maritime polar air mass. When the class is over they blow out of the room like a tropical depression that's intensified into a full-blown storm.

"Good job," I say to Mr. O. "I really liked your lesson and learned from it."

"Really?" says Mr. O. He looks like he's just emerged from a tornado cellar after a twister carried off his puppy.

"Definitely. Challenging three classes, wow. Nice kids but very distracted. You handled it as well as anyone could be expected to."

"That's not what I feel," he says.

"Well, I have to remind you what I tell myself. *We're* not the insane ones. We're only trying to teach. We just have to do the best we can and then go home and eat a full tin of rusty nails every night." He chuckles a bit. He's coming back to life.

"I've just returned to teaching after years of raising my kids. Mr. Mom," he tells me. "I've only taught in Jersey. This is my first year in a NYC public school. I had no idea it would be like this."

"Is the administration helpful?" I ask him.

"Well...they give out a lot of 'U' ratings." Ouch. *That's* unsatisfactory.

He tells me the rest of his remarkable story:

"I was one of three teachers in the US selected, trained and given a budget by NASA to teach a new curriculum on astronomy to teachers at the NASA Goddard Institute for Space Studies last fall. When I was hired here at BOSS, I told the principal that I'd need three days away from school for this. He initially agreed to it. Then I got sick. I was commuting one-and-a half hours each way from Jersey. I developed a bad cold. They're very tough about taking sick days here, so I kept coming to work. I walked in one day and the secretary looked at me and said, 'Go home. You look very sick.' By then I had pneumonia. I went home and stayed there for a few days until I was a little better. Then I dragged myself into school and started teaching. I wasn't really well, but I came in anyway to please them."

"By the way," he remembers, "every day I stayed home three different people called me at home from school: the secretary, the AP and the principal. Can you believe that?"

I shook my head sympathetically.

"My first day back was right after that big October snow storm. We'd had no power in our home in Jersey for a few days. It was freezing. But still, I came to school, anxious about missing time. On my first day back, the AP popped in on my class to evaluate me. She gave me an *Unsatisfactory* rating. Then it was time for the NASA event. I reminded the principal of our initial agreement but he said he would not give me the days off because I'd already taken them as sick days. So I didn't get to teach at NASA. This was a great disappointment."

"Did you go to your union rep?" I asked him.

"Yes. But he's very young and really scared of the administration."

I guess they don't teach "Keeping Your Word 101" at The Leadership Academy for Fear and Intimidation.

My next class is a French class. Credit recovery. I get to the classroom early. I write a large poster:

"Je m'appelle Mme. Rose. Je suis la mère de Derrick Rose."

"Fa real, Miz?" one of the boys says as he reads the poster. He understands! Voila! This is gonna be good.

The bell rings. I have a very neat lesson plan.

"Here's your do-now," I say. That's a task to focus students as they come into class. "Take out your French-English dictionaries and prepare to work on the essay you're writing about your family members in French." Four big boys walk into the class.

"Hey, ma nigga!" They strut around the room swapping high fives.

"Hi," I say to the group. "Are you in this class?"

"Yes, Miz!" One of them seems a bit offended by the question.

"Can you please show me your name?"

"Suck my dick, dickhead," one of them yells out to a boy across the room.

"You suck my dick, crackhead," the other one calls out.

"Guys," I say, calm and strong. "Let's tone down the conversation. Anyone who's not in this class, please go to your own class."

At this point, the two boys have met in the middle of the room. They start grabbing each other around the neck and shoving each other. Some of other boys surround them. Kids start yelling. I've got a situation here. I head to the phone. Darn. I can't find the paper I had with the dean's extension. I stand at the door, holding it open. The mêlée continues. A couple of students pass by in the hall.

"I need Mr. Z," I say to anyone who will listen.

"I'll get him," says a young woman.

The shoving, yelling and cursing continues. All the students are either watching or egging it on. I stay by the door. At least there's no punching yet. Mr. Z comes in with a large female security guard. He walks into the middle of the large crowd and pulls the two boys apart. He takes them out and stands in the middle of the hall talking to one of them. The other one has disappeared. The kids in my room are still in a highly energetic state. The security guard has walked out behind Mr. Z. "Guys, let's calm it down, OK?" I ask them.

"Crackhead!" somebody yells out.

"Awwww!" A big chorus. Loud.

"Guys, let's please keep it down." I'm calm but serious. My job: keep the room safe. "I could use a little backup," I say to the security guard as she is about to disappear down the hall.

"You have to speak to Mr. Z," she says and walks away.

"Mr. Z," I call to him in the hall. "Can you give me a little support?"

"Not till I'm done with this," he says, indicating the boy he's talking to.

I'm on my own. I walk over to the loudest kids and say,

"Guys. Do you mind returning to your seats?"

"Yo Miz. Chill. Chill."

"Gotcha," I say. The room settles down a bit. I walk from table to table and quietly say to the kids, "Hi. That was a little over the top. I just wanted to ask you to please be the calm in the storm if there's another outburst. Will you do that, please?" Every single one of them assures me s/he will be the one I can rely on.

"We're not the loud ones," a girl says, ripping into me as I visit her table. "Why you talkin' to us? We ain't the loud ones." She's outraged at me.

"OK. I'll move on," I say as she yells, "Shut up, nigga!" to a boy across the room.

Nobody comes in for support. I walk around from table to table.

"Would you like to work on your French essay?" I ask each of them.

"Naah."

"I did it arready...wanna see?" one boy volunteers.

"Sure." He hands me his worksheet. The pre-writing. No essay. The phone in the class rings. I walk across the room to answer it.

"Can you send Javier to my office?" It's a man's voice.

"Javier?" I look across the room.

"He's right there," a boy snitches.

"Javier. You need to go to…" I realize I don't know who is calling. "Where should I send him?" I ask the voice on the phone.

"Z. This is Mr. Z." I send a reluctant Javier out. A few minutes later the phone rings again.

"Z here. Can you send Eliseo to me?"

Eliseo doesn't want to go. I stand over him. Gently. Persistent.

"Eliseo. You have to go to Mr. Z's office."

"I'm not goin'," he says. But he does, very slowly. The class phone rings again.

"It's Mr. Z. Did you send Javier?"

"Yes," I say and we hang up.

The class continues with two boys playing a marbles game and ubiquitous conversations. There is absolutely no progress with the French.

C'est dommage.

Friday, March 9, 2012

Road Trip! St. John's University

It's a beautiful day today. 60 degrees. Yesterday, the principal asked me if I'd be willing to help chaperone some 23 students to St. John's for a sports management program this morning. We'd be back by 2 pm.

"That sounds like fun. That's where I grew up," I add.

"This is Ms. P," he said as he introduced me to a woman who works in the school office. A former sports management professional (whatever that is), Ms. P is a special hire, creating sports-biz programs for BOSS kids. Kudos for real-world enrichment. I tried to make small talk with her, show her how cool I am with the Mets.

"I sang the national anthem at Shea Stadium in September 2006, right after they clinched the National League East," I told her. The good ole days for my Mets.

"You need to get someone from the Mets in here to talk to our kids. Right away!" she commanded me. She continued to hammer me until her phone rang. Pushy.

A few minutes later I stepped into the principal's office.

"Would you mind if I left a little early tomorrow afternoon, after the trip? I have a long drive after school "

I don't see any problem with that," he said. He's a very nice fellow. Hard to reconcile this with the lousy review his administration received from Mr. O who got pneumonia and was not allowed to teach at NASA. Just goes to show, when you're in a school for only a week, it's unfair to judge...unless, of course, they put you in a marble dungeon.

Today, we're road trippin'. Ms. Pushy is shouting orders to the assembled students. Sit in your seats. Don't speak loudly. Act professionally all day while you're at St. Johns. Misbehave and it's detention. If you know any big shots in the sports world, make sure they come to this school or else. OK. I made this last one up.

We file into the cheese bus (so named for its cheddar hue) that's waiting for us outside the school. A small, middle-aged woman with a thick Hispanic accent is our driver. I have led student trips for years. But this one is Ms. P's responsibility. I assume she has handled all the details. All the students are in their seats, once Ms. P has barked them into submission. They're actually a very well-behaved crowd. Boys are dressed up in suits, vests, ties; girls in dresses. Professional-looking kids.

"Do you know how to get to St. John's University?" Ms. P asks the driver, as we're about to leave.

"No," the bus driver replies.

"Well, neither do I," says Ms. P. Perhaps as leader of the group she might have MapQuested it, like *yesterday?* It's right off the Long Island Expresway, one of the world's longest parking lots.

"I do." I butt in. "You know how to get to the LIE, don't you?"

"No," says the driver. "I'm gonna ask ma friend." We all wait as she calls her friend.

"I know now. I can get to the LIE. You will tell me how to get to... where we goin' again?" she asks me.

"St. John's University." We take off. She rounds 10th Avenue, crosses 57th, to 59th and finds the lower roadway. I settle into my ebook.

A few minutes later I look up and see we're heading to Brooklyn. Wrong way. After a long detour through Greenpoint, she gets us on the BQE and eventually the LIE. Once on the expressway, she pulls the bus into the middle lane and maintains a speed of 38 mph. Perhaps we will make it to St. Johns by nightfall, I'm thinking.

Finally, we arrive one hour late. We're ushered into the International Sport Management University Consortium whose topic is, "Facing Today's Challenges in the Field of Sport Management." Mark Fratto, St. John's director of athletic communications, is speaking. The other panelists are Bill Daughtry, ESPN host, and Alan Hahn, the studio analyst for the Knicks. Students ask a ton of very insightful questions. As it's winding down, one of our students, Matt, gets up to the mike. "I'd like to know what I should do to get an intern job."

Mr. Daughtry pipes up. "What do you want to do?"

Matt is rattled. "Well...I'm not exactly sure," he says, stuttering.

"OK," says Daughtry. "Just tell me...what is your wildest dream?" Matt pauses. "No really. It's safe to say it in here. What is your wildest dream? What would you like to do more than anything else in sports?"

"I'd like to be a sports writer for *Newsday,*" Matt confesses.

"OK! That's good. Now...what are you doing about that? Are you doing any writing?" he says pointedly to Matt, who's just let his dream out of the bag.

"Well...I've been writing a blog."

"Good! For how long?"

"About six months," Matt replies.

"OK. How many followers do you have on your blog?"

"About 150." Nobody was expecting this answer. Everyone's impressed. A few of us applaud.

"All right," says Mark Fratto. "Here's what I want you to do, Matt. And I want everybody in this room to help him. I want you to get 500 followers on your blog. Then, when you do that, I'm going to invite you to our October sports writers' event here at St. Johns. You will come here in October and you will not be able to ask any questions of the athletes. However, you will be able to hang out and observe all of the sports writers who will be there. And there will be a lot of them. I'll give you my email, right? OK. Then you know what you have to do, right?"

Matt thanks him and sits down. I feel like this kid's going to have a career. I'm proud of him.

"You know—this is a very competitive game," Alan Hahn tells the hopefuls in the audience. "You know who broke the story of LeBron James's defection to the Miami Heat?" he asks the audience. "Me! I did!" he says. Then he tells a ripping good yarn of his all-nighter when he got the news. Seems some of his news sources were NBA pals who were partying together one evening. He received several texts from a couple of them from the party, saying that LeBron had made his decision. After the third confirming text, he wrote the story and broke it online, the night before it was broadcast.

We make it back to school uneventfully. Our sweet lady driver manages to keep the bus at a steady 35 mph in the middle lane of the LIE all the way. Cars and trucks continue to pass us from the right and left. It takes her some deft maneuvering to get into the right lane as the Van Dam Street Exit approaches. Some of the kids in the back of the bus want me to battle them. "Come on, Miz. Throw down some rhymes." I keep putting them off. By the time we open the doors in front of the school, everyone has forgotten their hip hop dreams.

I'm hoping Matt will hold on to his dream: sportswriter for Newsday. Ray Barone lives!

Monday, March 12, 2012

MANHATTAN CENTER FOR SCIENCE AND MATHEMATICS (MCSM)

Boxing Matches

It's back to *el barrio,* to MCSM, an imposing school building on the FDR Drive and 116th Street. Built in the 1930s as Benjamin Franklin High School, it's my *alma mater,* Jamaica High School's twin, with 1650 students. Daffodils are blooming on Pleasant Avenue, across from its front door. Very pleasant.

"Soin ya name, print it, pud yer file numba. Go punch in ova dere," the secretary says, pointing. Her anti-depressants haven't kicked in yet. "Jus sit dere," she says, indicating a chair in the punch-card foyer.

"Hi!" A lovely lady explodes into the office. "I'm the APO! Just call me Janice. *I was an ATR, too."* I love her already! "I have nothing for you today. I need my coffee." She disappears. I find an empty seat in the adjoining office. A few minutes later she appears, buzzed with caffeine. "The art teacher can use your help."

"You know you get lunch," Ms. APO tells me after I return from helping the art teacher put a supply order together. "Thank you soooo much," she adds. I've saved her some work.

Where to eat in *el barrio?* I'm surrounded by pork, *cerdo.* Maybe I can find some rice and beans. Hey! There's Patsy's. The original Patsy's. The waitress sits me at the back where a giant picture of Frank is looking right down at me. It's me and Frank for lunch today. The pasta primavera? *Delicioso*. The rest of the afternoon, I chill in the library.

Tuesday, March 13, 2012

Here's what I do:

✔Organize old, dusty school files into new storage boxes.
✔Get dust all over myself.

"I'm off to lunch," I announce and head out. There's a pretty girl on the corner.

"*Hi, Elizabeth!!!*" she says. She gives me a big hug.

"You remember me, Miz? Right?"

"Of course I do. But, forgive me…I don't remember your name."

"Alexandra! Remember? I was in your class."

"Right. Autobiography class, right?" She nods.

"You wrote one piece—something very tough and beautiful about your life. It touched me. But you left school, right?"

"I'm getting my G.E.D. I went back to our school. They said they couldn't take me because I only have eight credits and I'm 19 now. I gotta run to the dentist. Sorry."

"Before you go…remember our principal?" She does. "Well, he also dropped out of high school and got a G.E.D. You can get your G.E.D. and become very successful, too." We hug.

"You know a nice restaurant around here?" I ask her.

"Caridad on 116th St…Second Avenue," she says and splits for the dentist.

That's exactly where I go. I settle down to a delicious *ensalada mixta* with fresh avocado, corn, and yummy red onions. Red beans. Yellow rice. Baseball posters everywhere: Mets win the World Series. Good times.

Back at the office, I tackle the last few boxes while the school aide is spread-eagled in his chair, fast asleep, snoring.

Thursday, March 15, 2012

Janice offers me a job.

"I wonder if you would mind going around to all the classrooms checking to see which clocks are not working?"

"Sure," I say. "I love to travel."

"I love you," she says.

So today I:

✔Checked all the clocks.

✔Organized Janice's closet. I volunteered. She didn't ask me.

I'm aware there are many teachers in the ATR pool who recoil at the idea of doing anything but teaching. I respect that. Teachers don't want to be janitors, secretaries and sentries. They want to teach. And, BTW, there are a lot of students who need teachers, while 2500 ATRs are on cafeteria duty or languishing in marble dungeons. But I'm glad to be out of the classroom for a week. Nice folks here. It might be another 60 years before my pretty MCMS files are unearthed.

Friday, March 16, 2012

Yesterday afternoon, just before lunch, I was in the library. Janice, my new BFF, spotted me there. I guessed she needed my expertise.

"This is for you," she said and she handed me a brownie she'd made.

Today, when I return from lunch, the school aide is standing by my desk. Unselfconsciously, he sings a few bars from a gospel song. He sings it with great clarity, pitch and soul. I'm stunned. He's hardly said a word to me all week.

"That's quite an instrument," I tell him.

"Wha?"

"I said you have a great singing voice."

"Wha? You heard me?"

"Yes. You just sang a little. You have a terrific, high, soulful voice and you sing on pitch." He collapses self-consciously on the couch.

"Go on," says the secretary. "Sing for the lady."

He can't open his mouth.

"He sings in church," the secretary rats on him.

"Naah. Naah. I can't," he says.

It's time to leave the school. Janice calls out to me as she runs to a meeting, "I gotta give you a hug. I love you. You're a real *schmoozer*."

"Yes, I am," I say. And she disappears.

"She used to be a wedding singer," says the secretary.

A wedding singer!! A woman of my cloth. That explains everything. She may be the assistant principal of organization in a school of 1700 students, but underneath it all she's a chick singer…

…and we chick singers really know how to harmonize.

Monday, March 19, 2012

HIGH SCHOOL OF ART AND DESIGN (HSAD)

The Icebox Cometh

My "greeter" is a large woman at her desk, suffering from post-St. Patrick's Day syndrome (PSPDS). Too many potatoes…Guinness. She hands me some papers.

"Here read this. Everything you need to know is right there." Except it isn't.

"I just have a question about the sign-in sheets," I say.

"Read the whole sheet first," she snaps. *Boy…Sister Mary McMean musta really given you a hard time in third grade. Who died and made you Pope?* OMG. Did I say that out loud? No? *Whew.*

"Your first class is in 607. Then you're to go to the Icebox."

"What subject am I covering? What's the Icebox?" I dare to ask. Now I'm chasing her into the hall. This bucket of bolts is in overdrive.

"Math," she spits. "The Icebox is the detention room. If no students show up, you must sit there until the end of the tenth period."

I'm glad I brought a sweater.

"May I please have a bathroom key?" I ask her politely as I catch up to her at the elevator.

"NO!! I am NOT giving you a bathroom key! No more bathroom keys for ATRs!!" Her rivets are loosening. "They keep walking away with them. You'll have to do without."

"Do I need a key for the elevator?"

"Yes. You have to ask somebody from the staff."

"One more little question..." She looks like she's considering hacking my body into bite-sized parts and serving them as blood pudding at her next full breakfast. "Do the bells ring at the end of each class?"

"There are no bells here. You're not going to get any *gong, gong, gong* at this school. We play music between classes. Today it's the *Pink Panther Theme*."

"Thanks," I say as the elevator arrives. Forget Guinness. This hangover's more Jamison's.

As the elevator door closes, the theme from *Peter Gunn* starts to play through mad distorted speakers. *Pink Panther*. *Peter Gunn*. Mancini. At least she got the right composer.

I have five classes today. Geometry and pre-calc. The kids tell me about their school. To get in, they have to submit a portfolio of their artwork and come for an in-person interview. These students are serious artists, graphic designers, filmmakers.

"May I take a look?" I ask Luke, a well-spoken boy with a sketchbook.

"Sure."

I open his book. The first page is a portrait he's sketched of one of his friends in school. It's amazing. The composition, shading, details and the look in his subject's eye. It's deep and soulful. I look through the rest of his sketches. He's created pencil portraits of his friends, family and a couple of well-known Jamaican dance hall artists.

"I made a nice one of Tony Bennett. He was here, you know. He went to this school."

"He's a terrific artist, himself," I say.

"Yes. When he came here, he was supposed to see my portrait of him but he never got to see it."

"Too bad. You are really, really talented," I say.

"Thanks. I'm a writer too. I'm developing a comic strip. See?" He shows me his characters. "I've copyrighted it," he tells me.

Tony Bennett's alma mater is *the* place for kids who want to go into fashion design, cartooning, photography, graphic design, video production and architectural design. "We don't just teach them how to paint, we teach them how to make a living," declares the school's website. These kids are highly creative. I'd love to work with them on creative projects. I wonder if the admin is as grumpy as the front office.

Five classes down. Time to go to the Icebox. The Icebox is just a room with chairs off the nurse's office. There are no students at all. I can write. I love the Icebox. Don't even need a sweater.

Tuesday, March 20, 2012

Restless night. I dreamed Ms. Snarl and I were locked in the boys' bathroom when the Northeast blackout struck.

"Happy spring," I say to her. "Top o' the mornin'." She stops what she's doing and looks up at me. Her mouth twitches.

"Right. I forgot. Happy spring." She's human! She has warmth! I've gotten in. I'm almost regretting the drinking jokes. Compassion rules.

I take a look at my schedule: Cafeteria. Icebox. Three classes. Two Icebox periods. Lunch and prep.

After doing solitary in the cafeteria, I head to the Icebox when the distorted *Peter Gunn Theme* over the PA rattles my spine. A thin boy comes in.

"Hi! What's your name?" He mumbles something. "Can you say it again, please? I don't understand you." Another mumble. "Can you spell it for me? N-i-c-o," I repeat. I give him a smile. He's all folded up in a blanket of sullen.

"So, Nico. You feeling all right?" He nods a little. I walk over and stand next to him. "So what are you in detention for?"

"I hit a teacher with a ruler," he volunteers.

"Did you hurt him?"

"Naah. It's a 'she.' It was an accident." *Yeah, it's always an accident.*

"An accident...and you got detention?"

"Yeah. I just pushed it off the table and it hit her."

"Come on, Nico. You gassin' me?"

"Naah, Miz. Some kid threw a ruler at me so I tried to throw it back at him but I hit the teacher."

"So...that sounds pretty dangerous to me. You could poke somebody's eye out." Nico is silent.

"So you understand that now, right?" I say it gently, respectful of him.

"Yeah, Miz."

"So in your own words, what would you say you've learned from this now that you've had time to think about it in detention?" He thinks for a second. Then...he gets it. His eyes light up as he says, "Don't get caught."

"I know you had to pass an interview to get into this school, right?" I ask him a bit later when I see he's just staring into space.

"Yeah."

"So what kind of artist or designer do you want to be?"

"An architect."

"Really! That's great. What kind of buildings do you want to design?"

"I wanna make my own house."

"So you want to do residential over commercial architecture?"

"Yeah."

"What grade are you in?"

"Ninth. The deans already know me here...and my friend too. He skipped out on detention. Ya know, last Thursday, they interrogated me for being in a fight. Then they put me back in the Icebox. I like detention. You get to sit in one room till noon and then go out and pick up girls. I did that yesterday."

Fascinated with his educational philosophy, I let him continue.

"Or you can go 'roofin'— that's where we go to smoke weed."

"Roofin'?"

"Yeah. The roof of the 24/7 parking lot a block away." He walks to the window and points uptown. "See, Miz? It's right over there."

I see it. It's right across from Bloomingdales, my house of worship.

Wednesday, March 21, 2012

Early again, I walk to school today, passing the Select Bus on each block. I'm covering two teachers. There's a note attached to my folder. "Last three periods, let students edit their documentaries." I need to wait until a staff member lets me go up the elevator to the fifth floor, locate somebody with a bathroom key and get to my first classroom by 9:20.

I stand by the elevator door until a teacher comes by. That gets me to the fifth floor. I head to room 501 for my first class. It's dark and it's locked. I look around for a teacher who might have a room key. No teachers in sight. I run upstairs to security on 6. "I'm gonna need a key to the bathroom, then to room 501."

"Oh, honey. We ain't got no keys for that. You have to go to the AP in room 311."

Patience. "OK. Could you please let me in the staff ladies room?"

"Sho 'nuff, Mami." A male guard standing by opens the door for me.

A minute or so later, I emerge, thank them and race down to room 311 to find the English AP with the key. Breathlessly, I find the room. Nobody home. That f'ing distorted *Peter Gunn* theme is blasting my ears as I charge back up the stairs. I trot down the hall towards room 501. Students are already gathered by the door. I see a teacher—a tall guy wearing a white shirt and tie.

"Hi…imasubtodaydoyouhaveakeyto501?"

He walks down the hall without a word and opens the door. I welcome the kids and give them their worksheet on Chapter 4 of *The Great Gatsby*.

After class, it's off to the Icebox. Nico is delighted to see me again. We are joined by a girl, Octavia.

"I'm tight." That's teen speak for "I'm angry."

"At whom?"

"Luli," she says.

"Wha'd she do?"

"She didn't come to school today and she didn't tell me. If I knew I wouldn'ta come. I'm tight." A tall boy named Marcus comes in. He's wearing bright new yellow Nike Foamaposite sneakers.

"They cost $239.53," he tells me. "I was so high when I got into the line at 6 am last week to buy them. I'd smoked some weed…man, it must have been laced. You like 'em?"

The kids get into a lively discussion about drugs. Evidently, Luli took Ecstasy and came to school yesterday. She had to cut out.

"I smoke every day," Marcus tells me.

"My sister's gonna throw me out and I'm gonna have to go to Staten Island to live with my friend," Octavia says.

"Why?" I inquire.

"Cause…I don't like her boyfriend. He takes a bath for two hours. I be knockin' at the door, lemme in, lemme in, but he don't care. He just smokes weed all day and doesn't do nothin."

"How old is your sister?" I ask.

"Thirty."

"Does she smoke, too?"

"Yeah. They all do. Her, her boyfriend, my brother."

"How old is your brother?"

"Nineteen. He dint finish high school so he has to go to some program one hour a week. He just sits around all day doing nothin'… They all so lazy. My moms is in Jamaica. You know…the island. I ain't going back there. She would kick the shit outta me."

This might be an ACS issue. As a mandated reporter, I need to mention this home situation to the dean.

The last three classes are on the seventh floor. I stand by the elevator. A woman comes by with a key. It's on three and coming down. I realize I've left my attendance folder in the office.

"Could you please hold the elevator for me?" I call out to the woman. I'm not sure she can hear me over the compressed Mancini crackling in the PA. I run, get it and hop on the elevator. I'm already late. Seven floors to go. The elevator goes down to the basement. Then it crawls upward. Somebody gets on at every floor. I settle into a time warp.

A cluster of students is waiting in the hall on 7.

"Is it locked?" I ask them.

"Yes," they tell me. A teacher is starting a class next door. I walk in.

"Do you have a key to 701?" I ask.

"No," says the teacher.

Another teacher is standing by the lockers. "You have to call Ms..." He mumbles somebody's name.

"Sorry. I didn't get that."

"I got it." And he goes to the classroom phone and punches some numbers. "I called. She should be here soon." We wait. And wait. The students are getting restless.

"Guys. Please keep the noise down," I beseech them. "We're in the hall. Shhhhhhh."

At long last, a gray-haired woman in a long hippie dress opens the door. I say "hi" but she doesn't answer. She disappears. The students file in. It's a wonderful iMac lab set up for making videos. It's strewn with posters from movie classics. The room is divided into three sections: pre-production, production and post-production. The kids settle down in their teams to edit their own documentaries.

"What's yours about?" I ask a smart little girl working in front of her screen.

"The Bronx."

"Cool. That's a pretty big topic. What's your focus?"

"You know…people have different attitudes about the Bronx. I wanted to get my mother to talk about what it was like back then… you know, when it was really all gangs and blowin' up and stuff… but I couldn't."

"Why not?"

"Cause she's working so much. She got no time. So I just asked some people about the Bronx. I'm a junior. I've been taking film class since ninth grade," she added proudly.

"Mine is a pseudo-documentary about Hide and Seek," another whiz kid named Edward tells me as I lean over his iMac.

"May I see it?" I ask him.

"Sure." He shows me his little film. It's very creative. He has four student actors, including himself, speaking and showing how they like to hide: under couches, behind blankets, in the woods. The students are all using Final Cut Pro to edit. This is my dream class.

Thursday, March 22, 2012

The secretary and I are now friends. Go figure. "I hope you can stay in this school longer," she says.

As my sixth-period math students enter, I hand them today's worksheet which deals with the access of symmetry. Just for fun, I spit a few bars. The kids explode. I quiet them down but all of a sudden, a young woman teacher comes into my room. She yells bloody murder. Everybody sits still in stony silence. She scares me. When she storms out, I say, "Guys. Let's really keep it chill, all right? That teacher scared me. I don't want her to come back here, please."

"Yo Miz. We chill. We chill."

Four of the girls come in dressed in total *fashionista* threads. They are all beautiful and exotic and have put together their outfits with great creativity. I take their pics. The *Peter Gunn* theme starts up and they leave, begging me to stay at the school and be their math teacher.

"I'd love to, but you won't learn any math." Except the axis of symmetry. I learned that formula today.

The first person to enter my class seventh period is a thin, blonde girl. She's clutching a doll with giant eyes. She walks right up to me.

"This is Blue Rock Shooting," she says. "I take her with me everywhere."

"She's beautiful," I say. "Did you make her?"

"No. But she's always with me." She smiles at my acknowledgment and takes her seat.

Next class a girl walks in with a cute doll as a backpack. She spins around like a model as I smile at her.

"I made it myself!" she says.

"It's amazing," I tell her.

"I've made a bunch of then and sold them to people. I put a zipper on them so people can store things."

Friday, March 23, 2012

I walk to my last day at Art and Design, wearing Betsy Johnson rose leggings, a white tunic and double strand of faux blue pearls. These student fashionistas have influenced my chosen apparel. I really hope they haven't given me any coverage for that nasty tenth period. It ends at 4 pm and I like to get out of town before the traffic.

The folder with my schedule is on the office table:

Period 3: cafe
Period 4: prep
Period 5: cafe
Period 6: Icebox
Period 7: lunch
Period 8: cafe
Period 9: Icebox
Period 10: AAJ4, room 701.

WTF?

I have no classes all day until 3:10. Then I have a technology class on the seventh floor. What hath the fates wrought?

Cafeteria duty is mad. Glad I brought ear plugs.

Back in the Icebox. An audacity of scholars has been assigned to join me. One boy is sitting all alone, his head in his hands.

"Are you all right?" I ask him.

"No," he says.

"Are you sick? Waiting for the nurse?" I'm still waiting for the nurse next door to disappear so I can use the students' bathroom she's been protecting from me all week.

"No. Somebody stole my wallet."

"I'm so sorry. What was in it? Where were you?"

"In the cafeteria."

"You left it alone?"

"It was in my bag."

"And you left your bag alone?"

"Yeah."

"Was there much money in it?"

"No, just two dollars. But it had my New Jersey Transit card. My moms is gonna kill me. She put like $100 on that card. And two weeks ago, I lost my phone."

I reach in my wallet and hand him a $5 bill. "Here. This will get you home. You don't have to pay me back. And who knows…somebody might still return your wallet."

"You sure?" he says as his eyes light up.

"Absolutely," I smile.

"Thanks, Miz," he says. A minute later, he's gone.

I give the rest of the students a cute hi and, after a few jokes, I ask them why they're here.

"I was intoxicated in school," a pretty raven-haired girl boasts.

"Intoxicated? What were you drinking?"

"Tequila. It wasn't watered down. I really drank too much. Couldn't stand up." She seems to be very bright and self-aware.

"Are you planning to become an alcoholic?" I ask her with a half grin.

"No, I'm not."

We go around the room. The rest of them have won Icebox time for cutting class or getting into fights. They're having a great time. The ones on suspension get to go home at noon.

"Bye, Miz!" they sing as they split the Icebox. The rest of them chill, listen to songs, sing, and talk about music and movie stars. The Icebox = teenage spa.

I head to my eighth-period assignment. Cafeteria duty. It's 1:30. The cafeteria looks like Times Square on January 1, just after sunrise. Refuse from student lunches decorates the foreground of a student mural. A few students are gathered around a picnic table. There is a school aide manning the door. A middle-aged man in a designer shirt and colorful tie walks over to me.

"Hi. I'm Irving." He has a friendly smile. We shake hands.

"Hi. I'm Elizabeth. Are you a teacher here?"

"Yep. I'm a science teacher. Are you working here?"

"Yes. Just this week. I'm an ATR. Today's my last day. Seems like a nice school," I add. "The kids are great. A level above so many. Talented."

"Yes, very talented. But I can't get them to pass the Earth science Regents. The principal is trying to get rid of me," he says. "My students can't pass the exam. No matter what I do, I can't get them to pass it. They talk constantly. They don't listen to me at all. I worked so hard last year. I made all new lesson plans. But it didn't make any difference. They just don't listen. The principal hates me. He told me he wants me to leave the school and he's going to do everything he can to get rid of me. I've been teaching ten years and never had a U rating. Now he's giving me U's all year. It's lousy."

"How about the other science teachers? Can they help you?"

"No. They don't talk to me." He pauses. "There's a lab practical, part of the Regents. One of the teachers…most of his students got 100 on the practical. That's unheard of."

"Why do you think that teacher is getting those results?"

"You're not allowed to let the students see the lab practical. It's against the rules. But we are given the test. That teacher must have shown it to his students and let them practice with it."

"Did you ask him directly about it?"

"Yes, and he said, 'Maybe I practiced too hard.' Meanwhile, I'm drilling my students and they're not getting any of it. They keep failing."

"So that's why you're getting U's? Cause the other teacher's students are doing so well?"

"Well…I went to the AP and told him I suspected that other teacher was cheating. He and the principal started yelling at me. They were unbelievable. They told me that they were going to get rid of me. So I called the DOE and reported it. Now they're going to have an investigation. Everybody hates me here. Every day it feels like war here. I can't take it. I'm a lover, not a fighter."

He exits the cafeteria to prepare for his next battle.

The Icebox is half-full with ten students. They are in a jolly mood. I greet them and we have a few laughs. It's a fun vibe.

Soon *Peter Gunn* starts playing. Tenth and last period for me here.

Outside the seventh-floor classroom door, a group of 15 or so kids are waiting. No key. Call to security. More waiting. Two of the boys decide to race down the hall. I can't stop them. They turn at the double doors and come racing right past me. *Swish!* I'm Natalie Wood in *Rebel Without A Cause*. They're a couple of 50s sports cars. It's really funny. For a film shot. Not an uptight school.

"Stop or I'll have to take you down," I tell them as I pantomime a karate chop.

"Ooooh. She's gonna take him down," the other kids chant.

Still no security guard with a key.

"Could you just take our attendance so we can leave?"

"Sorry. I can't do that."
"Why not?"
"Look. It's my job."

Another five minutes and a woman swishes around the corner with a key. No hello to me, she opens the door with her magic key.

"Thanks," I say. The students file in. "You're going to be editing your photos, right?"

They nod and sit down at their beautiful iMac workstations. This is a fabulous large, well-lit room.

"Take those out of your ears and give them to me!" The woman has turned on one of my student racers, a tall, well-built boy who looks like a young Denzel. The room silences at her mean voice. *"Give them to me!"* Reluctantly, he hands over his earbuds. She storms out.

He can't listen to music while working on his portrait? WTF?

This is a wonderful, large creative space. Two of the girls have taken over the photography studio in back. There's a stage with several dramatic chairs, high-end lights, a fan, and mannequins for students to incorporate into their shoots. One of the girls, a tiny thing, commandeers a high-end SLR camera. The other drapes herself over a chair and begins posing, as the tiny one shoots away. Everyone else is using Photoshop and Illustrator to edit and caption their portraits. BTW, with these skills, any of these kids can get cool jobs out there in the 21st-century world. *Anybody out there listening?*

"I love this class," I tell them. I'm glad I kept my integrity, I'm glad I stayed till 3:56 pm today. The music comes on, signaling the end of the last period. It's a Brandenburg Concerto. Mancini's out. Bach is in!

"Yo! Gangsta Teach!" A boy calls out to me as I pass him, darting west on 57th Street.

"Wha's up?" I turn around and wave back at him. As I bolt for the

4 train, I hear him say to his pals, "You heard her rap?? Yo. Fa real. She got *bars*!!"

Monday, March 26, 2012

RICHARD R. GREEN HIGH SCHOOL OF TEACHING (RRGHST)

The SAVE Room

I emerge from the Bowling Green Station at 8:10 am, 20 minutes early, and head to 7 Beaver, the school's address. At Beaver Street's northern pinnacle, the bronze tail of the Charging Bull statue wags at me. He's Wall Street's symbol of *aggressive financial optimism and prosperity*. I ponder the profound poetry of his 11-foot posterior as I proceed to my pedagogical post.

Richard R. Green High School of Teaching, with its 600 students, resides in a beautiful landmark building.

"Talk to Ian," I'm told as I enter. He's a cheerful chap who's standing at the doorway, welcoming students. He has a musical, thick accent.

"Are you a Glaswegian?" I ask him.

"Why, yes!" he says, rather surprised. "How would you know?" His patter is so thick, you could stuff haggis with it...along with all the other organ meats.

"My ear," I say. "Meet Professor Henry Higgins."

"I'll call Dean. He'll take you to your assignment," says Ian. Too bad. I would've liked to gab about Glasgow. A few minutes later, Dean arrives and escorts me up the beautiful staircase, down the hall, through the gym to the SAVE room.

"You are aware of the SAVE program?" he asks me as he unlocks the door.

"Not really," I say.

"It stands for 'Safe Schools Against Violence in Education.' It's a room for students who are taken out of class for disruptive behavior or who are already on suspension. Everyone here is on a first name basis." Cool. Just like my old school.

"But people call you just...Dean?" I ask.

"That's my name."

"Oh. I thought you were the dean."

"I am," Dean Dean replies.

"Students assigned to the SAVE room," he continues as he ushers me in the small room," are not to use the computer, phones or any other distractions. They can study, but they'll probably sleep." He opens another door. "This is the bathroom. The door's not locked but there's a dead bolt on the inside."

Wow! I have a bathroom. I don't need any keys this week.

"You won't start until 9 am. I think you will only have one student in here. So you have about a half hour. Just dial extension 1001 if you have any problems."

The SAVE room is empty. I sit down to an enjoyable respite. Six minutes before the end of the first-period, Dean Dean escorts two pretty girls into the SAVE room.

"This is Carolina and Mariaangeli. Just let them stay here until the end of the period."

"Hi, girls," I say. "Why are you here?"

"She was trying to help me in class. The teacher thought we were just talking." Six minutes later, they leave. A tall, quiet boy enters and sits down in the back. Another dean is right behind him. He's all business.

"He's on suspension for periods four and five." He leaves.

I introduce myself and ask him his reason for detention.

"I was play-fighting with some guy outside the school and they thought we were really fighting. I got five days suspension." Another boy comes in. I forget to ask him why. The three of us get into an extended discussion about drugs. They want to know more about "E" or Ecstasy. I go to Wikipedia and try to scare them with a selected list of its side effects (psychosis, anxiety, paranoia, insomnia).

"I just want to try it once," the first boy says.

After lunch, Ian the Glaswegian joins me in the SAVE room. An energetic, tanned, elderly man comes in. He greets me warmly.

"I work here. I'm their favorite sub." He and Ian get into a lively discussion about school trivia.

I wish everyone would leave. I wanna write.

Tuesday, March 27, 2012
I Gotta Run a Building

Bone-chilling cold this morning. Brrr. Early again. Brought my computer. This could be a great time to get my taxes organized. I hope I get the SAVE room. I hope I get the SAVE room. I hope I get the SAVE room.

"Good morning. We're having a fire drill," says Elvis, one of the young deans. The Young Deans. Nice name for a band. "Please go to the teachers' lounge and then meet me in the lobby at 9:30 and I'll give you your station."

I'm expecting the usual small space reeking of old socks and self-righteous indignation. But no! The teachers' lounge is beautiful. Light is pouring in from Bowling Green. I park myself at a table overlooking the green. People are scurrying below me at the tip of Broadway. My large window gives me a unique vantage point: tourists clutching the testicles of The Charging Bull for their NYC photo ops.

NB: Beaver Street begins just below the bull's testicles. Go ahead… make your own joke.

"Change of plans," says Elvis, as I finish a few entries in Quicken. "You can go to the SAVE room now."

"There's no fire drill?"

"No. We postponed it. It's too cold outside."

I pack up my accounting and roll my computer cart to the SAVE room. One of the boys from yesterday's drug cartel, Eugenio, a young man with hoop dreams, has already taken his place for suspension.

After some pleasantries, we both settle into our routines. He's scanning a tabloid. A few minutes later he interrupts my bookkeeping.

"Miz. You heard I won a scholarship?"

"No, how would I have heard that?"

"They announced it yesterday on the speaker."

"I didn't hear it. What kind of scholarship?"

"Georgia State College. Basketball."

"Really?? You won a scholarship to Georgia State to play basketball?" He nods.

"That's amazing. Wonderful. Congratulations."

"I can't believe it. I never thought I'd win it. It's like a dream."

"It is a dream. Your whole life can change now."

"My moms is so proud of me. You listenin', Miz?" he asks me.

"Yes. Is there something special you wanted to tell me?

"Where were you when 9/11 happened?" He switches gears quickly.

"I was home. At that time I was in Queens."

"My sister-in-law died. She was in the building. Thirty-second floor. They found her body in the rubble. Coroner said she killed herself."

"I'm so sorry," I say. "Do you know what kind of evidence they found that it was a suicide?"

"Naah. I think they look at the bones…something like that."

Just then, a smartly dressed, middle-aged woman comes in.

"Eugenio!" She gives him a work packet he must complete about the Crusades.

"Eugenio!" she snaps. "Five words! Let's have them! How do you describe yourself?"

"Uhhh….um…"

"Go ahead," she says.

"Positive."

"OK. But how are you positive? Give me five words that describe how you are a positive person."

"Ummm...I don't know...."

"Eugenio! Come on. Five words!"

"Mature," he says.

"OK. Good. Now give me another one."

"Hard-working." Right. For the hour we've been together, he's looked at the sports section, rolled himself around the room on the office chair and practiced throwing a large piece of Crayola Model Magic into the trash can. He's a regular workaholic.

"Do your work now, Eugenio, and I'll expect five words by tomorrow morning." She acknowledges me and walks out the door.

"I was thinking that you won the scholarship, Eugenio. So maybe you're a *winner.* Does that sound like a good word...*winner*?" I say when we're alone again.

"Yeah," he says. "*Winner*." He repeats it. "*Winner*."

"You just keep saying that one to yourself. It's true. You're a winner."

Together, we look at his packet with four illustrations. The Plague. Martin Luther. Galileo. The First Crusade. We discuss.

"You remember learning about the Crusades?" I ask him.

"Yeah. I learned it."

"So what can you tell me about them?"

"I don't really remember."

An hour later, Stan, yet another of the four deans in this school, comes in with a good-looking ninth grader whose name is Zyshonne.

"You have to stay here for the rest of the period," he tells Zyshonne. Then he leaves.

"Hi, Zyshonne. I'm Elizabeth. "So wha'd you do that brings you here today?"

"I dint want to sit alone."

"Where?"

"In class. The teacher made me sit alone. I don't like to sit alone. Hey, Miz, I hear you rap."

"Were you put by yourself because you were talking too much?"

"Yeah."

"What class?"

"Earth science. It's boring. I arready got kicked outta class maybe 15 times." He's getting chatty. "I was getting good grades. I had like an 85 average in sixth, seventh and eighth grade. I don't like this school. They're always writing you up."

"How'd you do this year with your grades?"

"Good. I only failed three subjects."

"Waitaminute....you failed three subjects and you think that's good?"

"But I passed before. Come on, Miz, rap for me."

"So...what's going on with you?"

"I'm messing up. I mean I was doing good. Playing football. Grades. Then my cousin got killed. I dunno. I just don't like this school."

"Whoa! Stop right there. Your cousin got killed? Maybe that's what's behind all this. Tell me about it."

"She was in all the papers. Tayshanna Murphy. Chicken Murphy. You read about it? That's my cousin."

His cousin, Tayshanna, a great athlete, was shot point blank in the projects last fall. ESPN ranked her as the 16th-best point guard in the nation.

Gangs breed in the projects. You live in Manhattanville Houses, you're required to hate people from the Grant Houses. Some dumb kids from MH got a gun and were overheard saying they were going to "smoke" somebody from Grant. It was 3 am and Tayshana and some friends were dancing in the courtyard. Kids just having fun. They saw the boys coming and ran into the stairwell, making it to the fourth floor. "I'm not with those kids," she told the three MH thugs with the gun. They shot her three times. Point blank.

"We grew up together. We're not really cousins by blood but we were besties," says Zyshonne.

"I'm thinking, Zyshonne, that the reason you're falling apart in school is that you're falling apart inside. You think I'm right?"

"Yeah, Miz. Look. The period's over. Can you rap for me real quick?"

Minutes later, on my way out to lunch, I run across Dean Dean.

"I think Zyshonne's grieving over his cousin's shooting."

"Maybe so, but I gotta run a building," he says.

"I know. I'm not being critical at all. I just think he's dealing with some powerful feelings and could use some help."

"You're probably right," he interrupts. "But I gotta run a building." And he walks off to detain another troubled teen.

Wednesday, March 28, 2012

They have four deans for 576 students. That's one dean for every 144 students.[12]

This morning I'm sent to the SAVE room. When I enter it with Eugenio, we are both overwhelmed with the stench of toxic floor cleaner. It's a small room with no ventilation and the fumes had been festering all night. Five minutes pass. As my eyes water and my stomach starts to turn, I say, "Eugenio. Come with me." I lead him to the cafeteria down the hall. You can usually find a dean in the cafeteria. I spot Dean Stan.

"Hi, Stan. I wonder if you can help us?" I tell him of the toxicity.

"Would you mind if Eugenio and I work together in the library for a while?"

"That's no problem."

We head into the beautiful library and find a great spot by the window with large, comfortable chairs. We open up Eugenio's work on the Crusades.

[12]144 = the only Fibonacci number that's a perfect square. The dean-to-student ratio here must represent the golden mean. After all, some of these deans seem pretty cranky.

"So, Eugenio. Did you write down summaries of the Crusades?

"Naah, Miz."

"OK. Let's do it now. Remember the two religious groups fighting?"

"Umm. Not really."

"OK. Remember the name of the pope who started the Crusades?"

"U-something."

"Urban," I remind him. "You know, like urban music?"

"Aiight."

"So the Crusaders were which religion?" He's stumped. I start hinting. "The pope ordered the Crusades. The pope is the head of which religion...? Remember we talked about this yesterday."

"Umm...Muslim?"

Long morning.

While Eugenio and I are in the middle of our scholarly skirmish, Dean Dean comes over to me in the library. "May I speak to you for a moment?"

"Sure," I say and he leads me out into the hall.

"I'm wondering why you are not in the SAVE room? That is your assignment." I give him my solemn face. He's got a building to run.

"I got Stan's permission to work with Eugenio in the library. Toxic fumes. It was closed all night so it didn't get ventilated."

"Oh. That's fine. I'll open it. Bring Eugenio to me at 10:45 in the cafeteria. I'm going to need you again in the SAVE room."

"Eugenio did very well today," I announce to the discipline of deans congregated at the cafeteria door. "He answered all the questions on the Crusades."

"All right," says Dean Dean. "Eugenio. This is your last day of suspension. Bring your work in tomorrow so your teacher can give you credit. You may leave."

Eugenio exits the school. Three hand-written summaries are in his backpack. The spoils of an ephemeral conquest. Ignorance retreats, licking its wounds as it plans its next campaign.

Lunch time. I've 45 minutes.

Dean Dean has come into the SAVE room so I can have a break.

"This building is run very well," I say to him. His eyes soften a bit.

"We try," he says. "We try."

After lunch, it's back to the SAVE room. Two boys and a girl. One boy is getting suspended because he refuses to take his ball cap off. He has to stay in the SAVE room until the end of the period and then leave school. He must bring a parent back with him in order to gain re-entry.

"I ain't doin' none of that bullshit," he tells Stan.

The girl is a beautiful, brunette Latina dressed in black tights, a very short black ballet skirt and a gray scoop neck top that falls off her shoulder, exposing her blue bra strap.

"I just left class myself. Nobody kicked me out. There are three girls here already who wanna fight me. I don't give a fuck. I'll fight them. One of them...Mexican bitch...she done some pussy shit, walkin' away from me. That same bitch wanna fight me again."

"Why are you so into fighting? It's so weird to me."

"I like fighting."

"Where do you get that? Is your family like that?"

"Oh, yeah," she says significantly. "Ever since my adopted father used to abuse me, I been fighting."

"Is he still living with you?"

"Naah. If he was still there, I'da killed that nigga by now."

The third student, a boy, refuses to do his homework. It's about Galileo and Copernicus. I take a stab at getting him excited about them as well as the artists of the Renaissance. His arms are full of elaborate decorative tattoos.

"I don' see what this has to do with anything. I jes wanna make money. I don' wanna learn this shit."

"You see those tattoos on your arms? They're really well done. Some of those designs, the lettering, the fonts, have been influenced by artists who lived during the Renaissance. Same time as Galileo. Someday, maybe you'll get the chance to visit Italy and see all that art. It will blow your mind. Promise! Then you'll see the connection with your tattoos."

After a few mellow periods with me in the SAVE room, the beautiful girl in her ballet attire and I have established a great rapport. We talk about her "stuff." She needs to vent. Eventually, after some coaching, she admits that acting out and violence don't make things any better. As the last school bell rings, I ask her, "So what are your plans for the rest of the day, my dear? Homework? A healthy meal?" She flashes a big smile, grabs her jacket, and turns to me.

"I'm going up to 5th and 117th. I'm gonna fight this nigga later today."

The door slams behind her.

Friday, March 30, 2012

Yesterday was a full day in the SAVE room. Me and my homeys just rolled a series of blunts and ate boxes of Mallomars. Dean Ian joined us. We laughed our asses off.

Yo—I be gassin' you.

Today is a short day. My suspended students get out at 10:45. My schedule says I'm to report to Elvis, the crabby dean, at 12:15. I ask Ian My Fav Glaswegian if I can work with him instead for my last few hours here at Richard R. Green.

"If I were you, I'd just leave when the students get out."

"Really?" I say. A dean is suggesting I cut out of school?

"At's whad I'd do if I were in your position. I'd just say, 'I'm headin' out for a spotta tea' and then just leave."

With some reservation, I go to the spacious cafeteria where Stan, the dean, is happy to see me.

"Good. I've got two girls for you," he says. It's back to the SAVE room with Esther and Ariana, sweet ninth graders who got caught cutting school.

"The security guard doesn't like Ariana," says Esther. "She should have said something to us when we cut out."

"The security guard is to blame, then?" I laugh. "It's her fault that you cut?"

Not a heck of a lot going on here in SAVE...just a steady stream of detentionees.

Yesterday, I spent the whole day with Teresa, the sweet girl with anger issues. She was happy and light yesterday. She didn't want to be in class so she stayed with me.

"You seem much happier."

"Yeah, Miz."

"So you didn't fight yesterday?"

"Naah. I went to my auntie's in Staten Island. I didn't go home. My adoptive father, y'know...he abused me. So I don't see him no more. Sometimes my moms sees him in the Bronx. So I just go to my aunties. I better not see him again."[13]

She morphed into a diligent student. She took her math test. She worked on her perspective drawing for her art class. She's talented and smart. I got to show her some pre-Renaissance and Renaissance paintings on Google images. We were both so excited. Having spent a winter week in Florence and Rome, I learned about this first hand in the Uffizi and the Vatican Museums. I attempted to teach her about the roots of the Enlightenment, too. It was challenging because Eugenio, my alleged b-ball whiz, stood outside our locked room for a long time, tapping on the window, trying to get me to let him in.

"You have to have a dean with you," I told him repeatedly without opening it.

"Lemme in, Miz."

[13] As a mandated reporter, when Teresa left for lunch, I immediately reported the alleged abuse to the school social worker who was already aware of her story. Good job.

"No! Go to class!" But he didn't. When Teresa went out to return a book to her teacher, Eugenio was sitting on the hallway floor, next to our door.

"Miz! Please!"

"Class, Eugenio." He looked at me like I'd just choked his chihuahua.

This is fun. I am really enjoying the asylum.

Except for the fact that this SAVE room has no ventilation or windows. Yes, it has its own bathroom, but I have to share it with the students. Let's just say that some of them have not quite mastered 19th-century sanitary technology. I'm an outdoorsy kind of chick. I love light, the sun, flowers, spring. I'll be glad to get out of the Batcave after today.

I'm assigned to Millennium High School for the next two school weeks. Recap: offered a job there, covering for a maternity leave... didn't take it because I was hoping to get a cool artsy-techy job at the iSchool...didn't yell loud enough at my interview...or else I was too loud. I felt guilty about turning down Millennium when they needed me. Now I'll be ensconced there.

At noon, the end of the student day, Teresa comes running in to me.

"I wish you would teach here, Miz," she says.

"Me too. Teresa, you are a brilliant and beautiful soul." She throws her arms around me.

I'm not cutting out. Ian's advice notwithstanding, I'm too much of a Girl Scout. My last duty of the day: handing out report cards in the cafeteria as the afternoon loiters on.

As I am leaving, I run into Dean Dean. He looks like he could be happier.

"Thank you for being such a gentleman this week," I say, shaking his hand.

"We try," he answers. I can see he's a little flushed with the compliment, but he manages to give a military reservist answer, devoid of enthusiasm. Still, he is a likable chap.

After all, he's got a building to run.

Monday, April 2, 2012

MILLENNIUM HIGH SCHOOL (MHS)

Class Act

Millennium is just around the corner from Richard R. Green on South William Street. Upstairs, at the main office, I make instant friends with Mrs. Stevens, the strikingly beautiful secretary, who seems to be running things. We're both wearing animal prints.

The teachers in the lounge are working diligently. Nobody is schmoozing. No one acknowledges my presence. It's a serious place. Students need a 90 average to get in. Millennium competes with the other top schools, like Baruch. They screen applicants, offering admission only to the highest achievers. I sit quietly so as not to draw attention to myself. That's funny when you consider that last month, I was the center of attention at the Cherry Lane Theatre. Here in the teachers' mausoleum—I mean lounge—I'm behaving myself. No showing off. No fidgeting. Speak when spoken to. These teachers are a little intimidating. I'm afraid I might be graded on my comportment, whatever the hell that means.

I have no classes to cover today. On my break, I go outside for a walkabout on Stone Street, one of the oldest streets in the city. New Yorkers have crossed it since the mid-1600s when it was Brewers Street. Today, in the shadows of the neo-Dutch Renaissance buildings which rise over the cobblestones, it's restaurant row...an outdoor gastronomic reading room. I return to the silent teacher space, where I remain undistinguished till day's end.

Tuesday, April 3, 2012

A full-size woman teacher enters the teachers' lounge. Soon after, a tiny lady who's sporting maybe an 8-month baby bulge joins her. They sit at the long table in the middle of the room, right across from me.

"Do you want me to talk about it now?" the plump teacher says.

"Sure. This is a good time."

"So his stepfather brings him to me. The stepfather seems a little crazy. You know, I told him, 'Ciaran is in danger of failing several classes.' 'He's just lazy,' the stepfather says, cutting me off. I tell him I don't think that's the problem. I tell him I keep seeing Ciaran in the halls with his phone. 'I wonder, at home...is he allowed to have his phone if he's not following instructions?' I ask him this in a normal voice. He starts yelling at me. 'You have no right to ask me about what kind of discipline we have at home! That's not your business!'"

The narrator is getting keyed up. She continues most emphatically.

"'Actually, when I confiscate his personal property and become personally responsible for it, it does become my business.' I tell him that and he starts walking around the desk. Towards me. He gets right into my face.

"'You are a major bitch teacher. You have no fucking right to know about what we do at home. That's none of your fucking business!' Now he's screaming at me." She pauses for effect.

"Was Ciaran just standing there?" the expectant mother asks.

"Yep. He is just standing there, his head down, in tears." She shakes her head.

"'All right,' I tell this guy. 'You have to leave.'

"'I'm not leaving until I'm ready to leave!' He's about a foot away from me.

"'Oh, yes, you are. I am finished speaking with you and you are going to leave.' I'm not yelling, but I think I've raised my voice a little. But I'm cool.

"'I am not leaving. You can't make me.'

"'Yes you are,' I say and I dial security. They come up and he leaves when he sees them. Ciaran's still there. I say to him, 'Ciaran. I imagine you think I feel sorry for you. Well, I do. But that doesn't mean I'm not going to hold you up to the high standards I hold all my students up to. You can still succeed. Do you hear me?' I make him respond to me. He just says 'yes' and he leaves."

"Wow," says the pregnant lady.

A few minutes later, when we're alone, I ask the pregnant lady what she teaches.

"I'm the guidance counselor," she tells me.

I wonder if Ciaran is going straight home tonight?

Thursday, April 5, 2012

Oh boy…last day before spring break.

Finally…after three days of solitary, I get to cover for an absent math teacher. I sit at a bench outside the next classroom. A number of students sit down next to me. We're all waiting for the bell.

"I'd be the first to die," says a pretty girl with long black hair.

"Not me!!" says another as she rushes to the bench. "I'm not going to die!"

"What about you?" says a red-headed boy who seems to be asking the mortality questions. "We should write this down. Who thinks they know when they will die?"

The Hunger Games opened last weekend. It grossed $155M. Biggest opening *ever.* Teens are streaming to see it. They imagine themselves as citizens of District 12, selected by lottery to fight each other. To the death.

The bell rings. Teens stream into the classroom.

"Are you the substitute?"

"Yes."

"Yeah!" They're so happy to see me. Must be my new blue capris.

"You guys were talking about *The Hunger Games,* right?" I ask them.

"Yeah!" the red-headed boy says excitedly. "Can we play it in class? We need to write it on the board."

"Yes," I say with a big smile. A number of students within earshot react enthusiastically.

"That's *awesome,"* says a short boy, a friend of the redhead.

"As soon as you finish your geometry worksheet." A collective groan ensues as I hand out a two-sided worksheet, "Working With Circles." I don't know how to solve the first problem. But these kids settle right down and work with each other at their tables. One of the girls finishes the first problem quickly. Some of them are stumped. I'm not alone. I ask her to come up to the board and explain it to everyone. She does. I ask her a few questions and then I get it.

These kids are so much fun. They work diligently and also help each other. A table at the back is having trouble getting started.

"Is there anybody in the room who might be able to help you?" I ask them.

"Yes. Xue. Over there." One of the girls points to a table with a number of boys.

"Him," she says. "The one in the gray shirt." I walk over to the anointed one.

"Would you be willing to help the kids at that table?" I ask him. I keep my voice very low. Don't want to put him on the spot.

"No," he says very quietly. He's very uncomfortable.

"That's fine," I tell him. I walk back to the other table. "Is there anyone else?"

They shrug their shoulders. I ask the girl, Claire, who wrote the solution on the board, if she would give them a hand.

"Sure." She walks over to their table and kneels down. She says something like, "You have to know that the inscribed angle is half the size of the intersecting arc..." or something like that.

Next class is advisory. They greet me politely and move the tables together.

"OK..." One well-dressed girl addresses everybody. "We are putting the blood drive together." She distributes all the materials next to the teacher's desk. For the next 40 minutes, these kids run their own humanitarian dot org.

"Remember, this year we're gonna do the work so Mr. O doesn't have to." The NY Blood Center is coming to the school for an all-day blood drive. There are posters to fill in, postcards to hand out. The kids are confidently in charge. I'm amazed.

BTW...Every class so far has perfect attendance.

Last class before break is coming up, eighth period. It'll end ten minutes early for a fire drill.

"When's the last time you ran down 13 flights?" the principal asks me as I hang with Ms. Stevens, waiting for the eighth-period bell. The hall is full of cheerful anticipation of spring break.

"What are you doing for break?" I ask him. He smiles down at me.

"OK. Since you asked...Friday night I'm going to a Good Friday Catholic wedding between two women. Saturday night I'll be at a second-night Seder."

I love this town.

One of my girl students has a free Mets app on her phone. Today is opening day and it's the bottom of the fifth, the score is 0–0 and the Braves have loaded the bases. There are two outs and Santana's pitching. We're under some pressure. Santana grounds them out. Whew. New inning. I show a few of them the picture of me singing the anthem at Shea. I got some Mets cred. They're impressed.

Ten minutes before three, two serious teachers open our classroom door.

"You take the front and I'll take the back," one of them states authoritatively. It's fire drill time. All the students exit the room in complete silence. Rules are taken very seriously here. We all stand patiently by the staircases until the go-ahead is given. Then we traipse down 13 flights and line up across Broad Street. A few minutes later, some invisible person gives a signal and everyone is dismissed for spring break.

I'm assigned to Millennium again after spring break. I'm already salivating for the Indian food truck I noticed Tuesday, when I brought my lunch.

Saturday, April 7, 2012
The Catskills
Aboriginal Wisdom

If you have come here to help me, you are wasting your time.
But if you have come here because your liberation is bound with mine,
then let us work together.
—Aboriginal activists group, Queensland, 1970s

This quote jumps off the page of *The Tao of Equus,* by Linda Kohanov, as I launch spring break with a good read.

"That's it!" I say to myself. "That's why I'm in the classroom! That's why I *teach*." It's not about *them*. It's not about *me*. It's about *us*.

An Aboriginal woman has looked up from her ancient fire. Some stranger has interrupted her ritual, offering her something unsolicited. A new religion? A new education? A new government? Perhaps. Surely it will improve her life. Or so the alien tries to convince her.

But she's too wise to fall for this perverse advertising campaign. She stirs the fire as she tells the outsider to go f*** himself, but in a much classier way. She smells his arrogance. She senses the spikes in his superiority complex. She hears the lies in his patronizing patter. She looks in his eyes as she stirs the red-hot coals. There's nothing much behind them. The vapid eyes of a salesman. She closes her eyes. Perhaps there's a portal to this stranger's higher self. She knows that if he would allow it to open, she could become his teacher. He might find a new religion, a new education, a new way to govern his life.

It's not her job to break down that door. It's his. She opens her eyes, looks into his, stirs the fire and speaks. Her words do not penetrate. He's not unlocked.

But I am. The sparks from her fire suddenly engulf me in a pattern of beautiful light, dancing around me until they swirl into my heart, causing it to open wider. *She is a highly effective teacher.* I will never meet her. I will never know her name. But with her words, she has allowed me to uncover a truth that has been lurking just under my own stream of awareness.

Most every teenager has embarked on a journey of self-discovery. *Who am I? What's life all about? What'll happen when I fire up this blunt?*

I get this. If they need a guide, I'm available. There are few finite, simple answers. We can help each other deal with uncertainty. We can draw from each other's creative expression. Writing. Making art. Music. We are each other's muses. And it's fun.

BTW...A word to "educators" who think you're out to *help* the poor kids...until you are willing open the door to your own liberation, I'm moved to tell you to go f*** yourself...in a classier way, of course.

Monday, April 16, 2012
Intelligence From Ghana

The cherry trees have started to bloom in Battery Park as I advance toward my second week at Millennium. It's going up to 86 today. A line of students stretches outside the school's entrance. The kids are subdued, happy to see each other, talking about what they're expecting today in school. They wait patiently as an adult woman checks them in. A dour, official-looking chap in a tie waves me over. He doesn't introduce himself.

"You need to go upstairs and sign the time sheet," he says. "You will be covering Woo in physical ed. Then you will cover math. Go upstairs, go to Woo's mailbox, take the materials, then come downstairs again and go inside to that room." He indicates the gym.

I assume he's an AP. I'll just call him "Grim AP."

The principal is in the elevator lobby, directing student traffic.

"How was the gay Catholic wedding and Seder?" I say.

"Fine." He smiles as some students appear. "You may go in." I go up, come down and have a quiet 45 minutes with Woo's wards.

Occupy Wall Streeters are supposedly sleeping outside but as yet, they're not in sight.

Fourth-period class is in the same room I demo-taught the Articles of Confederation last October. The kids are very excited to have a sub. One of the girls, a thin, dark-haired beauty named Gisele, starts doing some interesting African dance steps. I try to copy her moves.

"We just got back from Ghana," she says, showing me her brightly colored drawstring pants. The school had organized two trips during spring break, one to Ghana, another to China. Travelers to China will be back on Wednesday.

"Would you like to tell us all about your trip?" I ask her. She jumps up and gets another Gha-tripper, a boy, up in front of the class.

"Is everybody OK with this?" I ask the class. I get much affirmation.

"I have peer reviews for you to work on…but I'd hate to miss this chance to hear about the trip. How 'bout we hear about the trip and I'll give you the peer review form."

"Yes. That's great," they say. I know I'm supposed to have them work on their projects but I make a snap decision. These kids are right off the plane, full of the instant recall and passion from their exotic trip. A teachable moment is hanging in the air.

"Hey! You have to come up here with us," Gisele says to a girl sitting at her desk. The girl joins them. She's a tall blonde, also wearing the vibrant drawstring pants of many colors.

"So," I start the questions. "Please tell us about your trip. Start at the beginning. How long was your flight?"

"Eleven hours," says Gisele.

"What's the name of the city you landed in?"

"Accra," says the curly-haired boy. His name is James.

"There's no building when you get out of the plane," says Gisele.

"You just get off and they drive you to the terminal. It's really hot."

"What's it like for you when you first feel the heat?"

"It's so hot. Unbelievable," says the tall blonde. Her name is Phoebe.

"So where'd you go first?" I ask.

"We didn't stay in Accra. They took us to Tamale. It was like nine hours from Accra. We stayed there for most of the trip."

"We got to see some elephants and...we went to a monkey sanctuary. I held a little monkey in my hand. He was so cute," says Phoebe.

"What did you do in hot Tamale?"

"We were at the schools. That's why we went."

"What were the schools like?" I keep firing questions.

"Wow. They're sad," says Gisele.

"What's sad about them?"

"They don't have anything."

"There are like all different ages...from like two to nine years old. They are all in this hut together."

"Do they have books?" I ask.

"No. Only the ones we brought them. They don't even have paper."

"The teacher teaches them the same thing day after day. They can sing their lessons but if you put a 'G' on the board, they don't know what it is."

"They don't go to school after like 15 years old 'cause it costs money and they don't have any."

"Oh, yeah! It's like six dollars to go to school. Like for them...they don't have it so they don't go."

"Did you get to know the kids?" I ask them.

"Oh, yeah. We went to teach them. We'd read to them every day."

"You must have gotten to know them..." I said.

"Oh, yeah. On the last day when we had to leave it was really sad. It made me cry."

"Me, too. One of the girls...she was like a problem girl in school... all of a sudden she came running over to me and gave me this big hug. She kept saying to me, 'Don't go, please don't go.' "

"All the girls on the trip cried. I don't think any of the boys did." They look at James.

"I cried, but it was when I got to the end of my book...*The Amazing Life of Oscar Wao*."

"Oh. You don't get any time alone at all. You're always with so many people. Even in the dorm, you have a roommate."

"I didn't have a roommate so I got to read," said James.

"It was so crazy. When I got home I had to go to my room and just be by myself for a while," said Phoebe.

A girl at her seat raises her hand.

"What would you say was your defining moment?" she asks.

"I think it was when that little girl hugged me and didn't want me to leave," said Gisele.

"Dancing. That was mine," said James.

"Do tell," I say.

"There was this amazing moment when lots of people went outside and just started dancing. They wanted me to dance so I just joined in and we just danced for a long time."

"To Ghanaian music?"

"No. It was like our music. They like our music. They like Eminem."

"Were you dancing with the little ones?"

"No. They were like our age. It was really fun. Everybody was out there dancing at night."

"Did you learn anything about their tribal religion?" I asked.

"We met a witch doctor," said Gisele.

"Again, do tell."

"But it was boring."

"Why? Why was it boring?"

"Because...he just talked to us. 'I became a witch doctor because I had a dream when I was young that told me to be a witch doctor.' You know. Like that. It was nothing. Later he showed us his list of patients. Every one of them had written next to their name, 'mental illness.' That's the only thing that was wrong with them: mental illness."

"Did you see any hospitals?"

"Yes, they have one in Tamale," says Gisele.

"Actually, I think that there are three," Phoebe corrects her.

Gisele stands corrected.

"They have these really big umbilical cords. Almost like you can see their organs attached. They don't cut them so well."

"Did you see any AIDS patients?" I ask.

"No. But they have this disease." She holds her stomach. "They eat too much starch and their belly gets really big. All we had to eat was rice and chicken. With this fish sauce. It was nasty."

Phoebe's defining moment? "There are so many," she says.

"Do any of you have any questions?" I address the class. The clever girl raises her hand again.

"I don't mean to ask too much," she says with some hesitation. "I'm wondering, could you tell us what is your 'take away' from this trip? What the most important thing you've taken from going on this trip to Ghana?"

"Excellent question," I say. "Let's start with Gisele. What's your biggest take away?"

"I'm not going to complain about school anymore. After seeing what they have, it really makes me appreciate our school...what we have. They have so little."

"Wonderful. And you, James? What's your take away?"

"I'm just gonna do my laundry now. They don't have any machines.

They have to do everything by hand. It takes so long and it's hard work. All I have to do is put my stuff in a machine and turn it on. Which is nothing compared to them."

"And you, Phoebe?"

"I want to do more service. I would like to go back to Ghana. I'd also like to go to other places and help people. I want to do more like this."

It's time for class to end. Peer reviews did not get done but something bigger happened.

"I wanted to work on my project." A short, caustic boy criticizes me as he leaves for his next class.

"Oh, sorry 'bout that. I could have let you work on your project if I had known. Would you be interested in going on one of these trips in the future?" I ask him.

"No," he says. And he disappears into another classroom. I honor his feelings. Breaking academic routines can be tough for some.

Me…I wanna get me a pair of those great drawstring pants from Ghana.

Two more periods and the school day ends. When I arrive at my home station, a group of students from my old school is gathered, waiting for the uptown train. One of them, a boy with saggy pants, gives me a big hug.

"Why ain't you with us no more?" he asks. Another, rather quiet boy with giant headphones comes over for a hug.

"What are you up to?" I ask him.

"Nothin'…ya know…jes regula…regula." He hugs me.

It's the hugs. It's all about the hugs.

Tuesday, April 17, 2012

Grim AP gives me a serious look at the entrance. I'm three minutes late. "You will follow Ms. Zhu's program. Students are already waiting for you."

I face 28 ninth graders and a large whoop of excitement as I enter the room. "I'm already collecting the homework," says a big boy. I love this school.

Next I cover Ms. Zhu's advisory, a math class and then it's lunchtime. One more afternoon class and I head back to the office, my hands full of student worksheets. I wanted to clip them together for Ms. Zhu. The secretary is out to lunch. In her place sits Mr. Grim AP and his permafrown. I stand there quietly while he works on some papers with his head down. He doesn't look up. Finally, I speak up.

"I wonder if I might have a paper clip?" Annoyed, he reaches into a bowl and hands me one tiny paper clip. "I don't know if this will reach around all these papers," I hint, "but I'll try." No reaction. A second paper clip is not proffered. I try to force the paper clip around the pile of math papers and it bends way out of shape. Not wanting to bend Mr. Grim AP out of shape by asking for a larger paper clip, I wrap the sheets in a paper folded sideways and email Ms. Zhu, telling her how well things went.

Wednesday, April 18, 2012

"I am so tired," Ms. Stephens, the lovely school secretary, says as I come in. "Couldn't sleep for the last few nights. I'm worried about my daughter. She's flying back from China today. Her plane is going to land at 5 pm. She got sick over there and had to go to the emergency room. Somet'ing gastric. I am going to run out to the airport to meet her. I wish I could see her right now."

Both of her daughters attend this school. I am so grateful to her. She's treated me with respect and grace. No one has been rude here, but on the other hand, the welcome wagon must be in the shop.

"I'm going back to the teachers' lounge," I tell Mrs. Stevens after wishing her daughter well.

"If they didn't give you a program, then you don't have one," she says.

As I settle down in the teachers' lounge, the phone rings. It's for me.

"Hello?" I say into the phone.

"Ms. Rose? This is Mr. M." I recognize Mr. Grim's voice. "I must have missed you when you came in." *Yeah...probably when you held the elevator door for me and looked me right in the eye as the other AP called me by name. Whoops! Did I say that out loud? No. Whew.*

"Yes," I say. I'm happy he remembers my name. He could have just called me "ATR."

"The other ATR called in sick today. You need to take Ms. Wong's program. That's W-O-N-G. It's in her mailbox."

"Roger that." Second period, I head to Ms. W-O-N-G's Mandarin 2 class, 13th floor.

Outside, a young student teacher is waiting for the first period to end.

"I'm at NYU, finishing up my teaching program," she tells me. "I'm going to get my teaching license in ESL and Chinese."

After the bell rings, she sets up her projector and gives them a do-now. They have to translate two sentences from English into Chinese and two sentences from Chinese into English. This is a class of 20 or so students. Many of them are natives of China, but by no means all. They are very bright.

Next period it's Mandarin 3 class, 11th floor. I need to get to the ladies room first so I'm moving rapidly through the hall. Suddenly, Mr. Grim waves me over to him as I pass. He looks painfully serious.

"May I speak to you for a moment?" he says. Whatever it is, I'm not going to let him see me sweat.

"Absolutely." I smile.

"You took Ms. Schiff's math classes on Monday, didn't you?" The days run together.

"Yes, that's right," I say.

"Ms. Schiff told me that one of her classes did not do their work.

Instead, you talked about the Ghana trip. Is that right?"

"Yes," I answer humbly.

"From now on you need to follow the program you're given. If you want to hear about the Ghana trip, you could ask the students after class."

Busted.

"All right. Sorry about that," I say to him. He seemed satisfied with my apology. I smile on my way to the ladies' room. That was a bangin' class. Might have impacted a few souls in the room. Definitely worth the risk. I can understand why the math teacher complained about me. She has to catch them up now to her other classes *and* she's about to give birth any day. Irritating? You betcha. Do the math.

Thursday, April 19, 2012

There are no classes to cover today.

"I'm not feeling very well this morning. Maybe something I ate," I tell Ms. S. Mr. Grim is seated next to her. He's warmed up a bit to me. I'll just call him Mr. M, from now on. "If you don't mind, I'm going outside for a little air," I tell them. "Here's my cell number if you need me for anything."

I head out to the water. I'm thinking I'll stick my head into the air stream that freshens the Verranzano straits at the southern tip of the city. The sun is shining. It's about 60 degrees with a friendly breeze. I walk past the nautical landmarks: Governor's Island Ferry, Staten Island Ferry, Homeland Security/Coast Guard Station. Lavender tulips stand at attention, patrolling the walkway. I lean on the guard rail that frames Manhattan's downtown extremity. The waterways are vibrant with activity.

Two large ferries are loading tourists for their cruise to Ellis Island and the Lady. They'll head in the opposite direction my father took when he disembarked from the steamship that carried him, his mother and siblings from Vilnius. He was eight. Processed through

Ellis Island, the family arrived right here, where this international crowd is loading up in reverse.

"Daddy," I asked when I was little. "What was it like on that ship?"

"It was steerage." He'd give me a short reply. He was old enough to be my grandfather when I was born.

"You mean you got to steer the boat?"

"No. Steerage. We were treated like cattle. We sat on the deck. It was stormy. You couldn't hold on to your plate because the boat was tossing around on the seas."

"Were you scared?"

"If you really want to see what it was like, watch the movie *The Immigrant,* by Charlie Chaplin. Have your mother call me for dinner." And he descended into his basement shop to stick another resistor on his circuit board.

Crossing Battery Park, on my way back to school, I notice a flagpole that commemorates the selling of Manhattan to the Dutch in 1625. Given to the US by the Dutch government in the 1920s, the flagpole rests on a lovely stone sculpture of a Dutchman forking over the wampum equivalent to $24 bucks to a Native American. I wonder what this warrior, probably a Lenape chief, told his tribe when he headed back to the tepee the evening of the sale:

"Dudes! You're not going to believe what I just did! Some corny guy from across the big water, wearing a big stupid hat and some crinkly, smelly neck brace with about a gazillion layers, just gave us, like, 20 years' worth of beaver pelts in wampum. For Manhattan. Man, they could have had it for like…2 skins. Who needs it? It's all… you know…noisy and getting too full of white people. They're not gonna last. Too cold in winter. Too hot in summer. They're running all the game outta the place. Who needs it? We still got Brooklyn. We can hole up in Flatbush till the whiteys wimp out o' the island. Once they head back across the big water, we can take it back. We got $24 bucks. We can set up a Casino. We can rig the house against the Cherokees. Man! This is gonna be sweet!"

I cross over past the National Museum of the American Indian. It occupies the spot where the Wiechquaekeck Trail ends. This was a great Algonquin Indian trail, perhaps 10,000 years old. Amazingly, Broadway stretches north almost precisely over this ancient trade route.

Back in the teachers' lounge, I notice a staff list taped to the wall. Mr. M's title is "Administrative Assistant." *Not* AP. Today, he's wearing African drawstring pants. Turns out, he went to Ghana with the kids. He's cool.

Friday, April 20, 2012

"You have Mr. Bishop's program," says Mr. M, the administrative assistant. "In the art room." When the kids see me they run in cheering!

I'm back in the art room a few minutes before my sixth-period class. Most of the students from the previous class have left but one boy is just standing by himself. He looks troubled. He's a nice, clean-cut kid. I have a feeling he needs to talk.

"Are you all right?" I ask him. He looks up at me.

"No. Not really."

"What's going on?" If he doesn't want to say anything, I respect that.

"It's college. I have an 83 average and decent SATs but I only got into the CUNY and SUNY schools. Except for the one school I really want to go to...my dream school, the University of Illinois."

"Oh. You didn't get in there?" I say sympathetically.

"No. I got in. But I can't go there."

"Why not? That's great that you got in."

"Because it's too expensive."

"Did you get any financial aid?"

"Yes. I did my FAFSA and they gave me $8000. But that's not enough."

"How much do you need?"

"Well…for the first year with all my expenses, it's $40,000."

"How does that break down? What's the tuition?"

"$23,000. And I need $10,000 for room and board."

"Can your parents help?"

"My father won't let me go there."

"Why not?"

"It's too expensive. He only makes $40,000 a year."

"What about your mom?"

"My father's the only one who works in my family."

"What does he do?"

"He's an electrician."

"How big is your family?"

"Four. Me and my sister. My parents."

"Was your father born here?"

"No. He and my mother are from Kosovo. They had to come here."

"To get away from the war, right?" He nods.

We discuss options for him for a while.

"Best of luck," I tell him.

"OK. Guys. Please clean up your paints and brushes. Put your chairs on top of the tables. Have a great weekend."

And my Millennium days draw to a close.

Monday, April 23, 2012

MANHATTAN COMPREHENSIVE NIGHT AND DAY HIGH SCHOOL (MCNDHS)

My Very Own High School☺

I arrive early at MCNDHS, on 2nd Avenue and 14th Street to... practice piano.

"Just wait in there." The security guard directs me to the old-fashioned school auditorium. It's empty. A not-so-grand-anymore Steinway piano calls to me. I dust the filthy ivory keys and play. It hasn't been tuned since Herbert Hoover took the oath of office.

After 30 minutes of piano practice, a pretty young lady with dark brown hair and a form-fitting dress enters.

"Hi! I already have a program for you. I'm Roseanne."

I follow her out, making a quick stop in the staff rest room. It's from the Mc Kinley era, and I'm being generous here.

"You will be covering ESL in room 201," Roseanne says. Goody. "There is a student teacher. She will know what to do."

Upstairs in the classroom, there's a short-haired, thin lady of about 23 wearing suspenders, chinos and a white shirt, sitting at the front desk. As I draw closer, I see she has a nose ring.

"I'm Jiao. It's just a small class. There are about six students."

9:20. Class starts. I meet:

...a puffy girl of Hispanic origin. Not a morning person.

...Hao, a shy boy, recent arrival from China. I greet him with my Mandarin 101. "*Nihao* Hao," I say, kinda jokey.

...Yerem, a tall boy with a Beatles 1965 haircut from Armenia.

I help the boys with their English composition.

After we make some progress, I break it up a little. "How do you say 'hello' in Armenian?"

Yerem writes something down on the paper I hand him. I can't read it.

"You've written this in Armenian, right?" He nods. "Can you write it using the English alphabet?" He takes the paper back and writes *barev*.

"How do you say 'thank you?' " I ask him. He writes a very long word out using the Armenian alphabet. "Can you please write this in English letters?" He takes the paper and writes, *shnorhskslutyun*.

"How long have you been in the United States?" I ask him.

"Six months."

"How did you happen to come to this school? Where do you live?"

"Brooklyn. I went to Sheepshead Bay High School but they said I was too old so they told me about this school so I came here."

"How old were you when you came to the US?"

"Seventeen."

"What about you, Hao?"

"Same as him. Same story."

"Where did you come from?"

"China. Keelung City...north of Taiwan."

This is a two-period class. Jiao works with the other three students. A sweet boy drifts in late. Born in Thailand, he hardly speaks a word of English. I'm loving these kids. They are so motivated, cheerful. They just want to be Americans...instantly.

I have a two-period break between classes. Before going outside, I stop in to meet Mr. Huang, the business manager of the school. He greets me warmly and notices that I punched in at 8 am.

"You know it says on the website that you report at 8:30 am."

"I know," I say. "I'm a nerd. First-day jitters." He laughs a bit. "I need to explain to all our ATRs what the schedule is like for this school. We are the only school of our kind. We go Monday through Thursday, 7 am to 10 pm. Then we also go all day Sunday. The school is closed on Friday. So as far as ATRs are concerned, I contacted the DOE at the beginning of the year to see how to deal with ATRs. All they sent me back was a short email that said, 'Regular DOE schedule.'[14] Since we have to follow their requirements, we open the school on Friday only for you. On Friday, you will come in and sit in the library for the whole day." He stares, looking for my reaction.

"Just for me?"

"Yes. That's what we need to do. And for that reason and for your own protection, you need to punch in and out everyday."

"Will there be anyone else in the school on Friday?"

"Just one safety guard. And you. No students. No teachers. Nobody else." My mind spins. Six hours alone with a security guard on Friday. I gotta make a plan. Lessee. What will keep me occupied? Translate *War and Peace* into Swahili…?

That's all I can come up with. I'll work on this.

I feel a sense of guilt that they will be running electricity, heating and paying for a guard just for me. Extravagant. Not green.

"We maintain this schedule because our students are older and many of them have to work at jobs. We stay open till 10 pm so those who have to work during the day can finish high school at night," he adds.

Back in school, the next double period begins. This is a larger class. Only four absent. They are all ELLs, from all over the world. Here's the breakdown:

14 A typical warm and fuzzy communication from the Death Star.

Dominican Republic: 4
China: 5 (4 from the provinces, 1 from Hong Kong)
Haiti: 2
Liberia: 2
Ivory Coast: 2
Guatemala: 1
Bangladesh: 1
Tanzania: 1
South Korea: 1

This is an amazing group. They have read a short story, "Farewell to Zanzibar," a true story of a Japanese-American family's evacuation to a relocation center in California during WWII. Our Tanzanian student is actually from Zanzibar.

"Would you like to make up a 'do now' for them?" Jiao offers me.

"Sure." I think about it a minute. "How about we ask them what their first 24 hours coming to the US were like? " She likes this idea and suggests we have them make the connection between the experience of this Japanese-American family and their own experience. Bingo. Later in the class, I read their responses:

"I was excited." (Fujain, China)

"I met my aunts for the first time." (DR)

"I was scared to go out. They left me all alone. I felt like I was in a cage. Didn't have any English." (Haiti)

"I didn't like seeing homeless. They never show you that when you see movies." (Zanzibar, Tanzania)

The Bangladeshi girl asks me to read the story to them out loud. I do—with much drama. When I finish, they all applaud politely.

Seventh period the small ESL class from earlier in the day comes back to continue their compositions. This is a warm, friendly school filled with new Americans. I like it here.

Still no big ideas for Friday in a school of my own.

Tuesday, April 24, 2012

It's after 1 pm. I clocked in early this am. I have no coverages.

There's an hour and 14 minutes left until I can check out. The teachers have left for departmental PD meetings. I haven't been invited.

I'm feeling a bit excessed today.

Wednesday, April 25, 2012

I am filled with great joy. I have just come from subbing in two classes. I'm in love with these kids. I'm so lucky to have the privilege of spending a few hours with them.

I arrived early as usual and was sent to room 307.

Some students are already seated even though it's early: a bevy of Asian girls, a beautiful hijabbed Muslim girl from Africa in a gorgeous amber outfit, some European boys and some dark-skinned fellows.

"Hi—I'm Ms. Rose," I say. "I'm really thrilled to meet you!"

"Hi," they say. Yesterday's boredom is history. They've already energized me.

"So this is an English class, right?"

"Yes, Miss." Quite respectful, too. A few more dribble in. For starters, I greet them in what I guess is their native "hello" as I acknowledge each one with a wave.

"*Namaste. Nihao. Czesc. As-salam alaykum. Bonjour*...did I miss anybody?" I've run out of greetings but I've got their attention.

"I have to tell you guys something right off," I say. "You ESL students are really my favorites."

"Where you born, Miz?" a boy raises his hand and asks me.

"Queens." Everybody breaks out in laughter.

"Ok. First I want to take attendance." I look at the first names. They are:

Syeda, Gelson, Cui, Jianling, QianQian, Yan, Jardonna, Samantha, Asmaou, Jor, Bartlomiej, Satish, Meichai, Yacouba, Ravinder, Astride, Junzhang, Jingwen, Chu Ting and Mulin.

Never mind their last names. As I call them out, everybody laughs at me.

"See," I laugh. "I have a lot to learn from you. Like how to pronounce your names." I continue.

"Now we have to get to the reading, but first, for me, I really want to know what country you all come from." Wish I had a world map.

Here's how it breaks down:

China, Fujian: 4

Haiti: 2

Dominican Republic: 1

Ivory Coast: 1

Guinea: 1

Nepal: 1

Pakistan: 1

Poland: 1

India: 1

"OK! Now I want you to tell me which continent each of these countries are on. Only you can't raise your hand if you live on the same continent I'm asking about." A lively back and forth takes place. Lots of laughter. I ask the beautiful young lady from Guinea what her first language is.

"*Fulani,*" she says.

"Can you say something to us in *Fulani*?" I ask her.

"I don't know what to say."

"How about 'Hello, how are you?' "

"That's just *As-salam alaykum,*" she says. Everybody laughs.

"Well, can you say, 'It's nice to meet you, my name is...?' " She is a very composed young lady. She thinks for a moment and then translates it into *Fulani*. I can't understand the syntax, but I try to repeat it. So do a few of the other students.

"Now we have to do the lesson your teacher left. She says to read as much of the play as you can in class and we can check for comprehension." She did not mention which play so I ask them.

"*Death of a Salesman*," they answer.

"OK. We'll start here," I say. "But first I have to tell you that this playwright, Arthur Miller, used to live in my building, on the floor right underneath me."

"Really, Miz?"

"Yes. He's one of our great American playwrights. I was always afraid to be in the elevator with him. He was very tall and he didn't smile at me. I think he must have thought I wasn't very smart."

They're with me so I continue my true story: Me and Artie.

"So you know, I'm a writer. I really wanted to talk to him about writing. Maybe he could teach me something. One day I got into the elevator and he walked in. I looked up at him and smiled. He just kind of scowled." I imitate a scowl. "The elevator starts going up. I want to say something...*anything*...but I'm too intimidated. *What are your secrets? Bless me with a few magic words that will help me be a better writer*. But I can't find any words. The elevator arrives on seven and I walk out. Arthur Miller follows me. Why? My mind races. Has he decided to help me? Shall I invite him in? Is my apartment clean? *OMG!* I stop in my tracks. This is the seventh floor. I live on eight. I swing around, barely miss tripping over Arthur Miller, and run back into the elevator, turning my back until the doors close. Alone at last. Thank goodness." They laugh.

We read through a few pages. Then they start to get a bit restless.

"We have about five minutes left," I tell them. "Have you had enough reading?"

"Yes, Miz!"

The sound of a Chinese gong goes off in the hall. End of the period.

I walk across the hall to my next class. It's an ESL 2 class. Smaller. First names:

Hamdi, Mountakha, Avaz, Ridgery, Mamadou, Seriba, Randy, Yrrizarry (my personal fav), Katerine, Ignacio, Oumy and Nikola.

They laugh heartily as I attempt to call out their names. I have not been given the film they were supposed to watch but there's a map of the world on the back wall.

"Everybody! Come to the back of the room. I want you to show everyone where you come from."

There's something about maps of the world and ESL students that makes things come alive. The Haitian boy tells us his experience during the earthquake. He was 14 years old, driving his car outside of Port au Prince. That's right. They start driving young down there. His little brother was with him. He felt the whole car start to shake. He jumped out of his car and started running with his brother. People were running in all directions. Some of them went into buildings and got killed when they fell in.

"How long did it last?" I asked him.

"About five seconds." Luckily, his family survived.

The boy from Uzbekistan lights up when I mention that his city, Samarkand, was a very important trading post during the days of the Silk Road, when caravans, crossing to and from China, stopped there. Class breakdown:

Argentina: 1
Dominican Republic: 4
Haiti: 1
Ivory Coast: 1
Senegal: 2
Serbia: 1
Uzbekistan: 1

I ask the two students from Senegal to converse with each other in Senegalese. "Ask him what he is going to do this weekend. Then answer her," I say. They barely get through it with some giggles.

We point out how the Europeans, especially the Spanish and French, influenced their countries.

"My country is both from Spain and Italy," says Ignacio, a handsome boy from Argentina. After class he comes up to me.

"I give you a rose because you are a rose," he says in his musical Argentinean accent. He hands me a tiny rose he fashioned by folding a tiny gum wrapper. I'm melting.

Teachers are warm and chatty in the lounge.

"This is a good school," one of them tells me.

"We really like working with these kids," says another. I can dig it.

My last double period is AP English. But I don't know that at first. Big class. Here's the breakdown:

Dominican Republic: 1
China (Fujian Province: 12, Other Provinces: 3)
Guyana: 1
Nepal: 1
Peru: 1
South Korea: 1 (born in America)
Tibet: 1 (refugee)
Poland: 1

More fun with me calling out their names:

Dhurba, Leidy, Delon, Kimberley (!), Bin Bin, Quanhang, Victor, Qihong, Mujin, Chengfeng, Tenzing, Jie, Lin, Xiaolong, Xue You, Yi, Bin Jie, Qianhui, Sibin, Zitian, Marcin, Guangsong, Christina, Cunkui, Jia Rong, Wenjie.

They're reading *The Great Gatsby*.

We talk about the Jazz Age. They read. I sing "Ain't Misbehavin " to them. We bond. Bell rings. Nobody leaves. Whas'up?

"Our next class is in this room, Miz."

I'm done with my five periods. Outside for lunch and back to school.

Time to explore this aged building. It must be a contemporary of LSSS, where I spent that memorable week in the marble dungeon.

Perhaps I'll discover a teacher, frozen in a hidden marble dungeon. I research. Here's what I find—condensed version:

JIFF NOTES-MCNDHS:
Opened: 1906.
Founder: Minnie Louis, philanthropist of German-Jewish descent; 1880 founded the Downtown Sabbath School.
Why: "To assist the daughters of the city's poor Jewish families (read: Eastern Europeans), and turn them into upstanding American ladies."
Subjects taught: Hygiene, Self-Respect and Ambition
Regents in Ambition: None
Name change: New York's Hebrew Technical School for Girls
New courses: Sewing, Bookkeeping, Typing
Vocational Training Movement: Sweeps the nation.
My Mom: Graduate of Manual Training High School

That's my mom, Gertrude Raph, first gal on the right, spinning away.

Back to JIFF Notes:

A-List Celebrities:

• Mark Twain, who spoke at Sabbath School, January 1901, for women's rights:

If women had the right of suffrage such corruption as is said to exist in this city would be swept away. He predicted that the time would come when women in this city would be allowed to vote, and contended that it *would mean much for the purity of the city when such was the case.*

Gotta love him. Such a brilliant humorist.

• POTUS Grover Cleveland (Mrs. POTUS laid the cornerstone here)

• POTUS William Taft

Z-List Celebs:

Dennis Walcott, chancellor of the DOE. He spoke here this Monday, commending the school for its "green-ness." Guess he didn't know they were keeping it open just for me on Friday, via DOE directive.

1932: Closed due to the not-so-great Depression.

1989: MCNDHS, its current incarnation is founded by Howard Friedman, former teacher.

Thus, MCNDHS continues to cradle young immigrants from the far corners of the world. You have a day job? No problem, come to school at night. You have children? We understand. Too old for public high school? You'll fit right in here. Don't speak English so well? Welcome.

Thursday, April 26, 2012

After an American history class, I discover the gym across the hall. Kids are playing volleyball. And ping-pong. My fav game. Two Asian students are playing while three wait their turns. This is *extreme* ping-pong. Two boys spin the ball forehand, backhand, drive, push. I feel like I'm watching the Olympics. The winner plays the next student, a poker-faced girl. She crushes him. She hits every ball, slamming it back to the tippy corner of the table where it gyrates out of his reach. He loses. Another boy plays her. He's crushed. Another. Same thing.

"May I play?" I ask. The whiz girl nods yes. We play two games. I manage to get eight points off her eleven in the second game. Never mind the first.

Friday, April 27, 2012

The Enterprise Does a Fly-Through as I Play Hooky

This morning I have a "mandatory" job interview at the Facing History High School. The interview takes ten minutes. I'm supposed to report back to MCNDHS… and sit in the library alone for the next six hours. However…

The Enterprise, the prototype for the entire space shuttle program, is doing a fly-by up and down New York harbor on the back of a specially equipped NASA 747. Since I have no classes...

I high-tail it down to the tip of Manhattan. Just as I arrive, the crowd gasps as the double-decker airplane appears over Staten Island. The sun lights it up like a white eagle. It makes several passes. It flashes behind mirrored skyscrapers. The crowd applauds. Then it's gone.

Back to MCNDHS expecting an empty school of my own. *WTF?* The whole place is full of people. "There are a lot of things going on here today," a staff member tells me. Maybe Mr. Huang was having some fun with me on Monday when he told me I'd be solo.

"I thought you weren't coming in today," Mr. Huang says, coming out of his office. I thought he said he wasn't going to be here...nevermind.

At 1:25, I poke my head into the business manager's office.

"Bye now, thanks again," I say with a smile.

"OK. Please just leave your time card in my mailbox."

Outside, I turn around and notice the engraving at the center of the ornate Beaux-Arts entrance. It's a big H set over an TGS: Hebrew Technical Girls School. On the right side of the entrance is a bronze sign that reads, "Manhattan Comprehensive Night and Day School... Serving Students Around the Clock."

They're serving pretty *extraordinary* students, IMHO.

Monday, April 30, 2012

THE COLLEGE ACADEMY (TCA)

Upstate Manhattan and a Box of Colored Pencils

The Heights. I'm in the land of *mofongo, cuchifritos* and *"Mami."* Washington Heights. The beautiful George Washington campus looms up ahead of me, its ivory cupola stretching skyward.

There's a great stone sitting in the beautifully manicured front lawn with a bronze plaque:

In grateful remembrance of the patriot volunteers of the Pennsylvania Flying Camp led by Colonel William Baxter of Bucks County Pennsylvania who, with many of his men, fell while defending this height in November 1776 and was buried near this spot…this rock stood within the lines of Fort George…

Again, hallowed grounds. These brave Pennsylvanians saved our Revolutionary asses. And they died doing it. I bypass the long lines of saggy-pant-ers waiting to go through metal detectors and mount the stairs to the principal's office.

"Hi! Happy to meet you." The principal greets me with a warm handshake and introduces me to a lovely AP. I'm needed.

My second class, an art class, is on the fifth floor. I'm on the second floor. I've got to make it there in three minutes when the bell rings. Seems the elevator's too slow. I take the staircase. It terminates at the fourth floor. I jump on the elevator. It takes me on a slow ride to the basement, I arrive late and entertain my 25 new charges with the reasons I'm late. They applaud my stand-up routine. Just as they do, an AP enters.

"I'm just giving them their assignment," she says as she hands out papers with the outline of Piccasso's *The Old Guitarist*. "Have them color it in." A kindergarten-level task. Total art supplies? A few colored pencils in a cardboard box.

Last class of the day is an ESL history class taught in Spanish. They're a lively group, mostly Dominicans with one Ecuadorian. They have to work on some vocabulary lists and then answer *preguntas* about *La Segunda Guerra Mundial*. They're allowed to work together. Although I have to ask them to lower their voices about four times, they are collaborating well. I ask a couple of them how to say "too loud." I write *demaciada bulla* on the board. There are two minutes left to my last class. It's 1:05.

Suddenly, one of the boys in the first row jumps up and starts yelling at another boy in his group. He's angry. He runs out of the class and then comes back in shouting something to the other boy. Now all these kids have been speaking Spanish the whole period, so

I haven't been able to monitor the subject matter nor their language. The other boy jumps up and smacks him. This is what is technically called a fight. I'm a bit scared. The other boys are standing up and yelling at the two fighters. I go straight to the door, open it and call out into the hall. "I need some help in here."

Faster than a speeding bullet, a couple of adults come in. One's a dean. He takes the first boy out of the room. Another big burly man with a walkie-talkie comes in and takes out the other one. A young woman with an official looking set of keys around her neck comes in and helps me calm down the rest of the students until the bell rings. It's my longest two minutes since my last root canal.

"Please go to room 254 and write this up," another official lady instructs me after everyone has left. I am still a bit shaken. After weeks at Millennium and Manhattan Comprehensive Yada Yada, with their highly motivated students, this is a bit of a shock. Is this going to be a downer week? As I get ready to leave for some *arroz y frijoles,* I run into the same official lady.

"Gotta say, I was a bit shaken. I'm a pretty good class manager," I tell her. "But since they were speaking Spanish, I couldn't tell something was escalating."

"I know," she says kindly.

"I think these are basically good kids," I say.

"Oh, yes! They are. This same student returned a wallet he'd found on the premises with $25 in it. This is very unusual behavior on his part. He's a very good kid, generally."

I feel better as I sprinkle more tabasco sauce on my lunch in *La Caridad* on 191st Street. It's just small, high school stuff. Nothing like *La Segundo Guerra Mundial.*

Wednesday, May 2, 2012

Yesterday here at TCA, I got to explore the beautiful track that overlooks the Heights. I sat in the concrete bleachers after the rain stopped and watched the clouds blow over the East River valley. Walking around the clay-colored track, I discovered a number of windowless red trailers at the far end of the athletic field. Turns out, they house the Equity Project Charter School. Now, I know nothing about TEPCS. It could be a wonderful educational institution. But what I do know is once you are inside, there is no looking out. These red trailers look like containers, the kind that come into our ports from all over the world.

"They're really beautiful on the inside. They are painted with pictures—very artsy," the lovely AP told me at lunch. "You have to see them on the inside." Perhaps I shall. But here they are, sitting on these beautiful Heights. Sunshine and blue skies are breaking out. A glorious, clean wind is gently blowing across the fields. Everywhere, buds and wildflowers are displaying their perennial enthusiasm for the return of the light. And at the far end of the field, students and teachers are sealed into painted containers, advancing knowledge in artificial light, packed away from the natural energy surrounding them.

One of four small schools, TCA was designed to give kids from the Heights a head start into business careers. Several major companies, like Chase and Merrill Lynch, were partners. Once the recession set in, the big-gun partners split and most of the special business programs went with them. On the bright side, they just painted the halls yellow. It's fresh and cheery. Most of the staff, from the principal to the teachers' aides, is outgoing and friendly. It's a big-hearted school.

I got to sub in the "art" class again yesterday. Why? Because there doesn't seem to be an art teacher. Just an AP who, I believe, is a humanities administrator. Although I'd run into her several times in the office, as yet, she hasn't acknowledged my life form.

However, let's focus on the kids. They're supposed to be learning about art. Monday, this "art" teacher *cum* busy administrator ran into my first period class and handed me that Picasso picture. She forgot to make copies. She returned a few minutes later with copies, but they were done in landscape format and the Old Guitarist's bottom was chopped off as well as the instructions below it. Yesterday, I was given the same class. Although the kids were thrilled to see me, I had no lesson for them. I was about to improvise. I thought they could work on self-portraits with the colored pencils. Just as I was about to put that idea forth, a teachers' aide came in with copies of another Picasso outline.

"I assume she wants them to color this?" I said to the aide. The aide just shrugged, nodded and left. Each sheet showed an outline of another of Picasso's musical instrument studies. Trouble is, the copy machine had blurred all the copies. It looked like crap. I handed them out to each student and asked them what they thought it represented.

"Like a closet?" one said.

"Feelings," volunteered Brenda, a bright girl sitting in the front row.

"Why do you say feelings?"

"Because it has strings...you know...like heart strings...?" she added.

"That's a great insight," I told her. "OK, let's see how you color this in...what feelings you show with your use of color."

We had plenty of laughs as the period went on. As they colored, we talked about sports. The Mets. And that other NY-Baseball-Squad-That-Must-Never-Be-Named. But after two days with this "art" class, I get what's going on.

This isn't art. This is a coloring book with a sub. A three-year-old could color in outlines of Picasso. There are 35 bright, funny, creative minds in this classroom. Back at Art and Design, the art class couldn't wait to get to get into their classroom...at the end of the day on a Friday, yet. They enthusiastically booted up their computers, grabbed their cameras, all fired up about making art.

Here, they have a crummy cardboard box with a few colored pencils. Most of the pencils need sharpening. Someone's walked off with the sharpener.

Today I'm assigned SETTS groups fourth, fifth and sixth periods. This one's Special Education Teacher Support Services, in case your brain has room for another acronym.

The only girl in my first SETTS class, Jackie, tells me about her older sister who's in a charter school in the Bronx.

"It got no windows, Miz." Is this a trend? She says her sister got in through a lottery.

"Did you want to go there?" I ask her.

"No. They too strict." Want windows? Foggedaboudit.

Fifth-period SETTS, as directed, I take my two students to the music room. There are 15 lively students seated or walking around. They are loud, wild and can't sit still. Their class work: read a short article about Elvis Presley and answer five questions. The answers can be copied directly from the article. Is that a first-grade skill? No matter. They don't want to read. I deploy earplugs to calm the cacophony.

One boy is sitting alone and reading in the front row.

"What are you reading?" I ask him.

"Economics," he answers as he shows me his textbook. "I like finance."

"That's great." I speak loudly to be heard over the din. "You're a real student," I say. "What do you think of this school?"

"It's a terrible school," he says. "The teachers don't care and the students are knuckleheads."

"You're obviously focused on academics. Everyone else in this class is playing around. Have you thought of transferring?"

"Yes but the DOE doesn't let you transfer unless you have a medical or safety issue. I'm stuck here."

"Well, do you want to go into finance for a profession?"

"Yes. But I'm not sure what area."

"So maybe you can look on the internet and find some program where you could work with a downtown corporation after school or on weekends. That could lead to an internship and later a job, connections."

"That's a good idea." He is very mature.

"I'm only going to be here this week. Do you have a teacher who can help you with this?"

"Uh huh. The guidance counselor."

"Great. Well, good luck. You're going places," I tell him as I count the minutes until the period ends.

Later, the dean/music teacher explains that when he's there, he has them playing recorders. Great. That's called "music-making." When there's a sub, he explains, they read about music. I call that "baby-sitting."

Today's observation: there's no art in the art class and no music in the music class. Maybe it's just today. I'm merely a visitor, after all.

"I am covering the art class eighth period. I wonder if you know where I might get a lesson plan?" I ask the principal's secretary. She's just back from jury duty. She speaks to me as if I'm a convicted armed robber.

"She'll bring it up to you," she spits. *Yo. Miz Thang got her surly on.*

I'm ten minutes early for my art class on the fifth floor. When the classroom empties, I sit down in a chair in the front. A couple of students dribble in.

"You a sub?" one girl says.

"Yes." I introduce myself.

"Hey—we got a sub," a boy says.

"I know her," another says. "She raps."

"Fa real? Rap for us, Miz," another boy says.

"Not now," I say. "Let's wait until Ms. R comes up." Ms. R, their teacher, is supposed to bring me a lesson plan. I continue to wait for a lesson plan.

Twenty minutes go by. No lesson plan.

"OK. I'll rap for you. But you have to promise you won't make noise when I'm done." I do and they keep their excitement to a decent level. One boy says he wants to battle me. I sit down next to him and he spits a witty snippet of poetry about a rose, thorns, and love.

"You're very talented," I tell him.

"I killed you, Miz." Boys and their battles. It's all about winning.

"Yes, you did. I couldn't touch that. That was great."

We finish out the period with a game of hangman and some more rapping. It's fun, but the sound of the final bell is the best music I've heard all day.

Thursday, May 3, 2012

Nice and early for my second-period start. I head to the teachers' lounge. Tiny, it's like a teachers' closet. Today is Quality Review Day. Important people from Coercion Central…whoops…I mean Tweed, are here to observe and rate the school's data.

Room 249 is filled with students greeting each other as usual. Slapping, smacking, yelling. Their teacher, Mr. Delmonico, is preparing his handouts and projection for their Earth science lesson.

"Hi!" I say to him over the din. "I was sent to cover your class."

"Oooh!" he says, shaking his head. "I forgot." He is visibly upset. "I don't want to go to that meeting. I want to teach my class."

"What meeting do you have?"

"With the principal. It's about prom. I really don't want to go. OK, class!" he yells over the noise. "I have to go. Here's your work."

A few minutes later, Mr. D returns. "The principal was busy. They want you to go to room 511."

I head back upstairs to the "art" room. No lesson plan. No surprise. The kids are thrilled to see me.

"Miz!! Rap for us!!"

I go to the board and start up a game of hangman. My first word is "Foamposites," a coveted teenage sneaker brand.

"Miz!! How you know Foamposites??"

Most of them join in and we have a fun 30 minutes.

Next period is free. On my way to the library, I check out the George Washington High School Hall of Fame. Pictures of famous graduates hang on the walls. Harry Belafonte ('43), Alan Greenspan (also '43). Did these two have music classes together? Greenspan played sax and clarinet before he headed the Federal Reserve under Reagan, HW, Clinton and W. Belafonte is one of our greatest singers and civil-rights activists.

Graduate Henry Kissinger arrived from Nazi Germany in 1938. His moving letter to GWHS hangs next to his picture. In it he wrote:

> *When my picture is displayed in the Hall of Fame*
> *I hope it will say to some other person:*
> *In America anything is possible. It's up to you.*

Students are still lined up across the lobby from Kissinger, et al, where metal detectors scan them for weapons. Hey kids! Check out Dr. K. The most powerful weapon on Earth? Your education.

The library is closed. Upstairs, I find an empty desk in the administrative office. Melanee, the young and lovely AP, sits down for a chat. She's my new BFF.

"Just between you and me..." I begin, *voce sotto*, and I lament the "art" class. She is a good listener. Sympathetic. I go on. "You know, all you would need is a projector up there. You could show the classes episodes from Sister Wendy's PBS series about great art."

"I'm going to order it." I love proactive people.

"All a substitute would need is one or two questions from any episode. Knowing PBS, the lesson plans are probably all up on line. Then the kids could watch a section and do some high-level thinking and writing about the art and history." Who wouldn't love Sister Wendy?

Last period is that eighth-grade "art" class. Naturally there is no lesson plan. But I'm not going to go with the hangman. I wanna get creative.

"OK. Today let's do self-portraits. What do you think is the most outstanding feature of your face? Now draw it and exaggerate it."

I walk around and hand out white paper, asking each student what they think is their most outstanding facial feature. Their answers range from "my eyes" to "nothing, Miz." A couple of girls start working on the idea but it hasn't caught on. I go up to the white board and grab a dry erase marker. I start drawing sketches of the group of students on the left side of the class. Slowly, they start to catch on to what I'm doing.

"Hey, Miz! Who you drawin'? You drawin' me?"

"Yo Miz. You violatin' me." A curly black-haired boy is outraged that I am making a quick sketch of his hair and the outline of his face.

I just smile and keep drawing simple sketches.

"OK, Miz. Now I'm gonna draw you," he announces. He starts sketching away aggressively. Teenage retribution through art. *Yo! Snap!* I got him drawing.

"Great!" I say. "Be my guest." I'm a little concerned about possible placement of sexual organs.

As I continue to sketch them, they're starting to get more excited.

"Can I draw on the board?" A girl jumps up from her seat.

"Sure," I say and give them the remaining markers. Now we're having fun. The bell rings. The curly black-haired guy waves a paper in front of me.

"I drew you, Miz," he says, vengeance in his tone.

"Thanks," I say and I take the paper from him. I give it a quick glance. It's a face full of wrinkles. Eye wrinkles, cheek wrinkles, mouth wrinkles, wrinkles coming down from the forehead to the chin. It's hysterical. I break out in laughter.

"That's really good," I tell him. "May I keep it?"

"I don't care." He's a little deflated. Laughter was not the emotion he was hoping to evoke.

One of the kids, a strikingly handsome boy named Hector, doesn't want to leave. He continues to work on the sketch of him I had started on the white board.

"Do you think your eyes are your most outstanding feature?" I'd asked him when I went around the class. They are large, almond-shaped, dark brown and deep as a well.

"I guess so." He takes the marker from me and starts filling in the hair on his sketch. When he is finished, he stands in front of it so I can take a picture. Then we walk down four flights together as he spins his hoop dreams at me.

"I got moves like LeBron," he tells me, referring to the celebrated point forward of the Miami Heat who are creaming our Knicks. "Dat's what everybody says who sees me play."

Friday, May 4, 2012

I sub the morning away. There's a change in my schedule that has me finished "teaching" after sixth period. That means I'm free after 1:07 pm till school ends at 2:50.

Sixth period it's Living Environment. Big class. Worksheets. Some care. Some don't. I sit down next to a group of young boys who are not interested in learning the *theory* of sexual reproduction. They are far more interested in the *practicum*. I manage to get them on task after they quiz me on my personal experience "back in the day."

"Yo Miz, you ever smoke weed?" I'm honest and they hang on my every word. I leave them with this: "You never know what you're getting. It could be laced with gasoline or poison. Stay away from these things—be very smart about what you try. Really. You're probably going to learn what I did: that none of this stuff takes away the pain of growing. It just covers it up until you become ready to deal with it."

"Miz. You the best teacher ever!"

"Thanks, but you have lots of great teachers."

The bell is about to ring.

"Hey, guys. This is my last class at your school. I go to another school next week."

"Oh, Miz." A young girl jumps up. "I don' wan' you to leave." I give her a hug. "Why you gotta go? You should teach here."

"Because the Department of Ed sends me to a new school each week. So this is my last class." Some of them seem really sad. Some of them can't wait to get out of the room. As I get a few more hugs and well wishes, I notice Ms. Tetchy, the payroll secretary, is standing in front of the classroom. I walk over to her.

"You've been given one more class to cover. It's an art class, period eight in room 511. You will need to write that down on your schedule."

I'm a little taken aback. Despite the great conversations and mega love from the kids this week, I'm fried. I've had five classes and a short prep. I haven't eaten much of anything. I need these last two periods off. And anyway, by contract, teachers are not required to teach more than five periods a day. I need a break. I head to the teachers' lounge. Another ATR and a regular teacher are there.

"You don't have to teach more than five periods. I wouldn't," the other ATR says. "There are other teachers in the building."

"You want to talk to the union rep?" the other teacher offers.

"No. You're right, though. Asking me to teach six periods is going over the top."

I head back to Ms. Sulky's office. "Who is the person who you said asked me to take this eighth period class? I forgot."

"Mr. S. The principal," she mutters. Ever since she came back from jury duty, she's been the person who's told me where to go. On several occasions, I've felt like telling her where to go, but I zipped my lip. Now, I'm bypassing her, going straight to the top.

The principal's office is connected to hers. I look in the open door. He's involved in a conversation with a student. I catch his eye and then stand back. After five minutes, one of the fun APs comes in and waves at him. He motions her in as the student he's been speaking to gets up to leave. I move into the center of the doorway, still outside his office. He catches my eye and waves me in after the AP.

"Yes?" he says.

"Um...I just got word that you asked me to cover eighth period. I've already covered five periods. I haven't eaten lunch yet and I'm kind of wiped out."

"Why haven't you eaten?"

"Because I've been working straight through with only a short prep. Really, I've done five periods. Six is a lot."

"I know."

"You don't have anyone else to cover it?"

"No. That's why I asked you." He says it with sensitivity. He's a decent guilt slinger.

I take a deep breath. I'll probably never see these folks again. Once this little memoir goes public, I'll already be on the lam. What the hell? So I give a little extra with no chance of reward. He's appealed to my good nature. I cave.

"All right, I'll do it."

"Thank you," he says. "I appreciate it."

I have 40 minutes to eat lunch before my volunteer time triggers. Gotta get back early enough to wait for the elevator to the fifth floor. Today is Friday. I have my computer with me. That means I'm carrying extra weight. And my jacket. Not one time in this entire week did anybody offer me a place to hang my jacket or store my belongings. I have to take everything with me wherever I go. Substitute teacher = pack horse. Wait a minute. Maybe I can leave it hidden in the teachers' closet...lounge.

"It's safe here," a teacher reassures me. I head outside. My physical load is lightened, but in ghetto parlance, I'm tight.

And getting tighter. I'm angry they asked me to do extra duty when I'm fried like this. I'm angry that I've tiptoed around Ms. Petulant-Crabby-Sulky-Cross-Grumpy-Sneezy-and-Doc, hoping she won't blow up at me all week. Ultimately, I'm angry with myself for saying "yes" to the extra coverage. I'm not a confrontational type. I try to stay on the generous side of life. Another teacher would have said, "No," and that would be that. But not me. I said, "Yes." I should have known better. I know that "No" is a complete sentence. But I said yes because I'm a friggin' conflict avoider.

I storm down 191st Street to St. Nicholas Avenue, the center of the Heights. There is nothing to eat on this whole f***ing street except that damn pork. It's vegetarian hell. I'm hungry. I find a Spanish restaurant and order macaroni salad. It's not bad. Kind of vinegary and happily, porkless. But I'm still irritated. My anger and frustration craves revenge. Aha! I have an idea! Time to turn *limones* into *limonada*. This one's for the kids!

With the sweet sensation of retribution filling my heart, I return to the grocery store and grab two giant bags of Oreo cookies: one chocolate and one vanilla. Back at school, I walk up to the second floor teachers' lounge, pick up my computer case, approach the elevator and push the button for the fifth floor. Four students come running up to me as they catch me waiting there. Everybody knows this is a slow elevator with moderate-decline Altzheimers.

"Miz. You teaching our class?"

"Yup. I'm afraid you're stuck with me again."

"Can we ride up with you? Our teacher lets us." They look at me with great hope. It takes a nanosecond to decide.

"You betcha." Students are forbidden to use the elevators. "Come on! Everybody in the elevator!" Four kids and I smash that rule as we take the slow coach to the top floor. When we get out, there are about ten more students outside the classroom.

"Hi, guys. Sorry, but it's me again."

"Miz," says a girl from my sixth-period class. "You told us you were finished at this school."

"Yes, I did. But they just gave me this class at the last minute. I was pissed but then I thought of something that we could do for fun." I try to open the door. It's locked.

"The door is locked," I tell them. "Let's see if anyone has the key."

There's a very prim, well-dressed teacher in the next room, packing up her projector.

"Do you have a key to 511?" I ask her.

"No. Sorry." The kids are starting to get antsy waiting in the hall.

"Do you know if anyone might have one on this floor?"

"No. It depends on your school. Which school are you from?" There are four small schools in this building.

"College Academy."

"Then you need to contact the principal for the key."

I'm hip, Lady. Thought you might offer to pick up the phone.

"Just keep cool, guys, until I get a key," I tell the cluster of kids. "Hey! Close that door. That is off limits." One tall boy, whom I silently dub "Crackhead," has opened the door to the roof and is about to take his buddies out there. "If you do that again, I'm calling an administrator."

"OK, Miz," Crackhead promises me.

I walk down the hall to a small office. The sign on it says "School Psychologist." There's another prim woman sitting behind a desk. Seems the fifth floor is reserved for the prim.

"I have no key. You must go to the school you are working for and ask them." I don't mean to say that she's uptight, but you'd need a small caliber ice pick to penetrate that shrink-wrap. I head back to the kids. They are now jumping on each other's shoulders and we have the beginning of a slap fest.

"Yo!" I get their attention. "Chill, chill, chill, chill, chill." They calm down for a couple of minutes.

A female security guard appears on the floor. She is a beautiful lady weighed down by her unflattering uniform and regulation belt complete with walkie-talkie and ticket book.

"Could you please help us get the key for 511?" I ask her. She's on the ball.

"Which school are you with?"

"College Academy."

"OK. I'll call down." She disappears into the stairwell. You know, there's a terrible consistency to this. I tick off my list:

Facts: No art teacher. No lesson plan. No attendance sheet.

Rant: This is an ART CLASS!

- It should be a space where creativity and imagination thrive.
- It should be a space where students learn about the power of art throughout history, why artists are some of the first people to be persecuted when a dictator comes to power. Why art is meaningful, dangerous, subversive, truthful, empowering.
- The only art supplies are shoved into a small cardboard box, two-thirds filled with colored pencils that all need sharpening.
- *There is no f***in' sharpener.*
- And today, the door is locked. Thanks for the metaphor.

You think these kids are missing the message?

THE MESSAGE: Hey kids! You don't need art. It's just a stupid credit you must have for graduation. Basically…art is a waste of time for you. After all, how's art going to help you when you flunk out of your two-year college and go for a minimum-wage job? You're the underclass. Know your place. You are destined for more important things. You will have the opportunity to serve the 1%. Who knows? Maybe someday you'll get to mop the floors of the Metropolitan Museum. Yo, snap! That would be epic!

They get it. Believe me. They've gotten it most of their lives.

However, I have revenge in my heart. It's a small plan. But I believe it will get us all through the eighth period.

A pleasant man with some official tag hanging from a lanyard around his neck appears. I recognize him from the school. "I'll open this for you," he says.

"Thank you," I say. "OK, kids! Come on in. I've got something fun for us to do."

"What, Miz?" my girls from the elevator ask me.

"Let's wait a minute until we're alone and everyone settles down. I don't want anyone else to know what we're gonna do." The Keymaster leaves. The coast is clear.

"All right. Now everybody *QUIET!!!"* "Crackhead" has opened the back window and is hanging his head and shoulders over the chasm to the schoolyard five floors below yelling "Yo" to nobody in particular.

"Hey—what's his name?" I ask two girls. They shrug their shoulders. "Crackhead," I say quietly. "That's my name for him." The girls laugh. One of them yells, *"HEY!! SHUT UP CRACKHEAD!! LET HER TALK."*

"OK!! Listen. I have something for you." I take out the two bags of Oreos and hold them up. "I think you guys deserve a party."

"Oh my God!! I love you!!! You are the best teacher ever!!!" The kids run up to the desk. I figure they can distribute the cookies fairly.

I forget. I'm dealing with teenagers.

Crackhead races across the room and grabs the entire bag of vanilla Oreos. He runs to the back of the room, holding them like a football he's just caught.

"Hey!" I call out. I chase him and grab the cookies out of his hands.

"These are for everybody. Don't act like an idiot." *Crackhead,* I think. Did I say that out loud again?

From the front of the room I distribute the cookies from the desk, standing guard to see that nobody takes more than two. Time for my plan.

"OK, kids. I am really pissed at the way you are being treated in this so-called 'art' class. I've been here all week and nobody has given me a lesson plan for you." I start to raise my voice. They are most attentive. They are watching a bomb about to detonate.

"You deserve more than this shitty treatment." Cursing always helps keep a teenager's attention. They nod their heads. I pause. I look around. The room is lined with student-made origami birds. Maybe these kids made them and this is just a busy week for the APs. After all, Quality Review is a tense time. Let's find out. "Did you make these birds?" I ask them.

"No."

"Did you do any of the art that's hanging up on the walls?"

"No, Miz." That seals it. I'm mad tight.

"Listen!! This art class should be great. It should be your favorite class. I've been in 18 other schools this year. I've seen art classes, the last friggin' class on Friday, and the kids are dying to get in so they can work on their projects. They have great computers with up-to-date software, cameras, lighting, clay, paints, canvases." I raise my voice. "And what do you have but this stupid effin' box with a bunch of colored pencils that need sharpening. *AND THERE'S NO EFFIN' SHARPENER!!! NOW DOESN'T THAT PISS YOU OFF???"*

"Yes, Miz."

"That's not right, Miz."

"We should have computers and cameras." They call out their agreement as they scrutinize my controlled burn.

"So I would like us to create an art project that will express our outrage at this bullshit. You with me?"

"Yes, Miz!!" A chorus of support.

"OK. So we're going to create a political protest using art and photography. Check it out."

I head to the white board and write in big capital letters across the top,

WE DESERVE A REAL ART CLASS!

Underneath it, I write phrases:

Great materials!
Ideas!
Plans!
creativity!
computers!

I'm stuck. I turn around to them.

"What else do you want from an art class?"

"Trips," one little girl calls out.

I write on the board:

Trips to museums!

"All right. Now. I want to set up a photo. I'm not allowed to take pictures of kids in school but I'd still like you pose in front of this board with your back to the camera. And…I want you to raise both your hands and stick up your third-finger. Get it?" They start to jump up and approach the board. "We gotta be able to read what it says." As I place them around the writing, a couple of them grab markers and draw third finger icons around my writing. I head to the middle of the classroom and start snapping pictures of them with my iPad.

"More outrage!! You're pissed!!" I say. They shoot up their hands in angry protest.

"OK! We got it!!" I tell them. They run up to me and gather around the iPad.

"Lemme see, Miz. Lemme see!!"

"Oh! Tha's funny, Miz."

"I don't know about you but I feel better. Was that fun?" I ask them.

"Yeah, Miz. I wish you din't have to go."

"You should be our art teacher."

"Could you be our art teacher?"

"I'm sorry but I don't have a license to teach art. But I'm gonna put this in a book I'm writing and I hope you will read it and stay in touch with me. Whatever happens, don't ever let anybody make you think you deserve anything less than the absolute best of everything. Especially your education."

"OK, Miz."

"And don't you settle when somebody tries to give you a stupid effin' cardboard box with a few lousy effin' pencils and call it art supplies. You deserve a whole lot more than a stupid little box."

The bell rings and I head down the stairs with them. I've had them sign their names on a sheet of paper. In my last act of vengeance I write on the top of the page,

Attendance sheet eighth-period "art" class.

The quotation marks are probably too subtle for the administrator/ faux "art" teacher. Perhaps the kids will tear her another one next time she drops by. Perhaps Sister Wendy will hear her confession.

WE DESERVE A REAL
PLANS

Monday, May 7, 2012

SATELLITE ACADEMY HIGH SCHOOL (SAHS)

Healthy Curriculum and Junk Food Rewards

The Empire State Building rises in the morning light. Just under its radio tower, I notice, for the first time, its slender concrete ridges, molded in Cheshire cat smiles. That's the beauty of light. Always shifting its focus, it may reveal something new, even though you've looked at it hundreds of times.

Satellite Academy High School on West 30th Street, off Sixth Avenue, inhabits several floors in a rather nondescript office building.

"Just go to the second floor," the security guard tells me. She's very cheerful. Nobody's at the reception desk upstairs. A young secretary in an inner office finishes her phone call.

"Hi, I'm Jenny," she says and shakes my hand. "There's really nothing for you to do. You can sit in the conference room right over there or go to the teachers' lounge on the fourth floor."

"Thanks so much. I'll take the conference room. If you need any help with tutoring or anything else, please let me know. Oh, by the way, how big is the school?"

"We go to the sixth floor."

"How many students?"

"About 250. We're a transfer school."

A large lady carrying a number of bags enters the conference room.

She throws her bags down on the table and begins to rummage through one of them. She doesn't acknowledge me even though I'm two feet away. A tattooed man of about forty years bursts in and the two of them jump into a verbal headlock over last night's boxing match.

"Who you coverin' for?" a girl with chocolate skin tones and yellow hair held in a cheetah headband asks me. She's just come into school with her two gal pals.

"I don't know yet," I say. "Nice to meet you."

"It's probably Hector. She probably covering Hector," she says to her friends. Except for Jenny, the vibe here is tough-talking street slang. With a week of empty time ahead of me, my mind wanders to Mignon. I wonder how she's doing. Maybe I can visit her school before the summer break.

The large lady's name is Ms. Monroe. She's re-entered the conference room with two plastic bags filled with goodies.

"Am I in your way?" I ask her.

"No. Not at all. The students just come in here for snacks in between classes." She starts to arrange the snacks on the conference table. There are Doritos, Rice Krispie bars, Milky Ways, Almond Joys, M&Ms, Motts Medleys All Natural Fruit Snacks (no ingredients on the label), Twizzlers, Slim Line beef jerky and lollipops. Michelle Obama's nightmare. As the classes change (there's no bell), girls and boys line up for treats. She looks at each one and gives them their pick of two items. They thank her very politely and leave. A boy approaches, waiting for his turn to choose. Ms. Monroe looks up at him and folds her arms.

"You wasn't in time. You was late," she admonishes him.

"No, I wasn't, Miz."

"What time you got here?"

"I dunno."

"Well, I do. Eight-thirty-six. You was late."

"Aw, come on, Miz. Just some chips?"

"I'll see you tomorrow. You planning to be on time?"

"Yeah, I'll try."

"I don't want to hear 'try,' I want to hear 'yes!' " she tells him.

"What's your job here?" I ask her. She's become very friendly.

"I'm the attendance teacher."

"Just for this school?" The attendance teacher in my old school was split between several schools. She made rounds.

"Yes. I'm just here. You really see a difference. You can monitor their progress."

"So this is a transfer school, right? The students are here for safety or academic reasons?"

"Some are...but there are other students that just can't make it in big schools so they come here."

I ask Jenny for the class schedule. Here's what they are teaching:

Plays About Men, Literature Through Performance, Future of You, American Drama, The Novel Through Film, Ethics, Controversies in Society, Sadie Nash Women's Studies, 20th Century Liberation Movements, Legal Studies, Facing History, Leadership, US Immigration, Personal Finance, Chinese Language and Culture, Forensic Science, UN II, Currents.

Man! I would like to take all of these. There's also algebra, geometry, chemistry, environmental science. The Educational Video Center, upstairs, also offers courses in technology, documentary-making, immigration issues, advertising and marketing. This is a rich curriculum and, dollars to donuts, I'll bet the teachers are having fun with these courses.

Meanwhile, nobody seems to care when I come and go.

Half hour left till quitting time, 2:50. A kid comes by for chocolate.

"You'll have to ask Ms. Monroe," I tell him. The afternoon is moving along at a glacial pace. A man walks in. He looks at me and reaches for some candy.

"I need chocolate," he says and grabs a packet of M&Ms. There's no perceivable nod to me that we share a taxonomy (*H.sapiens*), so I decide to show him I am speech-abled.

"Hi. I'm Elizabeth Rose."

"Hi. I'm the principal."

"What's your name?" I inquire.

"Dave."

"Hi, Dave," I say.

He pockets his M&Ms.

"Guess I won't have to run it by Ms. Monroe," I quip. He is not amused. Nineteen minutes to 2:50, end-of-the-school-day...but who's counting?

Tuesday, May 8, 2012
The Big Sleep

I have a schedule: two homerooms and one class called "The Novel Through Film," where they are reading *The Big Sleep*. Homerooms are to continue their PBA work. Ah, PBA. Familiarity.

"Is this a Consortium school?" I ask a lady at the front desk.

"Yes," says Principal Dave as he walks into his office. He's overheard me.

You see me! *You see me! Did I say that out out loud?* No. Whew!

For the uninitiated, PBAs are requirements for graduation. They generally replace Regents. Students do formal research in the major areas and present their knowledge to a committee.

After a 5-minute homeroom, I wait for my novel/film class. Two girls and a boy come in. One of them sits in a chair next to my desk.

"Hi, I'm Elizabeth. Bill (everyone here is on a first-name basis) would like you to continue reading *The Big Sleep*...once you finish up that last text." The boy next to me is listening to music in his earbuds. I make a wild guess.

"Who are you listening to? Drake?"

"Yeah, Drake." He's impressed. Me too.

"So tell me, how come you transferred to this school?" I ask him.

"You know…at my old school there was a lot of distractions. It was in a bad area."

"What kind of distractions? Where was it?"

"You know…my friends. The South Bronx. So I failed all my subjects. If I had stayed there I would have graduated in June 2013. So I came here so I can graduate early."

"When will you graduate from here?"

"I dunno."

Another boy comes in wearing a hoodie and earbuds. I ask him to put his phone away.

"I'm not gonna do that," he says defiantly. Edgy dude. I back off.

"All right. Just get yourself settled. Do you have a copy of *The Big Sleep*?" He shakes his head. I retrieve one from the closet and give it him. He puts his head down on the desk and begins practicing its title.

A few more students dribble in, the last one three minutes before class ends. Three students are reading, eight are texting and two boys in hoodies are engaged in *The Big Sleep practicum,* their heads on desks.

One more homeroom, an hour and a half later, and then I get to go to *my* home room.

Thursday, May 10, 2012

Yesterday the English department took a group of 50 students to see the American Place Theatre's production of *The Secret Life of Bees*. I got to come along as their extra adult. We herded our troops down to Seventh Avenue. A soft rain was falling. I held my place at the back of the pack. As I am a pretty fast walker, this took a lot of braking energy on my part. In a walking race with nonagenarians, these kids would barely place.

Once at the theatre, a lovely teaching artist welcomes the students, asking them to take the seats up front. Many race to the back row.

"OK, I'm going to ask you to please listen up. How many of you have been to the theatre before?" A number of hands go up. She hasn't distinguished between movie theatres and live theatre. She introduces them to the play, set in 1964, South Carolina.

"What was happening in this country in 1964?" she asks them. They're shy at first but then a boy raises his hand.

"Civil rights."

"That's right! Very good. And do you know the names of any of the leaders of the Civil Rights Movement?"

"Martin Luther King," says one of the girls.

"Well, you're going to see a one-woman show about a girl named Lilly who was 14 years old in 1964."

The show is entertaining *and* redemptive. Midway through the performance a group of kids in the back row starts whispering to each other. Turning around, I notice that half of the kids are entranced by the show and the other half asleep. After the play, Lilly and the teaching artist lead a talk-back. Walking back to school, I follow the last two girls dragging behind the group. As we cross 32nd Street, a couple of snails overtake them.

The Met

Today one of the teachers is taking a group of students to the Metropolitan Museum of Art. I'd mentioned to the teacher that I'd be happy to go with them if they need me. However, no one seems to need me. I head to the conference room and stake out a chair. The group of students heading to the Met gathers in the lobby. That's all right. I can guard the candy.

However, two boys missed the group that left for the Met.

"I'll be happy to take them," I offer. Accepted.

"I didn't really fit into my last school," says Juan as we approach the museum. "It was too big. This school's much better. My counselor said she'd help me get into this science program out of state. That never would have happened at my last school."

"We're going to look at the Impressionists and the Post-Impressionists," Elaine, our guide, tells us when we meet up with the rest of the group at the Met.

Thank you, DOE. I love my job☺

In the Degas room, the kids are captivated by the bronze sculpture of *The Little Fourteen-Year-Old Dancer.*

Elaine explains, "Being a dancer was a very hard life. This girl, Degas' model, was a ballet student at the Paris Opera. Most of these girls were very poor. They had to work for hours, give performances, practice. For the first couple of years, they didn't make any money. Then they got paid. It wasn't very much money but it really helped their families who didn't have much of anything. Take a look at how she's standing. See if you can stand like that. You see how hard it is to maintain that pose for such a long time." They pay close attention to this story. They identify with her because they're close in age...and, shall we say, not of means.

At Van Gogh's *Wheat Field with Cypresses,* 1889, a couple of girls are texting. I interrupt their concentration.

"You know Van Gogh cut his own ear off and sent it to a priest."

"Word? You hear that?" one of the girls says to her friend.

"He put himself into an asylum."

"He was crazy?" one of them asks me.

"Depressed, bipolar...? Who knows? He had a very tough life. Check out what he painted even though he had all these demons." The girls turn to the painting as Elaine talks about his love of the cypress trees.

After Cezanne and Gauguin, the tour is over. We thank Elaine and head out to Mimi's Pizza on Madison Avenue. Everybody gets a good meal. I sit with Michelle, the art teacher who put together this program. She is a teaching artist who only works at the school on Thursdays. She loves working with these kids.

"I wish they could hire me full time. I would really love this job."

I tell her about last week's "art" class at TCA.

"Wow!" She lights up. "Maybe I could teach there."

Friday, May 11, 2012

The students and their teachers have split up for college trips today. They're going to Bronx Community College, Queens College, St. John's, plus.

"If you need any help with research or such, please let me know," I say to the principal.

"Not right now, thanks."

"If I can help you with any clerical work, I'm happy to do so," I say to Phyllis, the lovely school secretary.

"Maybe later. Thanks."

Next week, I'm assigned to the High School for Fashion Industries.

"Oh, you gonna love that place," says the security guard who has worked there. "The paintings when you walk in…they're like they're done by adults. Those kids are talented."

I can't wait.

Monday, May 14, 2012

HIGH SCHOOL FOR FASHION INDUSTRIES (HSFI)

Fashion Is Not a Luxury

I pack myself into the #6 train on 68th Street this morning at 8 am after running down the subway stairs. Just as I do, the conductor closes the doors. A crush of commuters remains on the platform. Inside, it's a monster mash. My backpack rests on the large breasts of someone standing directly behind me. I don't think the big guy minds the weight. A young man pressed up against my front torso gives me the impression he wants me to have his child. Happily, my new white Hue leggings double as a condom.

The train lurches. Breakdown. Guy with big bag at two o'clock—is he a terrorist? I was riding the London Underground during the second terrorist bombing attempt on July 21, 2005. That bomb fizzled. Nobody was hurt. London was shut down. I was lucky once.

Fortunately, I arrive at the High School for Fashion Industries safely and sign in with security. Everybody is sweet. The payroll secretary gives me a bathroom key and a plastic card for the teachers' elevator. *Awesome!* While she's giving me my program, the PA starts crackling and a perky man's voice comes on.

"Good morning, Fashion Industry students. Today's prefix is 'pro.' It means 'in favor of.' The word for today is 'profuse.' It's an adjective that means 'large amounts.' Students, please remember that Regents are coming up very quickly. Today we will have tutoring in geometry, trigonometry, global and US history. Take advantage of these tutoring sessions. Thank you."

Everybody's *stylin'* in this school. It's a fashion brigade. Color, form, accessories, hair, makeup…the hallways are like runway shows. They're lined with mannequins dressed in student creations. The walls are covered with student-created clothing designs. Every square inch explodes with creativity.

My first assignment is a global history class. I walk in, a little self-conscious. My lipstick has worn off. I rummage through my backpack trying to find it. Maybe Big Bazoomas Dude took it out of my backpack on the train. Students start to dribble in. This is Fashion High School. I am already decked out in my new Jones blouse and I've accessorized. I turn around to the four girls who have just entered.

"I can't start the class until I find my lipstick," I tell them. They laugh.

Next period, I'm to show the class episode two from the documentary, *Guns, Germs and Steel.* I look out at the distracted crowd and see something I've never seen before in a class. A lovely dark-haired girl with a bright-colored hair ribbon is seated next to an ebony-skinned beauty. They are engaged in deep conversation. The ribbon girl turns to her gal pal, takes one of her breasts in her hands and squeezes it three times. *WTF?* Can I ignore this? No. It's in my face. I walk over to the two girls. The classroom is crowded with maybe 35 students. I don't want anyone to hear me. I speak to the girl with the pretty ribbon in her hair.

"I need to ask you to please cease this interaction. I have seen what is going on and it is quite inappropriate."

"I don't know what you're talking about," ribbon girl says. I'm not going to spell it out.

"I think you do. It actually made me very uncomfortable," I say—

not with any attitude, but just to inform. "Would you please, just until the end of this class, move over to that chair?" She plainly doesn't want to, but I call her by name. She knows I can make something of this. I ask her again and she moves to the other chair. In the back of the room, two girls are holding hands and stroking each other's fingers.

"Girls," I say quietly. "Please watch the film. You're having a quiz tomorrow. And I need you to separate. Thank you."

Next period, I am subbing for the marketing teacher. This class is all girls. Twenty-eight of them. They are all *stylin'.* One of them wears a tight-fitting tee shirt that reads, "Fashion Is Not a Luxury."

"It's a free period for you gals. I have no work for you."

An exquisitely beautiful, tall girl comes over to me. She has a slight resemblance to Iman, the super model from Somalia, musician David Bowie's wife. She flashes a million-dollar smile at me.

"Hi. I'm Nadif."

"Are you planning a modeling career?" I ask her.

"No, I want to study fashion law or fashion editorial... publishing." She is very poised and well spoken. Beauty and brains. "Where are you from?"

"I was born in New York. But my father's from Somalia."

"Did he escape from there?"

"Yes. His father was a rebel. My grandfather. But he got killed. My father was eight when they gave him a gun. He almost had to kill someone but then he didn't so he was happy."

"How did he get out?"

"Well, he escaped to Mali. He's actually Fulani. That's a combination of African and Arab. He got out because ...what's that country...? I can't remember...they sent troops...was it Khadafi?"

"You mean Libya?"

"Yes! That's it. You know they didn't like Khadafi in the US but in Mali, he sent troops and helped them get out of Somalia. He built much in Mali, roads, things like that, and my grandmother and all her family except my grandfather escaped."

"Your grandmother. What happened to her?"

"The rebels took her and all her children. But they were lucky. They all got to stay together. Then they all got out to Mali when they escaped. My father was one of the little kids."

"How about your mother?"

"My mother is second-generation British, from London. She only learned a short time ago that her parents were from Nigeria. She's a psychologist."

"So how did they meet?"

"My father owns a bookstore in Harlem. One day she came into the bookstore. They fell in love right there."

"Do you speak any other languages?"

"Oh yes. I speak Fulani, French, English, Arabic and some Mandingo. That's the Mali language. It's also called *Bambara*. Oh!" she adds. "I'm also the junior-class president."

"I'm shocked. " I smile at her.

Next period I meet the marketing teacher who stops by. She's very upbeat and energetic. The students perk up at her entrance. She teaches courses in textiles, marketing and computer programming. This is her first year teaching here. Coming from a career in the fashion world, she worked for major labels and cosmetics.

"I give them readings from the news about these areas and ask them to underline words they don't know. We develop our vocabulary. I also let them know that in the real world they need to learn how to speak, how to network. I tell them that they should never post anything inappropriate on Facebook. When I was hiring for my company, if I saw anything on Facebook that looked strange, I would toss the application."

"Why did you start teaching? Was there a downturn in your industry?"

"I always wanted to teach. I really love it."

Tuesday, May 15, 2012

A lovely teacher from India comes into my class of five. "I'm teaching down the hall," she says. "I want to ask a favor. My classroom has a terrible smell. It's coming from the sink. I was wondering if it might be possible for me to bring my students in your classroom and teach them here?"

"Let me ask my students, all right?" I turn to my tiny crew. "Guys…" I explain the predicament. "Tell the truth. How many are OK with it?" They all nod their heads.

"You're sure?"

"Yes, Miz." I turn to the teacher. "It's fine, then." She thanks me profusely as she leaves to collect her class.

"OK," I say to my small group. "What do you want to use this period for?"

"Homework," two of them say.

"Can we use the computer?" another two girls ask me.

"Sure. Just make sure you're doing something related to schoolwork."

"Thanks, Miz," one of the girls says as she dashes across the room to the computer. Her exposed back is covered with a beautiful tattoo of a winged heart. She immediately clicks on a tattoo site.

The Indian teacher leads her seniors into the room. She passes out an article, "Marriage Is for White People," a provocative article written by Joy Jones from washingtonpost.com.

The students take turns reading out loud. They compete with each other for a chance to read. "Pick me! Pick me!" After reading it, the teacher asks them, "Do you agree with the author that black women don't get married so much because they decide they can do better alone, in many cases?"

One girl speaks out forcefully, "I don't want to take care of some guy who just wants me because I got myself together. I got a car and I got a good job. I don't need nobody trying to be with me just to get my stuff."

Of the two boys in the class, one, an African American, says he wants to get married someday.

The other says, "I'm engaged."

"Really? So when are you getting married?"

"Never!" says he.

After class, I meet up with the AP, Mr. R.

"So nice to meet you," he says, shaking my hand. "You know, my wife is a teacher, my sister is a teacher. I never want to disrespect teachers by asking them to sit at a door but..."

"It's no problem," I say. "I'm happy to do door duty. I'll stuff envelopes if you need it."

We talk for a few minutes. He's impressed by my background and fund-raising success for my old school.

"Hey, maybe we could have lunch? I'd like to hear more. May I take you to lunch?"

"That would be great."

"Not today 'cause I'm swamped. Before the week ends."

Sounds like a plan.

Wednesday, May 16, 2012

I head up the teachers' elevator to cover an English class in room 929. It's a wonderful, large, well-lit room. There are sewing machines on each table. The room is lined with dress forms. Student designs are taped around the necks of the dress forms.

I love this room. Displays of different materials hang on the walls: embroidery, plain-weave...students created them. Some of the dress forms are draped with fabric. Some are bare. They seem to be ladies-in-waiting, anticipating the next young designer who might approach them with tender confidence, certainly with some intimidation. They stand erect, the sole enduring canvases that inhabit this shifting world of fashion. They stand, graciously offering themselves to their young avatars, who dress them and leave them until the next cluster of delicate imaginations confront their infinite potential.

Thing is, no students are coming in.

Whoops, wrong room. I bid the ladies-in-waiting goodbye and it's off to 925, where a large middle-aged woman wearing a *dashiki* and African *gele* head wrap looks up at me from behind her desk.

"I've been assigned to cover this class," I explain. "They told me you have a meeting." She responds to me as if in mid-sentence.

"You see I don't like this at all. I don't know if he's going to show up. Do you know if he's there?" I shake my head. Who? What? Huh? "This meeting. I didn't even write him up. The assistant principal came in and he was rude to him. I guess I have to go." She exits. I cover.

Back on door duty, I explore the giant lobby. It's adorned with an abundant array of student fashions and art. Student posters contain numerous full-body designs with bell bottom pants, bikinis, formal wear, faces sporting tattoos, high-heeled shoes made to look like yellow cabs, butterflies, impossible high heels. Highly inventive. Ready for MOMA.

Door duty? More like gallery gig.

I have one more English class with no lesson plan, but we write poetry.

"Wanna hear what I just wrote?" I ask them. They do. I read aloud my scribblings from door duty. They listen politely and I ask them to journal about something that has impressed them.

As I walk out the main entrance, the sun shines brightly on this cauldron of creative energy.

Thursday, May 17, 2012

I'm sporting my vibrant pink Hue Capri leggings and a gorgeous ivory lace blouse with an Empire waist and three-quarter sleeves. I look pretty hot for an aging chick, I think to myself as I cross the lobby of my apartment building. I shiver as I hit the morning air and turn around. Back upstairs, I pull my short Lauren jacket with pink flowers out of the closet and descend for a second time. "Perfect," I think as I catch a glimpse of myself in a store window. Actually, I strain to find the right light so I can primp for the glamorous subway ride downtown. You never know who's going to crowd you.

Nobody. It's a slow day with only two coverages and a number of free periods next to each other. This gives me lots of time to explore Chelsea during lunch.

Last class is gym on the tenth floor. Earplug special. A small group of seniors stays after the talkfest is over and the other students have left. I sit down on the floor with them.

"I want to be a celebrity. How do I do that?" A pretty little girl who's going to the Fashion Institute of Technology next year wants to know.

"What do you love to do?" I ask her.

"Well, I love to design, but I want to be...you know...a celebrity."

I give her some suggestions: put together a short show, maybe five minutes long. Take a TV-production class in college. Get some people to help you. Maybe the school has a studio. Study other short shows. Write a script. Be the producer and on-camera hostess. Feature your designs. Feature the designs of your friends. Have a place on the web where people can interact with you. Don't be sloppy—make it tight and professional looking. Build it and see what happens.

Some of the others ask similar questions. One will be going to Howard, one to NYU. They are all poised for adventure.

We sit and talk after school. They air their dreams and I offer them an unconditional *yes*. After a while I say, "Guys. Sorry, but I have to go."

"Thanks, Miz. Wish you could stay till the end of the year."
"Have fun!" I say.

Friday, May 18, 2012

I'm ten minutes late today. My train was delayed. I tell you, I earned my subway ride this morning. The shoving match was between me and, my guess, a broker, strong-arming his way into the car. He pushed past (my guess again) an anorexic account exec, a retiree whose recent knee replacement is still on the mend and a burly house painter. Hey dude! I know today's the Facebook IPO frenzy. But I've got to get to work, too. I closed in on his big swinging dick-tatorial style by shoving my pink computer case right between his ankles. It worked. My case has a pop-up handle. As I put my finger on the pop-up lever, threatening to let it spring up in the direction of his private parts, he moved to the side. Swiftly. I swelled with pride as I seized my six inches of standing space. In the back of the car, a man's loud voice protested something in a garbled tongue, as yet unknown in Queens, where all the world's 6,909 languages are spoken.

I have a full schedule, covering for an English teacher. It's a small group of ELLs. Ten students.

"The sub's here," one of them announces. They all say hi. They are very polite. One of the girls is sitting sideways in the back, her feet resting on her pal's chair. She's showing her pal a video.

"May I help you get started on your essay?" I ask her sweetly.

"No. Why you asking me? I don't need no help. Leave me alone."

Is it too late to get a couple of shares of Facebook? LinkedIn maybe?

Second-period break, so it's off to the auditorium to check out the famous murals that line its long walls. They're treasures. They tell the dramatic story of the needle trades in the US. Painted by artist Ernest Fiene between 1939 and 1940, they have been granted landmark status. Both the murals and the school building were constructed as

WPA projects. My eyes rest on a large muscular man, naked down to just above his groin, pointing to some workers. Impressive abs. A trio of girls hanging out in the balcony snaps me from my reverie. They are laughing at me. Otis Redding comes over the PA and I strut back to the eighth floor.

One of the many charming bits here is that, instead of bells, soul music is played over the PA. Aside from Otis, I've heard Aretha, Sam & Dave and James Brown during this week. Old-school rules.

It's fourth period. My first period ELLs return. A para joins us.

For the rest of the period, she sits with the trio of former cell phone users. They speak Spanish *muy rapido.*

"They don' wanna work so I talk to them," the para says, a little guiltily.

I feel a disconnect. Shouldn't the para encourage the students to use class time for class work? Hey, *señora,* it takes a *pueblo.*

Feelin' a bit old school right now.

Eighth and last period at the High School for Fashion Industries. I have a small ESL class reading a Sherlock Holmes story, "The Red-Headed League." They're so nice, I spit a few bars. Most of them laugh. One of them, a large girl wearing a big black-and-white striped shirt down to her knees doesn't react. I look at her. She looks back at me.

"Yo. Tha's dope, Miz," she says in a dulcet tone.

The Beach Boys start singing, "Rah Rah Rah, Be True to Your School," as the period ends.

I'm off to the hills.

Monday, May 21, 2012

NEW DESIGN HIGH SCHOOL (NDHS)

Herding Cats with Cell Phones and Solving for Y

It's way downtown to Delancey Street. Formerly Seward Park High School, it was closed in 2006 and turned into five small schools. New Design is one of them. It's very clean and inviting. Today I'm subbing for a math teacher named Nancy. Everybody's on a first name basis here, too.

Students have drawn colorful anime characters that are hanging on the wall.

My first class sleepwalks into the room. The "N" word makes an early appearance. A pretty girl copies her whole worksheet from the boy next to her as they flirt. One little girl seems to be a serious student. She is wearing headphones and listening to her round cd player. It's kind of cute and old school.

"So why did you choose this school?" I ask them.

"I ask myself that question every day," says the pretty girl with the superb copying skills.

"I dunno. For architecture. But they don't have that so much," her flirting BFF volunteers.

"Did you have to submit a portfolio to get in?"

"No."

"I just came here because I wanted to get away from my neighborhood," another girl tells me.

"I hate this school," a young boy in the back says.

"You hate this school? Why?"

"I dunno, I just hate it."

"Did you come here for design?"

"I just like to sketch. But it's wack here."

"So 'wack' and 'hate' are pretty strong words. What exactly don't you like?"

"I dunno, Miz. Stuff."

By this time, we are all counting the days till Memorial Day and then, finally, the end of the school year.

I take a walk downstairs during my break. At the entrance to the school's auditorium, I notice some faded photos hanging on the wall. They have pictures of the men of distinction (only men) who attended SPHS before it was closed in 2006. Two of my favs: Zero Mostel, class of '31, and Walter Matthau, class of '33. I wonder if they were in drama class together.

One glimpse of me, and every student in my second class takes out a cell phone. "Do you allow them to use cell phones in class here?" I quietly ask a teacher who shares this room.

"If we didn't, I'd be collecting phones all day," he explains. *Huh? And...?* Might as well start up a conversation with the kids. These are nascent designers, after all.

"Last week I worked at Fashion High School."

Some of the girls call out excitedly.

"Oh!! I wanted to go there!"

"Me, too."

"I noticed you have a room with sewing machines," I say.

"Yeah. We have to take a class."

"What's it called?"

"Uh...sewing." They laugh.

I show them my pictures of the room at Fashion High with all the machines and dress forms. "They have to make gowns for their senior project."

"We do, too. Out of newspaper."

I laugh. It's a joke, right?

"No, they're made out of newspaper. I made one," says a girl.

"Just newspaper? What happens if it rains like today?" It's pouring outside.

"We wear them inside."

"Do you have a picture of yours?" She takes out her phone and shows it to me. Very impressive. Backless, it has a very short skirt, stiff, sticking out like a tutu on a ballerina.

Pleasantries completed, I get to help a few of them solve some $y=mx+b$ equations, solving for y. I feel a little more connected.

Last class.

Just a few kids. One is named Ares. He shakes my hand, very polite.

"Do you know the origin of your name?" I ask him.

"Yes. The Greek god of war." They are a nice group, not particularly interested in solving for y. We get into a rap session. Literally. Ares has recorded his own bars in his Pro Tools studio. He's very talented with words.

"I'm impressed," I tell him, as he finishes his first tune that has a repeating chorus line, *I don't wanna talk, I just wanna fuck.* "But you could take this to a whole new level. Instead of just sex, I'll bet you could spit some hot political bars about how you see things."

"I got that, Miz. Listen!" He plays me a beat and spits along with it. It's about drugs and gangs and wasting your life.

"That's what I'm talking about," I say. I let him soak in the praise. "I just have one little thing, if you don't mind."

"Naah, go ahead, Miz."

"I'm not crazy about you referring to women as 'bitches.' "

"Right Miz, I know. You're right."

"And I really like when you go beyond sex and all the cursing and rap about something meaningful that's going on in your life. Props. I really love your internal rhyme."

"Thanks, Miz."

"You're in eleventh grade, right? What are you planning to do after high school?"

"I dunno, Miz. I just want to graduate. College? I don't think it's something for me."

"I'm going to Penn State." His friend next to him pipes up. "I'm gonna be his manager. I'm also a hockey player. I'm gonna get a business degree and a law degree. If that doesn't work out, I'm gonna go with the NHL."

"Sounds like a plan," I say. "Why don't you both go to Penn State? Ares, you can study creative writing and learn how to think like a businessperson. The music biz is the worst business out there. You have to learn a lot to maintain success."

"Yeah, Miz. You right."

"You'll be a great team. And hey, do me a favor? We only have ten more minutes in the period. Could you please do the first page of math problems so I feel like I'm doing my job."

"You got it, Miz."

"You gonna be here tomorrow?" Ares asks me.

"Yes, all week."

"You gotta take this class, Miz."

"I wish I could but they give me a program every morning. I don't know what I'll be doing tomorrow." They are standing by the door. There are maybe three minutes to go. The MBA/lawyer/NHL guy takes out a wad of bills and gives them to Ares who puts them on a desk in piles of 20s, 10s and 5s.

"What are you doing? I would never display money like that," I say.

"Yo Miz," says NHL guy. "I carry around like $4000 in cash sometimes. My moms gives it to me. It's OK."

"I hope it's legal."

"Oh, Miz. This is all legal money. You got nothing to worry about." Ares finishes counting, wads it all back up and stuffs it in his jean pocket. The bell rings.

"Peace out, Miz." And they leave.

Tuesday, May 22, 2012

"You will be assigned to the library today," the principal tells me as I greet him at 8:35 am.

"If you need any help, research, envelope stuffing, please let me know."

"Thanks. Just ask the librarian. Maybe there's something you can help with in there."

Lunchtime. I decide to walk along Essex Street. Still looking for a salad. Hey! I smell pickles! Sure enough, it's the Pickle Guys. The sign here says they're closed next week for Shavuot, the Jewish festival of weeks when Moses received the Ten Commandments from God at Mount Sinai. For free yet!

Back in the library, things are very quiet.

Technology Trumps Earth Science

I have 23 students, with two student teachers. A few snippets:

"Get the fuck outta here!" A pudgy boy slaps a girl.

I walk over to him and quietly say, "Settle down, please, and let's stop the cursing, OK?"

"I wasn't cursing."

All the students have laptops and earbuds. They're watching You Tube. I ask them to put their earbuds away. They protest. "We're allowed to listen to music in this class."

Didn't I see this episode already?

"Is this true? Are they allowed to listen to music?" I ask Jo, a student teacher. She nods.

"I have issues with this kind of permissiveness," she says. "It's in the whole school."

I ask Margaret, the other student teacher, what school she's graduating from.

"NYU. I'm getting my Masters in Teaching."

"Science?"

"No. History."

"History?? So why are you student teaching in this science class?"

"I'm not student teaching. I'm a certified substitute teacher."

"So if you're a sub, why did the AP ask me to come in here?"

"I don't know."

"Are you planning to teach in the city?"

"I don't know." She looks out at the class. More girls in the back are singing and rocking back and forth with headphones. And so it goes.

Here's the uncanny part: Towards the end of class, Jo leads a discussion. Hands go up in answer to her questions. Ideas are shared. Students are thinking, participating and contributing good ideas.

"That's excellent, Jason," she says. "I think you've made a very interesting point, Kiara. Would you like to repeat it so everyone can hear it?"

How the hell have these kids grasped the material so well with all the incessant distractions? I don't get it.

Perhaps this crazy class is more evidence that the universe is expanding after all.

Wednesday, May 23, 2012

"Wednesday!" I greet the security guard cheerfully as I walk in.

"You got it," she replies.

"Goin' slow, right?"

"Oh my Gawd." She shakes her head.

"It's because of Memorial Day, right? It goes so slow waiting for Friday."

"You can say that again. I'm goin' crazy. I cannot wait." These guards work hard for the money. Their shifts can be extremely long, from 6:30 am to 10 pm, depending on the needs of the building. It's easy to walk into a school and see a couple of uniformed school safety officers laughing and "sitting around." However, they are the eyes and ears of the school. Everyone depends on them. Everything bumps up to their desks: flaring tempers, flying fists, crabby administrators, sobbing children, threats, litter, personal secrets from isolated adolescents. They don't get rewarded with long summer vacations like teachers. They have to keep up with their training sessions. They are serious guardians of the peace. They need to maintain their sense of humor. They have their own families with children, often students in the public schools. They are role models, adult confidants for kids who wake up in shelters or single-parent homes where parenting takes second and third place to survival issues. They keep the school safe. They help keep the kids straight. They are surrogate parents, psychologists, friends and nurturers. They are tough, strong and big hearted. When you visit a school, make friends with them. They might be the ones you call on in your moment of need. They got your back.

I'm assigned to another day in the library.

Wednesday. Hump day. Almost over. Thirty minutes left.

Twenty-nine-and-a-half minutes....

Thursday, May 24, 2012

I have one class today: design. It's been thundering outside and I got a *bissel* wet. This morning the librarian asked me to file piles of books back into their places on the shelves. That's what I did to earn money as a college student. I've come a long way.

It's lunchtime at the Shalom Falafel deli across the street. The little old Jewish characters come in and out. One fellow of maybe 85 is keeping up a running commentary on everyone in the news to who's not here yet.

"He's got 25 million. He makes $400 tousand a day. Vat do I care? If I had his money I'd know sumting, lemme tell you. You know his mudda lives on Park Avenue. Didja hear me? Park Avenue??"

After lunch, I have to stop by the main office to pick up a special key for the design room. A group of students has taken over the comfy chairs in the lobby. One of them, a pretty dark-skinned girl with long straight hair, is singing along with the music coming through her earbuds.

Gitchy Gitchy ya ya na na…

I can't help myself. I pick up on the jam and sing the next line of the chorus with her. She goes crazy so I stop before belting "Creole Lady Marmalaaaaade." I get the key and head down to 406. There are some kids sitting outside.

"Ares!" I say.

"I been sick, Miz."

"I've been thinking about you," I say.

"Yeah—I thought about some of the things you said."

"Great. When you guys graduate from Penn State, you'll rule the world." I know it's hype. But he could use some hype. I hope it sticks.

The big design classroom is filled with creative clutter. There are cut-out newspapers on the floor. Objects made from newspapers are all around. There is a chair made from rolled up newspaper. A sign taped to it says "Victoria, Vanessa and Kennaly's Chair." The frame of the chair is painted purple. It's taped with yellow and orange duct tape. Another display on an adjacent table is a woven newspaper sculpture. Its sign reads, "Team Members: Julia, Abigail, Tiffany, Elisa…The Potted Potter!" They've wrapped the bottom of it with a newspaper ad for the Potted Potter, whatever that may be. Tables and more equipment line the back wall, wood drills, clamps. The closets are labeled Face Masks, Goggles, Ear Protection, Gloves. One side of the closet displays ten wood files, long, short, fat and thin. A box is filled with acrylic paints. A tin holds watercolors. Everything seems to be strewn around the room with little attempt to organize or clean it up. I love this room. It's controlled chaos.

The bell rings and the students come in.

"Look!!! It's *her!!!*" It's the crew who had occupied the main office. The girl with the long straight hair starts singing, *"Gitchy Gitchy yaya."* This time, in the privacy of my own class, I pick it up and we start singing it together and doing some steps. I take it all the way to "Creole Lady Marmalaaaaade," and go up one octave. They go from giggles to silent. Then it's, "Yo! She mad cool." The usual props. I'm not lonely anymore.

"Guys! Chill. Chill." I read the instructions their teacher left for me:

> **"Over the past week and half [sic] students worked in groups designing and creating a chair. Each group received one roll of tape and unlimited newspaper to create chair [again, sic] that will support the weight of a person."**

So that's why the newspaper sculptures looked like chairs. Very cool. "Guys. Your teacher wants you to go back into your teams and make sure your chairs are reinforced. Then label them and write two or three sentences about what inspired the design, what it's for (lounging, work, etc), what makes your design unique?"

"Shut up!! She's trying to talk," a girl with tri-colored red hair yells out to her colleagues.

"OK—so you know what to do." I go to a couple of the girls and they help me bubble the attendance.

"They tore my mother-fuckin' chair!" a tall, thick dark-skinned boy yells in outrage. He starts using every Anglo-Saxonism known to man. It's an explosion. I walk over. I let him curse until he pauses.

"What happened?"

"See that???" He points to a newspaper chair on the floor. "They fucked it up. I'm gonna kill somebody."

"I'm so sorry," I say. I'd be upset too. He needs to vent. "Do you know who did it?"

"I don't know but when I find out, I'm gonna kill someone. I'm tight." Two other girls on his team are crestfallen. They start throwing names around. "I feel like tearing up every fuckin' chair in this room," he says. I keep my eye on him. He still needs to vent.

"That wouldn't be such a great idea," I say after a pause. He storms out of the room. One of the girls on his team takes their project, finds some tape and starts to repair it.

The boy comes back. He's calmed down a bit.

"You OK?" I say.

"I'm still mad." By now the other two girls on the team have attached the part that was missing. They're beginning to perk up.

"I need a marker. You got a marker? I'm gonna put a note on it." The Gitchy Gitchy girl grabs a yellow paper and writes a note on it. She pins it to the repaired chair. Together, she and I carefully move the chair way underneath a table. Her note says:

> Dear Haters AKA (MF's)
> If you touch our shit again,
> YO! shit will go missing.
> This goes to 9–11th grade hoes.

It could use a little polishing but her point is well made. We all get a laugh out of it. Things are getting back to normal.

I leave that team and ask the other students to show me their newspaper chairs. They're all clever. One adorable girl sits down in a chair that looks like it could be used for formal dining if you threw a silk cover over it. Another one, created by three kids who are pinned to their Blackberries, is a small pad made from a pile of newspapers. It's not particularly creative but it's a respectable attempt. One girl is taping, reinforcing a heart-shaped chair covered with musical pages. Her team members go out of the room and spray paint a giant cut-out heart, made from newspapers, which will serve as the back of the chair. It's dope.

I come back to the group of kids whose chair has been busted. They've already forgotten about it and are deep in conversation about social issues.

"Yo! He talkin' 'bout gay marriage. You buggin'!"

"Mind if I join you?" I ask.

"Naah, Miz. You cool," Gitchy Gitchy girl says.

"Whatcha think about gay marriage?" her girlfriend says.

"Me?"

"Yeah, Miz," says the big boy. Evidently, he's dropped his plan to tear up all the other chairs.

"Well…" I say. "For me, I'm in favor of it. But straight marriage? I'm completely against it. I don't think straight people should marry."

"Wha? Fa real?"

"Of course. Straight people shouldn't be allowed to marry. Just gay people. Then marriage would be much neater."

"*Yo!* She gassin' us! You heard?"

"Yo Miz…you buggin," says the boy.

"So…you're OK about the chair?" I cautiously open up the subject.

"Yeah, Miz. Course. It's just newspaper anyway. This school too poor to buy wood so we have to make everything out of newspapers. Chairs. Dresses."

"Actually, I think that's a good thing. You really learned something about construction with this exercise."

Class is over. The next class starts to drift in. A little girl with a bright-green tee shirt recognizes me from earlier this week as she comes in. She throws her arms open and gives me a big hug.

"Oh, Miz!! You taking our class today?"

"No—your teacher's here. I'm just waiting for him." She looks a little disappointed. No sub. That means she'll be held to a higher standard.

For me, it's nice to end the day with a hug.

Friday, May 25, 2012

Only have one class to cover today. On my way there, I walk past a large metal poster bolted to the wall. At the top it reads "College

Acceptances." Students' acceptance letters are posted for all to celebrate. The schools?

College of Staten Island, La Guardia Community College, BMCC...

Middle Tennessee, Morrisville State...

*City Tech, John Jay, Queensborough Community...*and so on.

This victory wall belongs to everybody who has been entrusted with these kids' success: teachers, administrators, parents, corporate givers, librarians, school secretaries, peace officers and custodial staff who keep the place clean and safe for thinking and learning. It's a village! This is a wall of winners, a wall of pride. This is a great wall.

The kids filter into the class and conversations fill the room. It's typical teen chatter: fuck this fuck that. Chill. You pussy, nigga.

"Guys, I have to congratulate you. You have squeezed more curse words into five minutes than any group I've ever heard. I can curse right the fuck along with you, but it's early in the morning. Could we attempt to refine our language?"

"You heard what she said?"

"Yo! Stop cursing, *niggas*!" a girl yells at everybody from the first row. Teacher's pet.

Library duty. Fire drill. Lunch. I grab a slice at Shalom Falafel. The owner is sitting to my left.

"Yer getteng to be a legula customer," he says, smiling.

"Hello," says an elderly man sitting at the booth right behind me. He's speaking to the owner.

"Good *shabbos*," replies the owner. They jump up, lock hands and give each other a vigorous high five.

Gotcha! Just wanted to see if you were still paying attention.

I'd love to leave but I have to get permission from the AP. Why not? It's a permissive school. She's been sweet, after all. I call her from Shalom F.

"What do you need?" she says to me sharply.

"I don't need anything. I'm finished with my coverages and wonder if you have any objection to my leaving early."

"So you'll take a half day?" She's going to dock my pay.

"OK. That's great. It was very nice to have met you," I say as she hangs up on me.

Shalom out.

Tuesday, May 29, 2012

MANHATTAN BRIDGES HIGH SCHOOL (MBHS)

Bienvenido

Headline from today's NYCDOE web page:

Chancellor Walcott Announces New Names for 24 Schools ...

He's changed the schools' names because they've been classified PLA, that is, Persistently Low Achieving. Shucks. Banana Kelly High School is on the list. It's my favorite name for a high school, *ever!* Banana Kelly is to become "The College Preparatory Academy at Longwood." *Boring.* Couldn't they have chosen another fruit and paired it with a different Hibernian moniker? How 'bout:

- *Mango Magee School of Excellence?*
- *Pomegranate Fitzpatrick Prep?*
- *Grapefruit Gallagher Leadership Academy?*

Maybe just call it: *We Hope This School Does Better Than The Banana High School.*

Hell's Kitchen is smoldering in the heat. Emerging from the E train, I push through the heavy hot air. It's several long blocks down 50th Street to the large brick building that houses Manhattan Bridges High School. Formerly Park West High School, it closed in 2005 and reopened with five small schools including Manhattan Bridges and another called Food and Finance. What do you learn there…how to swallow your portfolio? Or just pay for your food?

Manhattan Bridges High School is on the third floor. With some navigational assistance, I locate the school office. At a long bar which separates the office space from the waiting room, there's a pile of small booklets: "A Guide To Free Food and Assistance: Chelsea/West Side 2011." I wonder how many people who come to this office wait until there's nobody looking and stuff one of these in their bags? Hunger is ugly.

"Hi, Ms. Rose!" Olivia, an extremely friendly secretary, greets me. "Here's your program." I have three classes. Ms. Fernandez had a baby boy over the holiday weekend. I'm to teach her ESL students.

"Here's the bathroom key," says Olivia. "I'll show you Ms. Fernandez' classroom. It's 339." She walks me into a vast corridor.

"This is the AP's office," she says. The AP looks up. She's a blonde lady well dressed in subdued, classy neutrals. "Please come in," she says to me. "I'm Ms. Segal. Please sit down. We're a bilingual school. Do you speak Spanish?"

"Not really," I say.

"Many of them are struggling with the English language. What's your background?" she asks me. She actually listens when I give her my elevator pitch.

"I used to work in a Consortium School," she tells me. "We're not with the Consortium. I wish we were."

She leads me down the hall. "Here's the teachers' workroom. They insist it is *not* called a lounge!" I go in and sit down with some friendly teachers. We chat. We laugh. We swap stories. I don't have to teach until 9:59. It's 9:05. Ms. Segal comes back in.

"Oh. I just realized. You have an advisory. Now. Please follow me. We really don't have a program for advisory here…it's a shame."

Earplug time. Advisory is chaotic. One boy's acting up. He's smart, full of energy. He settles down.

"What's your name?" I ask him.

"Darling," he replies. No wonder. His name's a life sentence in humility.

Advisory chaos goes on...and on. Please end. Please end.

A large boy comes in with the key to the laptop cart in the back of the room. He opens it and distributes tiny Lenovos laptops to the throng. In two minutes, the place is silent. Although You Tube is blocked, the laptops take over. Aaah. Quiet. Laptops are great babysitters.

Three more minutes of advisory. A teacher enters. She turns on me, her incisors flashing.

"Who gave them the laptops?"

I indicate the large boy.

"Who gave him the key?" she snaps. "*You need to put back your laptops*," she shrieks across the room to all the students.

"I'm not sure who authorized this," I say.

She hisses. "*They can easily slip them into their bags. You lose any of them on your watch and it's your responsibility.*"

"Sounds like a threat," I say out loud. *Yo Miz! Quit gankin' ma shit! You violatin' me. I will take you down, beeshay!* Did I say that out loud? No. Whew.

"I don't mean to make it a threat." *Yo. Snap. She backin' off ma grill.* She turns to the newly arrived young teens, struggling to learn our complex language. Applying the Gilbert Gottfried approach to sensitive language erudition, she screeches, "*Make sure you turn in every single laptop.*" I duck out for my next class.

It's an English class. As the kids come in there's the usual excitement at seeing a substitute.

"Where's Ms. Fernandez?"

"She had a baby."

"You our teacher?"

"Yes." I give them a few minutes to settle down. It's a small class. Very sweet kids.

"Please take out your books." I go around the room and make sure each of them has a book to read.

Shortly, everybody is reading. Ms. Segal enters and speaks to them: "I just want to tell you that I know you've had different teachers and that's hard on you. I'm sorry about that. But you have your reading and paperwork, so please keep on going. Ms. Desheraud is going to grade you." She is very sympathetic and they seem to appreciate it.

Lunchtime! Class blocks are almost immeasurably long. One hour and fifteen minutes. Lunch? Incredibly short. Forty minutes? Must forage. *Rapido.* Outside, it's *muy caliente!* Must find food. Nearby. I turn right on 11th Avenue and walk north. Irish pub. I peer in. Nobody home. I look across 11th. A building is draped with banners. *OMG! It's the Daily Show.* Faux News Central. For so long I have dreamed of being their Senior-Senior Correspondent. Sigh.

I choose a veggie salad at the corner deli where I can sit by the window, hoping to catch a glance of Jon...

"Hi, guys," I welcome my new class after lunch. It's a lovely, small group of eleven tenth graders learning English-language skills.

"Miz. You know Spanish?"

"Not much," I say. "*Unas pocas palabras*. Maybe a few bad words."

"Oh, yeah. You learn bad words first. *Malas palabras*. You know this one? *Asaroso? Malnacido*?

"No. Write it down. What does it mean?"

"Lowborn," she says.

Our class is reading and working on their projects. Ms. Segal the AP comes in and says she'd like to talk to me.

"I understand you didn't have all the laptops put away."

"The other teacher came in and took over. I thought she wanted to supervise getting them all put back."

"All right. I understand. The English Department is really stressed out these days. I see that you have got this class reading. We may be able to have you come here until the end of the year. You'll have a home. I just need you to understand the importance of controlling the technology and to see that you are up to the task."

"Absolutely," I smile.

So...Ms. Uptight snitched. *Gonna hafta muster ma crew fer round two.*

Meanwhile, the AP is offering me a temporary "home." It's tempting. Nice kids. Screeching teachers. Naah. Homeless = more appealing.

This block is going slow. Half hour left. I'm aging. My skin cells have already grown a new elbow. Three girls come over to me.

"You remind us of Rose from the Titanic. You saw the movie?"

"Rose? She was young and very pretty. It can't be me."

"Your eyes, Miz."

"Well, that's the nicest thing anyone has said to me in a long time."

"I mean the one who tells the story."

"Ooooh. You mean Old Rose. That makes more sense." We start singing "Near, far, wherever you are..."

"I'm from DR," she says. "Salcedo, DR. Really Puerto Plata. You heard of the Mirabel sisters? They were from Salcedo. Trujillo killed them."

In 1960, these brave *hermanas* were clubbed to death by henchmen of Trujillo, the brutal dictator of DR. They called themselves *Las Mariposas*. This young lady from Salcedo is rightfully proud of her brave butterflies.

Wednesday, May 30, 2012

I was up all night. Called in sleepy.

Thursday, May 31, 2012
Soy Tu Madrina

Arrived 45 minutes early and punched in. Lovely Olivia gave me my program: *Historia Global Y Geografia* taught in Spanish. Took a walk past the Daily Show, my ashram of political vitriol.

Regents are eight days away. ELLs are allowed four hours to take the three-hour exams. My job: continue Regents prep. Most of the exams will be in Spanish. Herewith some vignettes:

"Miz, me puede ayudar por favor? I go over to a boy who's stuck on a practice question. I look at the question he's pointing to.

"Que es esto?" He's pointing to a specific word. The word is "*Hsia*."

"No se," I say. I try to read the long quote it's taken from. The quote is from *The Shu Ching Book of History*. Happy as I am that we have gotten away from the Eurocentric teaching of world history, I'm still not sure what the hell is *Hsia*. Guess it has something to do with Asia. My tourist Spanish will not fly in this situation. *"No se,"* I say again. "I wonder if it's a misprint…for the word 'Asia,' " I say to myself out loud. I call out to the class. Some of the students are working together which is fine with me.

"Excuse me. *Número ocho*. Does anybody know this *palabra*?" I write "*Hsia*" on the board. *Nada*. "OK. I don't know either. Skip this question and ask your teacher tomorrow, *por favor*."[15]

Hoping to redeem my pedagogical potency, I walk around the room, checking on students' progress. Some of them are hunkering down on the practice Regents, some are getting bored. Two boys are playing with two-inch toy skateboards.

"Por favor," I say to the boys, sticking out my hand. "Give them to me please. *Como se dice?"*

"No, Miz, *please*," one of them says to me very sweetly. He's such a charmer, he almost breaks my heart.

[15] Later, I googled it. It's the name of an ancient Chinese civilization. Who knew?

"Como se dice, Give them to me!"

"Entragalo, idiota!" a girl behind them yells out. She's on my side... or maybe just not on theirs.

"What she said, *por favor,*" I say, smiling, holding my hand out. Sadly, with profound separation anxiety, he puts the tiny skateboard in my hand.

"Muchas gracias," I say. *"Ahora, examen de practica."* I walk over to the globe sitting on the teacher's desk. I carefully place the toy skateboard on the North Pole. "Do the *examen ahora.* I will leave this right here and you can have it back at the end of class. *Comprenden?"*

"Yes, Miz." Everyone in the class has enjoyed this little diversion. Regents practice is about to turn into a *fiesta* if I don't play my hand well.

"Guys. I'm sorry. *No habla español muy bien."*

*"No habl***o** *español, Miz!* Speak English, Miz!" A few of them call out. I'm annoying them with my Spanish.

There's a commotion on the right side of the room. Two boys and two girls are yelling at each other. I can't understand a word they're saying. I walk over with a little smile. Don't need to pour any more salsa *picante* on their *acalorada disputa.*

"Que pasa?" I ask.

"Miz!! *Mire!* What's right?" She points to a graphic diagram on the exam. A boy yells something at her and she counters back. It's intense and I don't understand their words.

"OK. A little *mas tranquilo, por favor,"* I say sweetly.

"What is it, Miz? This...right? Number one!" She is passionately defending her choice of an answer to question #20. I look at the diagram. It shows the social hierarchy of the *imperio colonial español en el Hemisferio Occidental.* Answer number one shows the following order from the highest to the lowest class: *peninsulares* (born in Spain), *criollos* (born in Spanish America), *mestizos/mulatos* (mixed Indian and Spanish race) and *africanos/nativos.* It's probably a necessary over-simplification, but...

"You're right," I say to her. She fires some extremely self-righteous bluster in Spanish back to the boy.

This racial stratification issue is always *muy caliente* with kids. Skin tone and its relation to social class? An extremely hot topic and, I might add, a great place for teachers to ignite thoughtful discussion and scholarship. The Regents is eight days away. Right. No time for thoughtful discussion and all that crap. Teach to the test...teach to the test...

Sat in "my" room for a leisurely forty-minute lunch. The next class is about to come in. I grab a pile of Regents practice exams *en español* and stand at the door, ready to greet them.

"Hi, Miz!"

"Hi," I say to each one. "I'm Ms. Rose."

"Very nice to meet you."

"Hello, how are you?"

They are gracious...charmingly old fashioned.

"You know... I'm very impressed with how polite you are. You come from a very lovely culture."

"Oh. thank you."

"*De nada,*" I say and do a little flamenco step.

"She dancing!" I do one complete pirouette. A couple of the girls get up and do a few *salsa* steps. I grin at them.

"OK. So everybody...*siéntense*! *Por favor*!" They sit down and look up to me. "You know," I say, "when my generation is gone, you will take over for us. You can be the next Justice Sotomayor."

"Sotoma*yor*!" a girl calls out, correcting my pronunciation.

"*Gracias!* I'm learning. I love to learn. I hope you do, too. I can see how possible it is for you to be very successful. Today we have to practice taking these exams. Most of us don't like exams, but we have to take them. I want you to get high grades, not just pass. So do your best. Use today as an opportunity to learn how to take the test. See what you know and what you need to learn. You still have eight school days to practice. I really want you to do great. That's in my *corazon."* Something amazing happens. They all applaud. I wasn't expecting that.

"Muchas gracias." Now write your *nombre* on the practice test and go to the first question.

"Miz. You're like *madrina*. Can you say *madrina?"*

"Madrina," I say and they all laugh. "What? Did I say it wrong?"

"No, Miz. Say *tu madrina*."

"I don't know what I'm saying. Is it a bad word?" I pick up the Spanish dictionary.

"No, Miz. It means...I don' know how you say..." A girl comes over to me and tries to explain. "It's like you know...somebody when a baby born...some woman comes over after and..."

"Like a family member?" I ask. She nods. "So it's a good thing."

"Si," a boy calls out. He points to two girls working on the test across the room. "Say *tu madrina* to them." His friends all laugh. There's more to this word than I understand.

"Is it 'godmother'?"

"Jes! That's it! Godmother!"

"I'm very honored by your calling me *Madrina. Soy tu madrina. Soy tu* teacher, too, and now I want you to do all these *preguntas* on your exam. *Esta bien?* So you succeed!" They start their work.

"It's all right if you collaborate. Don't copy—learn. You won't be able to work together on the Regents."

"We know, Miz."

"OK. Go ahead and start. But first...tell me where you're from?"

The breakdown: DR: 11, PR: 1, Ecuador (Quito, Cuenca) : 2, Peru (Lima): 2, El Salvador (La Libertad): 1, Mexico (Puebla, Guerrero):1.

"Miz...you always so happy?" a Peruvian girl asks me as I walk around the room, checking their work.

IMHO, MBHS is doing a great job providing a safe launching pad for their *sueños,* their dreams. A dual-language school has its critics. "You wanna be a real American, *speak English!"* To them, I say, *Hau kola washichu.* (That's Lakota Sioux for "hello friend." "Washichu" refers to white man, literally, "bad medicine.")

As the class ends, one of the talkative girls runs up to me.

"Miz—I have to give you a kiss," she says. I get a gracious peck on my cheek and she heads for her next class.

After school, I walk across town with a young teacher who's got four years in the NYC public school system. I can tell he's highly creative. He came up with some unique programs for his students. Then last year a new administrator at the school started doling out U's to many of the teaching staff in pop-in observations. It was deflating, to say the least.

"Still…I love the kids," he tells me. "The kids are the juice."

Friday, June 1, 2012

8:45. A cluster of students is waiting outside the room I'm assigned to cover.

"*Madrina!*" I get a few hugs and a kiss on the cheek from a girl.

They are writing fables about their own lives. One is by a girl whose name is Garleney. It's called "The Annoying Teacher."

> *Once there was an annoying teacher. He was my English teacher. My classmates and I were angry with him because he insulted us because we were many Latinos and African-Americans. That day we decided to go to our Principal to talk with her, because he was not supposed to talk with us like that. Our Principal talked with him and she said that all people are the same no matter who we are. Next day at school our teacher said, "I'm sorry. I was not supposed to talk with you guys like that. So with all respect, you guys have the opportunity to have a better future in this country."*

I check the progress of those smart little girls in the back of the class. I bring up that word again. I don't completely understand its usage.

"*Madrina* can be an insult sometimes, Miz," one tells me. I look at her quizzically.

"If I insult you then you might insult me back by calling me *Madrina,*" the other girl says.

"Why is that an insult?"

"It just is, Miz."

"But I'm just calling you 'godmother.' Why is that an insult?"

"It depend on how you use it, Miz. You need to learn more Spanish."

Tienes toda la razon!

Monday, June 4, 2012

Murry Bergtraum High School for Business Careers

(MBHSNYC)

Nothing Short of a Professional Attitude Will Be Accepted

Not one but two rainbows arched over the sky as we headed back from the mountains yesterday. It wasn't easy to drive and gape. My husband drove. I was the designated gaper.

Today, a large brick building stretched between two round silos rises in front of me. On it is written "Murry Bergtraum High School for Business Studies." I'm way down south near City Hall. Everyone in the school office is friendly. June. It's almost summer.

"Let me know if you need anything," a kind AP says.

"Here's your program," says Elaine, the secretary. Her voice is low range, with a rasp. In musicological terminology it would be classified *basso molto profundo rasputino*. She's definitely got that Selma Diamond thang. "You're subbing for two teachers. Usually we try to give you one, but not today."

I'm given a bright orange paper entitled, "Substitute Assignment Form." It makes for an amusing morning read: no bathroom passes first and last ten minutes of classes, no hats, coats, iPods, Walkmans (what is this, 1990?), beepers (1983?), yada yada. The last paragraph is adorable:

> *All teachers should walk about (1897?) the classroom when delivering the lesson for the day.* ***Sitting at the desk is not considered acceptable behavior and is a poor classroom technique****...We will not accept anything short of professional attitude and effort. Failure to comply may result in your dismissal.*

It warms my heart to belong to our esteemed and highly respected profession.

My first two classes are held in a computer lab. Labeled "FL," foreign language, on my program, the students are a mix of Asian and Hispanic. They're supposed to work on the Castle computer program where they make progress in English.

There are 19 students. I visit two boys. One is playing cards. The other is looking at sports.

"You should be working on your Castle," I say sweetly.

"I'm not doing nothin' until my teacher comes back."

"Miz, go sit down," says his friend, giving me the evil eye.

A woman comes in the room with long black hair and a long black skirt. Gen baby boomer. She gives me a friendly smile.

"I need to talk to two of your students."

"Absolutely."

She goes over to two girls. "I need to know where you are going to college," she tells them. "You are seniors. You have to decide between these two colleges. They're both in the city." The girls just shake their heads.

"OK. I'll fill out the forms for both colleges and then when you decide, let me know." One of the girls takes out her cell phone and makes a call. Gen baby boomer turns to me. "I gave her permission to use her cell phone." The girl hands her the cell phone. She speaks into it.

"Your doctor says you're all right? That's great. You have to come back, sweetie, and take the English Regents. OK? All right, then. I'll see you…tomorrow? I miss you." When she's finished, I ask her what she does.

"I'm the bilingual guidance counselor."

She's what we need. She's what we have. An abundance of love for the kids. Going the extra mile to make sure they get into college. Yay, team. She's special but lemme tell you, schools are full of this kind of "special," I'm proud to say.

Next class is in the same room. Kids sit in clusters, self-defined by ethnicity and language bonds. The Hispanic kids are ebullient, loud, confident, sassy. The Asians are quiet, but highly energized together.

One of the girls in the Hispanic section is yelling at a boy who is talking a blue streak. I go over to manage the explosion.

"Fuck off, asshole!" she yells.

"Why not just use initials like FOA?" I ask her sweetly.

"You heard what she said?" She turns to the boy and yells, *"FOA!"*

"That's better, don't you agree? Later, we can find some great curses from Shakespeare."

"Suck my dick!" she yells back at the boy who has continued to chide her.

"Why not try SMD?" I suggest.

"Yeah! Hey, asshole! SMD!" she yells. She swells with pride, looking to me for acknowledgement. It's so gratifying when your students learn quickly.

I'm in the basement, looking for B37, my next class. A towering boy suddenly jumps out in front of me from a room on my left.

"Whassup?" he yells. He waves and shakes his hands at me. A short, stocky adult man carefully ushers him back into the room.

"Steven…come back inside," he says patiently. Steven goes back in and the man closes the door. Boy, am I glad I'm not teaching in there.

"You just passed B37," says an adult whom I've just asked for directions. The bell rings and Steven bolts out. Thank God he's not in my class.

"It's a small class," says Joey, the para inside. "Special ed."

Suddenly, Steven comes bounding in. He's six-foot-two. He flies over to me, totally hopped up.

"I told you I knew her, Joey!" he says as he gives me a high five. Then he begs Joey to let him leave again. I walk over to the girls.

"Hi. What's your name?"

"Maribel."

"Gabriella."

"Beautiful names. Beautiful girls. Ms. Garcia wants you to work on your DBQs. Do you know where they are kept?"

"Second drawer, Miz." Gabriella helps me find their Document Based Questions.

Another highly energetic boy leaps into the room. He and Steven butt into each other. His name is Davin.

I realize I am facing the classic pedagogical recipe:

(Ninth graders + special ed) x one substitute teacher = the seventh circle of Hell.

The DBQ is a cartoon about the Articles of Confederation.

"Naah, Miz. We ain't doing' nothin." I need a strategy to prevent impending mayhem.

"OK. Let's put our papers down. May I ask you a question?"

"Sure, Miz."

"OK. What do you want to do after high school? Steven?"

"I want to be a vetanarian."

"You stoopid!" says Davin, the boy sitting next to him.

"Please let Steven speak. That's great, Steven. Big or small animals?" Davin starts making humping movements with his butt.

"Settle down, please. Steven?"

"Pit bulls. Me and my dad and my uncle were breeding them."

Just then another young man saunters in late. He raps loudly as he crosses stage right.

"Yo bitch, yeah bitch…"

"And you are…?" I say to him. He looks at me.

"Frank."

"But I mean, what's your real name?" I know it ain't Frank.

"It's Frank."

"It Marcus," says Davin. I walk over and look Marcus in the eye.

"I just want you to know that it hurts my feelings when you use the word 'bitch.' "

"Aiight..right, Miz. I ain't talkin' bout you."

"Doesn't matter. It hurts me when you use it."

"Aiight. Aiight, Miz. I gotcha."

"Thanks, Marcus." I turn back and walk to the front of the class.

"Yo bitch, yeah bitch…" Marcus starts up again.

"Marcus…please."

"I ain't mean you! *Yo bitch…yeah bitch…"* I ignore it and continue with Steven.

"So you, your dad and uncle are still breeding pit bulls?"

"Naah. My uncle died last year. He got shot five times. I think it was over some girl."

"Well, I'm really sorry." I pause for his loss, then pick it up. "What about the rest of you? Gabriella? Please put your phone away. What do you want to do after high school?" Gabriella picks her head up from her desk.

"I dunno."

"You have no idea of what you want to do?"

"No." She puts her head back down.

"Maribel?" She just shrugs her shoulders.

"Hey, Miz, we special ed!" Marcus calls out. He's stopped yo-bitchin'.

"What do you want to do?" I've still got some focus with this group. I'm feeling pretty slick with my classroom management technique.

"B-ball. I wanna go to LA!"

"OK. You hold on to that and be respectful to women." Just then, a horrible gaseous odor permeates the room Everybody gets up and moves away. Steven laughs his head off.

"I farted."

"You asshole!" Davin shouts.

So goes the focus. Steven goes over to the large trashcan in front of the room and sits on it.

"I'm taking a shit," he says and groans like he's constipated. Joey and I just stand by, asking Steven to stop. Eventually, he does. Davin runs into a closet. Marcus and Steven start moving large metal desks in front of the closet. It's getting dangerous.

"If you don't stop, I will call extension 1000 and there will be serious consequences. Marcus! Put those chairs back." Surprisingly, he does. The bell rings and they fly out of the room, heading towards their next academic encounter.

Ladies and Gentlemen....*drum roll...*

This is the worst class I've ever had.

And there were only five of them.

I have lost my sense of humor.

I run up to the third floor. I am covering two classes for Ms. Garcia. A small group of older students is standing by the door. It's locked.

"What class is this?" I ask my students when someone opens the small seminar room.

"Marine biology," says a girl.

"That is so cool. Do you go out on the river? Field trips?"

"Naah. We don't go nowhere."

They are juniors and seniors. About seven of them. They're a nice group, a welcome change from the last class.

"What are you going to do next year?" I ask the only girl in the class.

"I'm going to college."

"Great. Which one?"

"Hunter."

"That's terrific. So you're already accepted?"

"Naah. I still have to apply." *Yo.* It's June 4, girlfriend.

My last class only has one student, a girl who's so exhausted she just sleeps the whole time. It's been quite a day: five classes, no lesson plans and a few boys who are in need of extreme wrap-around services.

"How many students go to this school?" I ask a teacher as I'm leaving.

"Two thousand." I'm going to keep an open mind. Remember, this is my first day, first impression and I'm a sub. No need for snap judgments.

I google the school later in the evening. Headlines abound:

> **"Halls of Hell at New York's Worst High School" screams the headlines of The NY Post...posted March 11, 2012.**
>
> "It was on You Tube for only a few hours, but in that time, to the mortification of city officials, it went global: the sight and sound of at least 100 students at Murry Bergtraum High School, located just next door to NYPD headquarters, rioting in the corridors, wrestling with officers who patrol the campus and one student punching a police sergeant in the face."

Come on...it's the Post. Whaddya want?

Tuesday, June 5, 2012

Mondays can be hard. Tuesdays can be better. Big "hi's" from the secretaries. I have math duties but can't understand the lesson plan.

"Go see Ms. Jones," says Elaine.

Outside Ms. Jones's room, an excellent student poster grabs my eye.

"*Misogyny:* Why are woman [sic] used in hip hop as misogyny?"

I show Ms. Jones the confusing math lesson they left for me.

"They should be doing Regents practice" she says, shaking her head at the pile of busy work the teacher left for his three math classes. "This is not going to help them." For the next half hour, she finds a master copy of a recent Integrated Algebra Regents exam, warms up the copy machine and carefully and painstakingly creates 80 two-sided copies I can distribute to the students. Her care and diligence may make a difference to quite a number of these students who will be facing the exam next week.

Have you met Ms. Jones? You should. Dedicated. Focused. Devoted to these kids' success. *The kids are the juice.*

Three classes in a row. Highlights:

Only a few students show up for my first class. Three girls take over the back of the classroom. They sit there texting, brushing each other's hair. A couple of students, a boy and a girl, have already started on the practice test. Ms. Jones comes in and works with them individually. The salon girls are annoyed with me. I let them continue. Entropy wins. Headline: Teacher Gives Up on Students.

My next class storms in. Loud. One girl, in particular, is very boisterous. She gives me a big "hello" and tells me her name: Brittany. I hand them their Regents practice exam with a word of encouragement.

"We are not taking this, Miz." Student after student gives the exam back to me.

"Why not?"

"We're a geometry class. Not algebra." Ms. Jones saves me again. While she's copying practice exams, the girls teach me the "Cat Daddy" dance.

I run to my fifth-period class. It's a wonderful group of 27 bubbly young students, recently arrived from China. Someone is supposed to stop by with a lesson. The girls in front help me with the attendance sheet. They hardly speak any English at all.

"Do you like this school?" I ask them.

They look at each other. One says, "Yes."

"You can tell me the truth. You don't have to say 'yes,' " I say.

"No. I don't like this school," she says. They all giggle. For fun, I run down the last names on the attendance sheet very quickly for them and they get hysterical.

> Xiaomin, Xingwei, Weijie, Yu, Yu Jen, Jun Wei, Yanning, Yunshi, Jun Yao, Chaocheng, Shumei, Jianyong, Chen, Zhangsong, Hui Fang, Jinghong, Yao Zhuo, Quing, Fadong, Haoliang, Mingcun, Runnan and Xiuying.

"Guys! A little quieter, please." A group of boys is playing cards in the back of the room. The girls are laughing. All of a sudden their teacher comes in. She says one or two strict-sounding Chinese words and everyone freezes. You could hear a chopstick drop. She gives them a 100-word essay (your favorite sport) to write in Mandarin in preparation for their Chinese Regents. They do not mess with her. She's scary. I'm ready to crawl under the desk, myself. Then she says something and laughs. They laugh. After a few minutes, she leaves.

They write their essays in Mandarin. Their characters are so neat and well drawn. I spend some time walking around the room, looking at the beautiful art work on the walls. One girl is too distracted to write.

"What's your favorite sport?" I ask her.

"Sleeping."

"OK. What's your second?"

"Eating."

"Well, you could write about either of those for the Regents, but you probably won't get any credit." She laughs and starts to sketch Chinese characters for her essay.

"You know, I'm Derek Rose's foster mother," I say, trying to get some boyz to break up their crew ninth period. Derek = Chicago Bulls NBA Most Valuable Player.

"Fa real?"

"Yep. I've fostered him since he was five."

"Can you get me his autograph?"

"He gives you money?"

"No. It's not like that. We're still close but we talk on the phone. I'd never take money from him. I like making my own money." All the guys have perked up. Half of them believe me. A big boy in the back is skeptical.

"How's he doin'? He gonna play?"

"Well, you know he tore that ACL so he's taking it easy. It's hard on him but he's got a great attitude."

"Where'd he go to college?" the kid asks me. I'm busted.

"OK. You got me. I don't know. I'm not really his foster mother."

"Damn. She got me. I believed her," one of the older kids says.

Memphis. He was a University of Memphis Tiger. Looked it up.

Wednesday, June 6, 2012

It's D-Day. We are all here today enjoying our freedoms because of the sacrifices made on this day in 1944. Hold that memory.

It's S-Day at Murry Bergtraum. Skinny Wednesday. Classes are 30 minutes long. It's a half-day. I've got the same math classes plus two creative-writing classes for special ed. I pray to the gods of special ed:

Please let them be sweet, cooperative, ready to learn or absent.

My prayers are answered. Only three students come to class and they're lovely. My next two classes are the same ones as yesterday.

The first class with the salon girls doesn't like me. The second loves me. We do the Cat Daddy Dance and spit some bars.

I have an hour break. I walk across Rose Street, narcissist that I am.

School ends at 12:38. I disappear into the South Street Seaport and hop the ferry uptown. It's a perfect ride.

Friday June 8, 2012

Yesterday was a lovely "personal" day. This morning I'm back at school. Selma gives me my program, saying, "I wish you were going to be with us until the end of the year. In case I don't see you later..." and she gives me a big hug.

I look over my program. Five social studies classes, no lesson plans attached. The day slinks along, moving its slow thighs. I'm in my last class at Murry Bergtraum.

2:29.

Class ends at 2:54.

One hundred bottles of beer on the wall,

One hundred bottles of beer...

If one of those bottles should happen to fall,

99 bottles of beer on the wall...

2:30.

"Can you please help me with this paper?" Leslie, a bright girl, is writing about how the clothing you choose affects how you feel and how you are perceived. It's extremely well written.

"I can't think of a conclusion. I need a closing sentence." She's stuck.

"If you don't mind, I might have one for you."
"No, Miz. Please." I pause and say…
"You only get one chance to make a first impression."

I'm leaving this school impressed with the students, the staff I've met and the fact that some students showed me a video game where you can build your own taco.

My week at Murry Bergtraum comes to an end. What did I learn? You can't judge a school by one downer story in the Post. You have a pretty tough crowd here in this school of over 2000 students. Lots of diversity between these silos. Many students need a great deal of attention. The teachers I met seem to be collegial, upbeat, and full of humor. They take their enormous challenges in stride as they plan the next day's lesson or call home to make sure their senior finishes her college app.

Yes, I had my worst class…ever. And…I got beautiful hugs and learned a couple of dance steps. Lesson plans often went missing. Entropic forces are persistently poised to annihilate structure. However, the Mandarins, misogyny poster boards and math coach held tight, putting students' needs and safety ahead of every other concern. Each day, I witnessed small conquests, which, as anyone who can count can tell you, add up. Battles are won, here and there, and for some, Murry Bergtraum High School is a safe passage out of the war zone.

Monday, June 11, 2012

HIGH SCHOOL OF ECONOMICS AND FINANCE (HSEF)

Graveyard Shift

Today I am doing everything I can to ignore the papers. That Squad-Which-Must-Never-Be-Named swept my Mets in the first game of the subway series. I am trying to avoid their fans.

From the Wall Street subway station, I walk west alongside the Trinity Churchyard to Trinity Place. A number of elderly gravestones in the churchyard call to me. I'll come back at lunch to mine their mysteries.

It's a short walk past the American Stock Exchange and the High School of Leadership and Public Service to the lobby of my last school this year. A few students are walking in. They're quiet and serious. Or groggy. Conspicuously absent are metal detectors, a cadre of guards, saggy pants and ghetto speak. I'm sent to the tenth-floor office.

"Hi! You must be Ms. Rose!" Several people introduce themselves. One of them, Gabriela, the school secretary, takes me under her wing.

"Looks like you're going to be with us until the end of the year," she says. Tomorrow is the last day of classes. Regents week starts Wednesday. This is a good-vibes, clean, friendly school. I lucked out.

This is school #25. Twenty-five schools, ten months, forty weeks, fourteen hundred class hours take away 300 hours for lunch and prep. That's 1100 hours of substitute teaching. Excuse me. I need to pat myself on the back for a moment. Darn. Can't reach it.

I'm assigned to the library, helmed by a friendly and exceptionally loquacious librarian. A tall, dapper chap with a big smile comes in as I'm standing at the library entrance, checking students in as per the protocol.

"Hi, Ms. Rose. Nice to meet you. Guess you'll be with us for the rest of the year."

"So I hear."

"I just want to go over the protocols."

"Are you the principal?"

"I'm the APO, Mr. Johnson." Affable chap. "Sometime this week, let's sit down and talk. Maybe we'll have something for you next year."

My two periods in the library go well. Occasionally, the librarian crosses, center stage.

"I have to teach these ninth graders...there is so much work piled up on my desk...I'm wearing this shirt because my daughter left it out it on my bed last night saying it wasn't hers..." She continues toward the shelves, airing out her internal dialogue.

My first math class is on the fourth floor. Six students get in the elevator with me.

"Are you allowed to ride the elevator?" I ask them. A couple of them smile. Two boys nod. I let them in.

"Everyone out!" a teacher orders them when the doors open on nine.

Mondays...I forgot over the weekend what it feels like to be a chump.

I hand out a worksheet of quadratic equations left for me. Most of them ignore it. They pull their chairs into small circles and start the hang. "Guys! Can you please keep it down so I can take attendance?" I'm tired. They are wearing me down.

Back upstairs in the library, I think back on this long year. Mignon. Her laughter, her beauty, her impossible trials…they haunt me. On impulse, I call the latke-making AP at AES.

"How is Mignon doing?" I ask her.

"She didn't pass her Regents in January. We'll see how she does on them again next week. It's sweet of you to call and ask." That's it. Just the facts, ma'am. Our connection is lost…except for the one I feel in my gut for Mignon.

I'm walking about the sacred graveyard of Trinity on my break. The news about Mignon has left me feeling blue. I'm just a voice from the past inquiring about a student. A student I knew for two months. For a moment, I felt…necessary…to her success. That's the thing. I felt needed. Even if it was only an illusion, it propelled me. I certainly needed her. I had a reason to go to work every day. I could help her…and the other ELLs. I could offer them a path, some skills, a set of ears. We could laugh and we could grow. It's a "we" thing. We are two equal sides of an equation. We balance each other out.

There's nothing as sacred as being needed. There's nothing as necessary as serving another. There's nothing as rewarding as making a contribution to another soul that allows it to expand. The soul doesn't like being placed in a box. The soul needs to expand, to connect with its highest self. It must have freedom to do that.

Freedom. When I have freedom to be myself in the classroom, my soul reaches upwards. I am content. I am happy. The energy is infectious. There is love in the classroom. Sometimes it's tough love...but...it's love, nevertheless. Love is the current. It's a complete circuit that flows when everyone is connected...when all the souls are expanding. When the energy is flowing, there is no effort. It's love in action. Unfold a world map and set it down on a large table in front of a small group of ELLs and they get excited, connecting with the visual. Wow! You came all the way from there? What's it like? Are those mountains? Everybody's flowing, reaching out to each other. It's infectious. It's fun. It's learning. It's sacred.

Like this hallowed spot. All these souls in this graveyard spent their days in early New York City, when Trinity Church towered over all the other buildings in the young city...when Spirit transcended Commerce. I sit among them on an old wooden bench. They are all facing Broadway, standing in clusters, like students facing a whiteboard. I am looking at their backs, an observer of their class, thinking about who they might have been, what they might have learned during their precious time on Earth, what we might learn from them.

It's a graveyard. I'm sad. Twenty-five hundred DOE teachers like me are ending their first peripatetic year. Tweed hopes to wear us down, capture our souls and restrain them in a box till we can't stand it anymore. Teachers holding regular jobs...their spirits are being boxed in, too. Too much condemnation, criticism and judgment. Too much testing. Choke creativity in the teacher, the child's spirit cannot breathe. Instead, children are reduced to "data points," mere receptacles for information, parrots with a test. The soul of a generation of students struggles to expand from the innards of a tiny dark box.

I have a few minutes before I assume library duty sixth period. I walk between the gravestones. Something draws me to the one at the end of the last row. Its brown slate shines in the sun. Its edges are frayed. But the engraving is perfect. In a determined scroll it reads,

In memory of
Elisabeth Rose
adopted Child of
James & Hannah Welsh
who departed this life
Nov. 7th 1795
aged 9 years and 5 mon

I wipe some tears from my eyes for my tiny namesake and head down the back stairs of Trinity. Tomorrow is the last day of high school classes for the year. Regents start Wednesday. Game over.

Tuesday, June 12, 2012

Everyone needs a tombstone with their name on it. Motivating? *Word!*

Last day for classes. I'm subbing for a social studies teacher who left Regents practice exams for her global and American history classes. I wax nostalgic.

Library duty…easy.

Economics…a wonderful group of 11th graders with excellent taste in music. *They like me*☺

One more break, one more class to go.

My last class of the year. Ninth graders. Global history. They're supposed to read and answer questions about Louis XVI and the storming of the Bastille. They're not excited about this. The class clown has arrived, a tall boy who is wandering around, speaking loudly. A few boys in the back are trying to choke each other with a tee shirt. Girls have taken out cell phones. Boys on the other side of the room are firing up their video games. A couple of Asian students have taken out loose-leaf paper and are picking up the book to complete the assignment. *Mis en scene.*

This may well be the last NYC public high school class I have the privilege to address. As crazy as they are behaving, I feel a sense of responsibility. I want to engage my highest self. I take a deep breath. I summon all the gods. I ask them to let me become a channel for the wisdom, truth and love I have been chosen to impart to them on this, my last day. I take a deep breath. Over the din, I turn my attention to the boys who are still trying to asphyxiate each other. Summoning my inner guide, the words rise effortlessly to the surface as I call to the young pranksters across the room…

"Hey! Crackheads!"

"You heard what she called you???"

"She called you 'Crackhead!' "

"You nice, Miz."

"Thank you. It's good to have your attention." One of the boys in the back smacks the other with his rolled up shirt. "Pardon me, boyz. I was hoping you could defer from violating each other until I could make my announcement."

"Hey! You heard her!"

"Shut up, crackheads." A couple of burly girls appoint themselves my posse.

"So…Ms. Donnelly left you this work. It will count as a quiz. The instructions are up on the board. If everybody finishes it, I'll spit some mad bars for y'all. Everybody grab a book."

Nobody moves. I hand a few copies to the students near me.

"Miz. Will you bring me one?"

"What am I—your waitress? You want coffee, too?"

"Yeah, Miz. You got coffee?"

"Come up, get your books, do the reading, answer the questions and we will battle. Fair enough?"

"OK, Miz." They get the books out. There aren't enough to go around.

"Can you share?" They're fine with the sharing. A boy and girl sitting next to each other way in the back of the room seem to be swapping spit. I walk over to them. They are so absorbed they don't see me coming.

"Get a room," I say. They break apart, embarrassed. The four girls at the next table crack up.

"You heard what she said?" And so it goes. Video games still appear. No one seems to know what the Bastille is. I coach them table-by-table.

Time goes slowly. Five minutes left.

"Miz. You said you'd spit bars for us."

"OK. Hand in your papers. Would someone please collect the books? OK." And I sit on top of a desk where everyone can see me.

"Yo…yo." I start my hip hop engine.

"Shut up! She gonna rap!" They get very quiet. I start quietly and, for the last time in a NYC DOE high school class, rev up my hip-hop groove forthwith:

I'm your Gangsta Teach
It's you I want to reach
And I don't want to preach, screech or beseech
Cause when you're playin' me
You think I'm old and thick
Well I can whip you with words
I don't need a stick

"Whoop..." I've paused for a little reaction from my adoring fans. "Shut up! She got more," the girls in the back yell.

So roll the dice
Cause my words can be nice
Or they can bloody you like lice
And leave you sliced and diced
So don't drizzle on my frizzle
Try to give me the slip
I'll cut you with my lip
Now let me rip

I'm Elizabeth
Not Betty, Beth, Liz
Eliza or Lizzy
Call me that you'll wake up dizzy
Cause I ain't a one-syllable old-timey chick
I'm a four-beat woman
Stand back while I flick
My rhymes on you
Cause I got the name
That's Izza Izza Izzabeth
You wanna get maimed?

Shorten my tag
I turn into a hag
I jump on my broom
So give me room
I'm Elizabeth
Two, three, four beats
You try to shorten that
I'll turn you into chopped meat
I'm a four-syllable woman...
I'm a four-syllable woman...
Word.

Much applause, laughter. The bell rings and they storm the Bastille hell out of here. *Fin.*

Wednesday, June 13, 2012
Relieving the Regents

Yesterday as I emerged from the subway at Wall Street and Broadway, there were four bodies sprawled out in front of Trinity Church. Their hand written signs were lying next to them. OWS, no doubt. Sleeping close to Alexander Hamilton's grave. Are they dreaming of the golden days of Federalism? Or do they want to break the Bank of New York, Hamilton's creation?

It's the beginning of Regents week.
Today I'm a "relief" proctor.
Global at 10:35.
Physics after lunch.

Upstairs, I head to the office and talk to Gerry, the principal's secretary. She sits ten stories over the site where the big black Deutsch Bank was ruined on 9/11. I look out over the streaming tourists, the ongoing construction, the Hudson River.

"What an amazing view you have."

"Do you really think so? I guess so."

"Were you here on 9/11?"

"Oh, yes. The worst day of my life. I don't look out the window."

"What happened to you?"

"I really don't like to talk about it."

"I totally understand." It's still all too real. "Have you been at this school for a while?"

"I came here three years after it opened in 1992. Before that, I was at Murry Bergtraum. That used to be a great school."

"Why? What made it so great?" I didn't get much chance to hear about the good old days while dodging special ed explosions there last week.

"At one time we had ten secretaries and all of them were great. Great administration…great principal."

"Was it serving the same students…from the projects, Chinatown?"

"From all over. They were able to pick the best. Just like this school. Until they stopped letting us."

"So this school used to select the top students, too?"

"Oh, yes. But now…I don't know if it's because of the break up of George Washington…but we have to take students who have no interest in business careers."

"So that's why this school was founded? Did it have partnerships with banks and other Wall Street businesses?"

"Oh, yes. We still have it. WISE Institute. They set it up for that."

"So your students get internships in these companies?"

"Yes. Unpaid and paid."

"It's a real connection."

"Oh, yes. The principal who started this school…she passed. That's her picture." She shows me a large color photo matted into a golden frame that's leaning on the wall, waiting to be hung. "She was wonderful."

Thursday, June 14, 2012

With American history in the am and integrated algebra in the pm,

I have lots of time on my hands. I discover the teachers' lounge for the first time. Whoops. I mean "Teacher Center." It's huge. There's a large central room with long wooden tables. It's lined with two comfy faux-leather couches, two loungers and a big, soft, cushioned chair. One teacher is stretched across a couch, covered in a blanket, sleeping. Four offices, designated Math, Spanish, English and History, break out of the large central room. Every one of them has a spectacular view of the Hudson River and the new World Trade Center construction. The center area has a large stainless steel refrigerator, vending machine for water and soda, coffee maker, bookshelves, mailboxes...all it needs is a masseuse and juice bar. The walls are lined with the official DOE announcements, but someone has gone to the trouble of hanging up large Chagall and Picasso posters. Good vibes.

Back at school, kids are lining up for the Integrated Algebra Regents. POTUS is due at the WTC Memorial. I wish he'd get here already. I've got a seat with a great view.

Friday June 15, 2012

I missed the president. He arrived after school. Today I've only got one Regents to proctor: the ELA. I do the last shift, 12:15 to 1:45. The test started at 9:15 am. These kids get an extra hour and a half to take it. That's five and a half hours of concentrated test taking. As with all Regents exams, they are being taken simultaneously across the state. Mignon, Akram, Tavio...Dhurba, Tenzing, Guangsong...young people from all over the world who have come here to realize their dreams, are sitting for five and a half hours, staring at the packet of papers written in a difficult language. High stakes. You fail? Take it again and again 'til you get that 65. Or turn 21.

There are five students left in the exam room when I arrive. Papers are piled up from students who finished early. The young teacher I'm relieving is happy to see me. She gives me detailed instructions about how to proceed.

"Essays must be in pen, scanatronic answer sheet in pencil, four piles, they must write their ID number on top of each piece of paper, including their scrap paper. If they go to the bathroom, they must sign out. You walk them to the door and the hall monitor will escort them there." I notice a student ID card sitting on the desk.

"Does this card belong to a student in the room?"

"Yes. She's sitting right there. I gave her a pencil." She had to trade her ID card for a pencil? Wow. That's OD ID policy.

Half an hour before the official end of the test, there is one student left: an Asian boy. I've tried to abide by the rules after being "busted" earlier twice by Mr. Johnson, the APO, for writing in my iPad and reading a book. My mind is restless. Oh sweet, dear boy. Please finish your test so we can leave. Please. He sits with his test, carefully jotting notes on his scrap paper and writing in his essay booklet. He is very careful. He is very diligent. I respect his work ethic.

But...I can't take this any more. I could die in this room before he finishes. Please. *Please*. I beg you. I don't want to die here. In a classroom. Proctoring the English Regents. Oh, cruel irony. Headlines spin, newsreel style in my imagination: *"Teacher Expires from Ennui...English Regents Blamed."*

I write "1:40" on the board. I add, "5 minutes till the end of the test" underneath the time.

"You have five minutes," I tell him sweetly. Did he just fold his essay booklet? Maybe he's ready to leave. No way. He just opens up the question booklet and starts reading it from the top. This kid is thorough. Maybe in a few years he can be my accountant. Or mortician.

Three minutes left.

Two minutes.

One minute, thirty seconds. He stands up! He carefully arranges his papers. I check them for ID, signature and collect them.

"Best of luck to you," I say. "Where do you come from?"

"China. Beijing," he says with a cultured accent.

"You speak a bit like someone from Great Britain."

"I have been in this country four years. I have watched a great many British movies."

"That's wonderful." I've collected all the paperwork, paper clips and exam paraphernalia. I start walking towards the door.

"Have a lovely weekend," he says to me as he carefully arranges the contents of his bookbag.

"Thank you. Actually, I have to be the last person out the door. You have to go before me."

"Very well, then." He politely holds the door for me.

"Have a nice weekend," I say as I run into Mr. Johnson, the APO who had busted me.

"Sorry about that," I say, referring to my fall from grace. "We didn't give many Regents in my old school. Didn't really know those rules... but they make sense," I add.

"We do it by the book here," he says. He's sweet.

And he lets me leave a little early for the weekend.

Monday, June 18, 2012

My early morning subway skirmishes leave me weak. I could barely get down the stairs at 68th Street, blocked by battalions of ascending caffeinated commuters. Suffering from PTSD, post-traumatic subway disorder, I'm grateful for today's light schedule of relief proctoring. During a break, the APO tells me not to hang out in the office. Feeling momentarily like a leper, I remove myself to the teacher center.

Tuesday, June 19, 2012

I hump books for two hours in the library, helping the librarian.

"I'm heading out to get something to eat. Then I have to proctor at 12:15," I tell the librarian.

"I have so much paperwork to do. There's a great deal to clear on my desk not to mention the back office. Do you have any idea where

I should put a smart board...?" Her voice trails off as I back into the elevator.

More afternoon relief proctoring in the sub-zero air conditioning. At 3:15, I head out into the sun.

Wednesday, June 20, 2012

The tabloid weather forecasters on TV are preparing us for hellfire and brimstone. They're predicting we might melt. It's going to 98F. Maybe higher. The apocalypse is imminent. Personally, I can handle it. Mets pitcher R.A. Dickey pitched his second straight one-hitter on Monday. In the last two months his ERA is 0.92. Now *that's* hot.

The news also reports that several OWS protestors were convicted of misdemeanor trespassing on December 17 when they crawled under Trinity's chain-link fence to camp after being kicked out of Zuccotti Park. They've started a vigil for a comrade who had been arrested. When I emerge, there are even more OWS sleeping bags lined in front of Trinity Church. I engage the protestors in conversation while my iPad video rolls.

The school is cold. The office folk are warm.

"Have you met my staff?" The perky payroll secretary indicates a congregation of stuffed creatures on her windowsill. Monkeys, a leprechaun, several teddy bears, Humpty Dumpty, twin puppies, two mice (or are they moles?) wearing ski caps, a chartreuse pig and a pink rabbit. "They assist me in many clandestine endeavors," she adds.

"I need you to proctor on five," the APO interrupts us. He's changing it up again. I dutifully head downstairs. There is one girl left in the room. She's working diligently on her test.

"I got it," I tell the APO.

"Take your time. You have until 3:15," says the APO to the girl as he leaves us. He's right. She deserves all the time she needs.

She should feel comfortable taking the time she needs. Just like the diligent Asian boy. I know. *I know.*

Thursday, June 21, 2012

Sick. The air conditioning has made me sick. It's 98 outside. Inside, an artic wind blows. I'm closing the RCT Writing Regents. There's only one beautiful little girl, with purple hair extensions, left in the room, taking it.

"I had to take six Regents." She smiles at me as she hands in her test. "They wanted me to take three over again." She leaves the room momentarily free from academic torture.

"In order to take the RCT, students have to take the regular Regents first and fail them. They can't just sign up for an RCT," a teacher explains to me in the lounge...uh...center.

Oh—I get it. You have to take all the Regents exams and fail. Then, and only then, do you earn the right to take the RCT. Interesting educational philosophy: build self-condemnation by scaffolding failure.

What I know for sure...this beautiful young soul is going to need a miracle if she's ever going to discover the joys of learning.

Friday, June 22, 2012

Home. Sick. The AC took me out.

Monday, June 25, 2012

The six-game subway series ended last night. I couldn't take it. I switched to Seinfeld reruns. My Mets went one of six against The-Lineup-That-Must-Never-Be-Uttered. I consider myself lucky. After all, I'm not a Cubs fan. Anyway it's over and I don't want to talk about it.

Still have the bug but I make it to school, dodging some forked lightning as I cross Trinity Place. I have five classes to cover.

Holding classes after Regents? *Wack.*
First class gets brain teasers.

Only two boys are present (out of 21) in my second class: a muscular Asian boy and a rotund chap with a thick Spanish accent. They're swapping war stories about their Regents.

"I got a 72 in Algebra," the Hispanic boy says.

"I got a 79," says the Asian boy.

"So that's not so bad," I say.

"It's bad," says the Asian boy. "I'm Chinese. My father expects me to get 90. 79 is definitely not OK. Also, you don't get to take a good trig class unless you get an 85 on your algebra Regents. So I'll be put in a worse math class next year. It sucks. We have a pool. My father makes me swim every day. Even if I've been in the park for eight hours and I'm tired, he makes me get in the pool, anyway. We live in Bay Ridge."

He shows me a picture of himself as a six-year-old standing in front of the Forbidden Palace in Beijing.

"I'm going back to DR for the summer," says the other lad. "Santiago."

Third class in a row. Sixteen ninth graders are attending. One boy, Nicolas, wearing a red tee shirt, baggy pants and stylish sneakers, gives me his ID in exchange for a Rubik's Cube.

"I can solve that," he says in a low voice. Decked in hoodie and saggy pants, he looks like he's from central casting, "ghetto" from *The Wire*. I hand him a scrambled Rubik's Cube. He starts manipulating the pieces. Expertly. In a little over a minute, he solves it. He's a Rubik's genie. Never judge a hoodie by his sag. Teachable moment.

Last class. Only three kids. They chat and draw on the board. My day is over. Why are we all here? Maybe I'll sleep outside at the Trinity vigil. Naah. I'm heading home. Two more days and the year ends with a whimper, I hope.

Tuesday, June 26, 2012

Today is graduation day. I have been planning to make myself invisible. I don't know any graduating seniors. I'm proud of these kids in spirit, but a bit removed. They've handed out gowns to all the teachers…except me. After all, I'm merely the ATR.

"You going to graduation?" one of the teachers asks me.

"I wasn't really planning on it." A highly animated teacher with lots of years in her pension fund turns to me and exclaims in her raspy voice, "Oh but this is not like any other graduation. They line up and walk down Broadway. They aren't astronauts. They aren't heads of state. But they get to parade down Broadway, escorted by a fire truck. All the tourists just step aside and stare. Then they parade over to Trinity Church. That's where they hold their ceremony." Wow!

I'm going to stick around. I love a parade.

I have three classes today. Nine out of thirty-two students show up.

"We can just chill," I announce to them.

Romeo and Juliet in the first row cup each other's faces in their hands.

"Guys…*please*…this is a classroom."

"You can watch Justin blow-dry his hair on You Tube. I saw it on MTV…" A cute little girl hangs with me, wanting to talk mad Beebs.

My very last class as an ATR, as a NYC public school teacher… ends. I'm going to graduation right after lunch. This is the most beautiful day of the year. I'm outside. The sun is shining. A pigeon is stalking me for crumbs. Graduation day = perfect.

Graduation

Back at Trinity Place, a few people are standing in front of the revolving doors at the school's entrance. They look like family members, holding a garment bag and an air of expectation. The lobby is packed. There must be several hundred people in long black graduation gowns. All the faculty and staff are wearing long hoods to distinguish them from the graduating seniors. The APO towers over the crowd. People are hugging, trying to get each other's attention. A teacher is helping adjust a student's cap. There's a great buzz of anticipation.

The march is scheduled to start at 1:15. It's about 1:20 and there has been no signal. As I open the revolving door to the street, the sound of a bagpipe fills the air. A piper, his long black hair pulled into a ponytail, is warming up on the sidewalk. He is dressed in a black watch kilt, green military jacket and black Glengarry feathered hat.

As he squeezes the air from the bag under his left arm, he exhales into the blowpipe, fingering a melody on the chanter. The melody dances above the drone. This is the air of the Scottish war pipe. It augers something sacred. While the song flirts with Terpsichore, the drone upholds, sustains and protects us from crumbling. Why? Do spirits journey into our world on that drone? Can anyone say for sure they don't? We are a few steps from hallowed ground where three thousand souls were lost to a monstrous deed. Time and again, the pipes have returned to this spot to honor them. The bravest. The finest. The heroes. Summoned by the drone, it seems a portal has opened. Anchored to that drone, their spirits ride its muscular energy. They help us transcend our grief, our outrage, our desire to even the score. They are ready for us. We summon them on the drone. They canter in, ready to serve us, accepting us right as we are in this moment. Today it's a celebration. Today they are laughing.

"We're waiting for the fire engine," a dean explains. Traditionally, a NYFD engine leads the graduation procession. It's 1:30. Sirens are heard from the south, getting louder and louder.

"Sounds like the fire engine is arriving," says a teachers' aide. "Look!" A fire engine on full alert races by. Then another. "Guess they ain't stoppin' for us," she figures. I wonder what's going on?

Two fire trucks have just raced toward One World Trade Center. I feel a sense of dread. It's *deja vu* all over again.

"There must be a fire," says a bystander. The fire engines disappear. A moment of quiet. An invisible signal is given. All traffic is stopped, the piper steps into the middle of Trinity Place and begins to drone. It's a B flat. A NYPD School Safety van has taken its place in front of the piper. The piper plays a slow melody above the drone, gathering the spirits again, summoning the ceremony. The honor guard lines up with its three colorful flags flying in the breeze. Behind them, a girl and boy hold a hefty maroon-and-white banner which reads, "The High School of Economics and Finance." Behind them, the school leaders, faculty and students form a line, two abreast. The piper holds the melody. The drone continues. Another invisible signal and the entire procession moves north. It turns east, up Cedar Street towards Broadway. Tourists have stopped in their tracks. People are lined up on the sidewalk, taking pictures.

"Look, Mom!"

"This is a *high school* graduation?"

All of a sudden, another siren pierces from the south. The graduating boys, emerging from the school and turning left on Trinity, are oblivious. They wave at the shutterbugs on the sidewalk, speaking into their cameras in their triumph.

"Kristen, baby, I love you, Kristen," one of them yells. "You too, Isabella!" Another boy does a perfect chimpanzee cry. "Eee, eee, eee." Their party has started, but right behind them, a man wearing a hard hat and reflective vest stops the graduates who have not yet stepped off the curb.

"Everybody has to stop!" he commands. The siren gets closer. It's deafening. Cars that have been stopped at Thames Street, right at the edge of the school building, are now blocking whatever is blasting its siren. The hard hat runs over to the stopped traffic. Two lanes of giant buses, two lanes of cars and taxis are in the way.

"Do not move!" Someone barks at the graduates who have clogged the sidewalk.

"Here! Move!" The hard hat yells and points at the cars directly in front of the siren, now bleating angrily. Insistently. *"Move!"* He's joined by a NYPD uniformed officer and another hard hat. Together, they are trying to keep graduates and pedestrians at bay, move cars out of the way and let the siren through. It's life and death. *People! Think! Yeah, you! Move! NOOOOW!*

The front of the procession has disappeared on Cedar, the drone lost beneath the siren. Buses, taxis, cars are directed forward, left and right. Out of the way. Anxiety builds. Why here? Why now? *PTSD.* Horns blast, the siren becomes painful. Another taxi. Another bus. A red-white-and-blue ambulance emerges. It screeches toward One World Trade Center. *Deja vu,* indeed.

Graduates are still standing on the sidewalk, waiting to join the others who are, by now, way ahead of them. Buses and cars have started to roll down Trinity Place. As every NY driver knows, if you follow an emergency vehicle whose siren is going, you can really make time. The APS, bulked out in his graduation robe and hood, steps into the street and morphs into a traffic cop. He plants himself in the middle of the ongoing traffic, yelling directions as each vehicle approaches. It seems like a dangerous occupation, especially considering a NYPD van has just pulled up to do its job. He points at a silver GMC SUV and yells, "Go over there!" pointing to the left. "There! Go over there," he yells at a black sedan, indicating the right. The police take over the traffic control job and the APS turns to the rest of the graduating seniors. Now that traffic has been stopped again, the seniors start to file out in that direction. He is not satisfied with their progress.

"Go! Go! Go! This way!" he yells at them, pointing, running back and forth, showing them the way. *"Let's go! Let's go! Two lines, let's go! Quickly!"* Grads speed up a bit, smiling, girls rocking on their 5-inch heels, still besotted with the party atmosphere. *"Quickly!*

Quickly! Quickly! Come on! Let's go!" His face has taken on the hue of the fire engines.

As he wrangles the last of the spike-heel draggers and joins the dean at the rear of the procession, I cut across the small alley called Thames, heading for Broadway. Up the hill, I see the color guard emerge in front of me, heading south down Broadway towards Trinity Church. I turn around and glance at 4 World Trade Center. Its windows gleam in the sun, mirroring the puffy clouds and perfectly blue skies that surround them. It was only yesterday that the highest beam was anchored into place. I notice that the two exterior elevators, the ones that transport workers up and down the 974-foot structure all day long, are not moving. Could that be related to the ambulance and fire trucks?

Horns behind me are still honking, but the sound of the drone and its marching song echo in the cavernous alley, louder and louder. I stride up the hill alongside men decked out in pressed blue shirts and light pants, the uniform of lunchtime in the finance district.

The pipes, the pipes are calling.

On Broadway, the sun hits with full intensity, lighting up the happy parade of graduates. Tears begin to run down my cheeks. I can't help myself. Traders, secretaries, tourists, families, friends, bankers, the curious, loved ones, complete strangers, have all stopped their routines and stepped aside to honor this milestone. One hundred seventy-one graduates confidently stride down Broadway, waving to the crowds, smiling, eating up every second of this pageant. I'm holding up my iPad, capturing the moment on video as tears continue to cleanse any doubts I may have held about donating some of this incarnation to the service of teaching. I don't know any of these students. I haven't fostered them, challenged them, supported them, praised them. I don't know their names, their families. I am not apprised of their struggles, their triumphs, their future plans. It doesn't matter. At this moment, I am filled with pride. I share their joy. I revel in their accomplishment. I am profoundly moved. I am exquisitely happy. I walk next to them as they proceed to the church.

I finally made it to Broadway!

Trinity's entrance is clogged with students. They're gabbing happily, anticipating the upcoming ceremony. I slither past the waiting grads, making my way up the stairs into the church's vestibule.

"Are you part of the school?" A female security guard stops me. "Yes. I'm a teacher." She allows me to slither on. As I reach the last door to the sanctuary, it suddenly opens and the graduates begin to file down the long aisle toward the altar. I begin walking in with them but quickly realize that I've stepped into the procession. I move swiftly inside and to the left of the sanctuary. The giant organ resounds with the first strains of "Pomp and Circumstance" as the place bursts into applause. It is packed. There are more than a thousand people standing up in the pews, snapping photos, smiling, waving. Tears. I've heard this song played by fifth-grade bands. I've downloaded the orchestral version for my old school. I marched to it myself when my Jamaica High School orchestra played it on my graduation day. But I have never heard such a magnificent performance. The giant pipes resonate through the nave of this beautiful Neo-Gothic church. Joy permeates. Tears continue their track down my cheeks. It's standing room only. The graduates take their place in the 171 folding chairs behind the altar. A girl grad leads us in the Pledge of Allegiance. Another graduate sings the national anthem, receiving thunderous applause. I stand in the back, admiring the giant, happy throng crowding this exquisite church, first chartered in 1697, for the price of one peppercorn per year to the King.

I can't take it anymore.

Outside, excited tourists are pressing their cameras up against the door to film this celebration of strangers. They're hooked on a grand occasion in the lives of ordinary people...in the greatest city on Earth.

On this penultimate day of my public school teaching career...

I am blessed with this brilliant sendoff.

Wednesday, June 27, 2012
Last Day of School

Something strange happens this morning as I look down the subway steps at the ascending crowd at 68th Street. Nobody is blocking my way down. Everyone is keeping to the right, leaving a clear path for me. Is this a sign? A message? If so, what? That my path is obstacle-free? Is this parting of the Sea of Commuters a sign of emancipation? Am I free now to leave the classroom and follow my heart? Perhaps. Or...the message might be that I'm overdoing this whole message idea, I'm a pompous ass and just lucky that I don't have to swat angry commuters with my Metro tabloid for a change.

When my train arrives at Wall Street, I get out. I'm further back in the station than usual. I hear a woman's high voice singing above me. Commuters have piled out of the train and they pass me, filing up the stairs toward the voice. The train leaves for Bowling Green. The station is empty. The voice continues. I climb a back stairway that I've never used before. The voice gets louder. At the top of the first stairway platform, there's a thin, middle-aged woman, dressed in a long-sleeved, black jacket, black pants and a baby blue hat with a small rim. Next to her a small suitcase and a backpack are set neatly on some old newspapers. There is no place to leave donations. She is not collecting money.

She is singing a beautiful hymn.

Hold me in my heart...I'll be there.

I stop and listen. I video her on my iPhone. She perks up for the camera. Another train comes and goes. Passengers climb the stairs, keeping to the opposite side of her. She sings to them. It's beautiful. She's an angel. When this group has passed, she turns and smiles at me. Her song continues. She raises her arms in devotion. I feel a Great Presence in her music. She is not crazy. She is *Connected.* I hate to leave but I have to report for my last school day. I smile at her and begin to back up to the next flight of stairs to Broadway. She turns to me and sings the last few phrases of her hymn. When she gets to the last notes, she slows it down to a *recitative*…

Always remember
Feel despair
Hold me in my heart
I'll…be…there

"Beautiful," I say to her.

"Have a beautiful day," she calls back to me and folds her hands in an "amen." I leave her with her worldly possessions…her loyal audience.

Today, my path is clear. An angel sings to me. I'm in my sacred space: the subway.

Upstairs, the OWS vigil has grown substantially. Many more bodies are wrapped in sleeping bags, lining Trinity's cemetery.

"We're here for *you*," a well-dressed middle-aged man calls out to me from his sidewalk perch.

"We need you in the lobby," says the school secretary. We collect books and hand out report cards. Back at the teacher center I look over the Hudson River and listen to the angel sing again on my iPhone.

The library is packed with the staff reflecting, coping with common core curriculum on the fall's horizon. My mind is turning to jello. At some point the principal announces, "You may go to lunch." The APO suddenly comes over the PA. "Attention, everybody. There has been an accident at the World Trade Center. The police have roped off the street in front of the school. They will not let anyone back in the building without something that proves that you work here."

Another accident? That's two days in a row.

"A crane hit one of the windows way up there where you see that orange strip," a policeman tells me outside. "No one's hurt but we don't want anyone to get hit by falling glass."

"There was an accident here yesterday, too. Was anyone hurt?"

"Yes. One of the construction workers got hit in the chest with shrapnel from the broken window. He's gonna live." Thank God. Seems like it's 9/11 PTSD every day around here.

After a while, the police let me back into the school.

Back on the tenth floor, the sun pours in the window, warming the river, a shimmering teal. Lots of boats on the Hudson today. Since I arrived here three weeks ago, a new floor has been built on the parking lot going up below. Today, a glass window has cracked high up on 4WTC. Everything around me has been shut down as prevention. The usual long lines of tourists winding through back-and-forth barriers to honor Ground Zero have vanished, construction workers evacuated. Everything is still below me.

Ground Zero is still.

In the stillness lies the path. The path is clear. An angel sings to me. This day is the end of something special. I've been graced with this incredible opportunity to tell a story about 25 schools where I've been lucky to serve this year. I've tried my best to tell it well, responsibly. I've tried to be fair. I've met brilliant teachers, caring administrators and a few crazies. And…I've fallen in love with the students. Rich or poor, top or bottom school, day after day they've made me laugh and they've moved me…especially a boisterous, bubbly spirit named Mignon. I cheer her on.

Plus, I've been to the best high school graduation *ever!!*

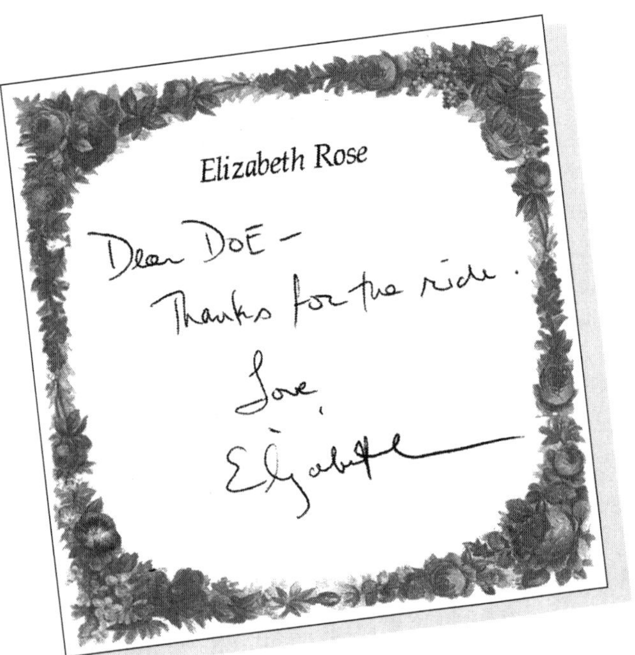
Elizabeth Rose

Dear DOE -
Thanks for the ride.
Love,
Elizabeth

Message to Readers

Thank you so much for reading *Yo Miz!* If you laughed, if you cried, if you feel these kids deserve the best...then together, we have energized Hope, which very well may evolve into Action.

If you would be so kind as to spread the word about *Yo Miz!* by leaving a review at your fav retailer, that would be amazing.

Special Message to Teachers

You're a teacher. You've got so many stories. You could write a book.

But who's got the time?

I do.

For my next book, I'm compiling great stories...from great teachers. Like you.

"We need more teacher books filled with the kind of love & compassion displayed in *Yo Miz!*" Dr. Mark Naison.

Interested? Please go to yomizthebook.com and click on *Yo Teach!* for more information.

For Music Teachers

PennywhistleBand.com

For the cost of ONE student instrument, 30 students can enjoy a rich music program. For students age 10 and up. Fundamentals of instrumental music and ensemble playing with an emphasis on learning through playing, using the pennywhistle. Full disclosure: my husband, Don Castellow, created this pedagogy while teaching in the South Bronx and, later, rural Pennsylvania.

Whaddyawaitin' for?

About the Author

ELIZABETH ROSE swore she would never follow the advice of her parents, both teachers, and become a teacher, too. But in between creating music and comedy for stage, film, and TV, she took a gig teaching songwriting in a NYC public high school. Her students, mostly from the projects, ignited her with their energy and raw creativity. Frustrated by the school's outdated technology and lack of a music program, she raised hundreds of thousands of dollars in tech grants enabling her kids to create DVD yearbooks and record original songs. When her job was cut, she was given the choice of substituting in a different school each week—or resigning. She almost resigned. Then she realized that this assignment would give her access to a unique story. So she stayed. And wrote it. She hopes her late parents are having an unearthly chuckle.

Connect

Email: yomizthebook@gmail.com
Website: yomizthebook.com
Subscribe to my blog: yomizthebook.com
Twitter: twitter.com/yomizthebook
Facebook: facebook.com/yomizthebook
Linked In: www.linkedin.com/in/eroseiserose

For Laughs

"Leave Me Alone" http://goo.gl/JVaWFQ
Hilarious music film about caregiving, honored by NYC Family Caregiver Coalition, starring 96-year-old Gerry Rose (Mom) and a cast of nona- and octo-genarians.

"Back Seat Driver" http://goo.gl/zlqKXF
Wild ride through the west of Ireland with crazy back seat driving Elizabeth Rose.

Acknowledgements

It's
About
The
Kids.

Two years into the writing of *Yo Miz!*, my editor, Jennifer Sawyer Fisher, delivered these four words to me after pouring through my protracted piles of poorly processed prattle. Thanks to her stamina, insight and carefully-crafted critiques, she inspired me to do something that I had been meaning to do since this incarnation began: get myself out of the way and tell the story. Thanks to her, these kids, whose voices are rarely heard, have a path into the hearts of readers who, if we are lucky, will be moved to help them reach their American dream. My friend from Rowe Camp, Katherine Hall Page, now the famous author of the Faith Fairchild Mystery Series, sent me to Jennifer saying, "She's the best in the business." Thanks to both of these remarkable women for their generosity and guidance through my first venture into the arcane world of publishing.

Three-and-a-half years into the writing, just when I thought I had a polished manuscript, I met Marileta Robinson, a writer and former editor at *Highlights Magazine*. Kindly offering to proofread, she found hundreds of places to improve *Yo Miz!* She's a major literary talent; a cultural polymath elegantly bundled into a soft-spoken dynamo. Many thanks to my friends who encourage me to write, especially Katharine Houghton, my steadfast cheerleader as we've churned out screenplays, songs and musical comedy; and novelist Molly Turner, who encouraged me to join her at the Yale Writers Conference. I so appreciate my first readers, Deborah Meier, Ken Jenkins and Mark Naison, who see the big picture. During this wacky year, I got to chill with Angela DeSouza, my rotating ATR pal, where, as outcasts, we found laughs in lonely teacher lounges. BTW, she's a great teacher… as is my fav husband, Don Castellow.

Thanks also to my pal, adventurer, author and TV host, Francis Tapon, for coaching me long-distance from his 4-year adventures in all 54 African countries and for connecting me to Yasamin Rahmani, our lovely book-cover designer. Also, thanks to Karen Hudson, interior design, Jonathan Fox, photo editor, Gloria Tabares, who fixed my broken *español,* Jody Kihara for her digital prowess, Dave Justice for digital production and Alexis Siroc for her peerless polish.

Paying it forward…thanks to those of you who allow these kids into your hearts. You realize they too deserve no less than love, support and a first-rate education that challenges and prepares them to participate in our democracy. Therein lies *our* freedom.

Glossary

4WTC = 4 World Trade Center (the building's address)
ACS = Administration for Children's Services
AP = Assistant Principal
APO = Assistant Principal for Organization
APS = Assistant Principal for Supervision;
ATR = Absent Teacher Reserve, aka, "Excessed Teachers" = a pool of about 1500 to 2500 full-time tenured teachers whose positions were cut due to budgets or school closings.
AYSOATI = Aren't you sick of all these initials? I am.
CTT = Collaborative Team Teaching
Consortium School = NY Performance Standards Consortium: Progressive, authentic learning communities that oppose high stakes testing. www.performanceassessment.org
DOE = New York City Department of Education
DR = Dominican Republic
ELA = English Language Arts. This is the New York State Regents exam.
ELL = English Language Learners
ESL = English as a Second Language
Excessed Teachers = see **ATR**
Gassin' = I'm playin' you, not telling you the truth...for fun.
G.E.D. = General Education Tests which, when passed, certify that the test taker has high school-level academic skills.
IEP = Individualized Education Program, mandated by law for any child labeled with a disability, as defined by the feds. The IEP is designed to help them reach their goals more easily while being able to participate in the normal school culture.
IMHO = In my humble opinion
OD = Overdoing
OWS = Occupy Wall Street
Para = Paraprofessional teacher. Teaching assistants who serve under the supervision of a certified teacher. Many are assigned to one student with special needs.

PBA = Performance Based Assessment. They're cool. Also called **PBAT**, PBAs could have been a win for Mignon, et al. Look 'em up: www.performanceassessment.org

PSPDS = Post-St. Patrick's Day Syndrome (Don't bother looking it up.)

PTSD = Post Traumatic Stress Disorder

PD = Professional Development

PR = Puerto Rico

RCT = Regents Competency Test. It's not exactly a Regents exam. In order to qualify to take the RCT, you have to fail the Regents in a subject like ELA or math. Failure is not an option…it's a requirement.

SETTS = Special Education Teacher Support Services

Sempre librea degg'io, Folleggiare di gioia in gioia. = Free and aimless I frolic, from joy to joy…(*La Traviata)*

Spit some bars = Rap

Tight = Angry. I'm tight = I'm pissed.

Transfer Schools = Small schools designed for students who have been unsuccessful at traditional schools.

U Rating = unsatisfactory

Xie Xie = Thank You

School Initials

AES = Academy of Environmental Science (Secondary School); also **AESSS**
BCCHS = Baruch College Campus High School
BMCC = Borough of Manhattan Community College
BOSS = Business of Sports School
CPE = Central Park East; **CPEHS** = Central Park East High School
HSSIS= Henry Street School for International Studies
LSSS = Life Sciences Secondary School
MBHS = Manhattan Bridges High School
MCNDHS = Manhattan Comprehensive Night and Day School
MCSM = Manhattan Center for Science and Mathematics
NTHS = Norman Thomas High School
SPHS = Steward Park High School
TCA = The College Academy
TEPCS = The Equity Project Charter School
UA Green = Urban Assembly School for Green Careers

For the erudite only:

Fashion Is Not a Luxury (page 319)

In this chapter, the school-wide English language announcement comes over the PA as follows: "Good morning Fashion Industry students. Today's prefix is 'pro.' It means 'in favor of.' The word for today is 'profuse.' It's an adjective that means 'large amounts.'"

To be technical, "pro" as used in "profuse" does not mean "in favor of." It means projecting forward or outward. Thanks to wordsmith Marileta Robinson for enlightening us.

APPENDIX

The appendix is a narrow, dead-end tube about three-or-four inches long that hangs off the cecum.

ATRs

ATRs are a group of several thousand highly experienced teachers, now assigned to dead-end rotations as substitute teachers via NYC subway tubes. Most of them lost their jobs due to budget cuts and school closings. A principal, who might want to hire an experienced ATR, can hire two newbie teachers for the price of one pro.

In the past, the appendix was considered an evolutionary leftover.

ATRs are usually portrayed negatively in the media. They are considered evolutionary leftovers.

Now, however, scientists acknowledge that the appendix helps support the immune system in two ways: it tells lymphocytes where they need to go to fight an infection and it boosts the large intestine's immunity to a variety of foods and drugs.

Now, however, educators acknowledge that many ATRs have been valuable in their schools. Scores of them are wise in the ways of classroom management. A considerable number are African-Americans and Hispanics, role models and inspiration to many children from our most underserved areas. Turns out, ATRs, when used wisely, have helped support the "immune systems" of their schools in many ways: by tutoring, raising funds, initiating engineering and technology programs as well as producing plays, concerts, art galleries and love of learning.

The latter [boosting the large intestine's immunity...] helps keep your gastrointestinal tract from getting inflamed in response to certain foods and medications you ingest.

Despite the high-stakes testing epidemic that has inflamed our educational system, devouring joy and motivation while reducing our energetic, inquisitive kids to simple "data points," most ATRs, if you allow them, can boost pride with even small victories, helping to decrease the burn.

PRAISE FOR YO MIZ!

"Despite the fact that there's never been a sub quite like Miz Rose, she manages to capture what it is about NYC schools that we both love (and occasionally hate). I love it. It's a masterpiece. I couldn't put it down."

Deborah Meier, author, *In Schools We Trust*

"Yo Miz!" is a love story—not a "summer romance," not a fling," not a "brief infatuation"—but a real love story where the stakes are high and lives are at risk...you'll love the teachers and you'll love the kids!"

Ken Jenkins, actor, Dr. "Bob" Kelso, *Scrubs* (ABC-TV)

"Elizabeth Rose's *Yo Miz!* is hands down the best book ever written about the experience of being an ATR (rotating substitute teacher) in the nightmare world of Michael Bloomberg's Department of Education. Following her journey from school to school is heartbreaking and infuriating, especially because this is an incredibly talented teacher who LOVES young people. Her portraits of the students she meets are filled with empathy, humor and an incredible ear for dialogue. But the treatment she receives, along with thousands of others in her position, is a sure sign of an education policy that has gone off the deep end, at the expense of children as well as teachers. This book takes an awful subject and brings it to life in a way that will make readers laugh and tug at their heartstrings. A must read!

Dr. Mark Naison, author, *Badass Teachers Unite*

Made in the USA
Middletown, DE
02 September 2015